RELEASING THE CHURCH FROM
ITS CULTURAL CAPTIVITY

RELEASING THE CHURCH FROM ITS CULTURAL CAPTIVITY

A REDISCOVERY OF THE DOCTRINE OF THE TRINITY

Siew Kiong Tham

Copyright © 2015 by Siew Kiong Tham.

Library of Congress Control Number:	2015917975
ISBN: Hardcover	978-1-5144-4224-1
Softcover	978-1-5144-4225-8
eBook	978-1-5144-4226-5

All rights reserved. No part of this book may be reproduced or transmitted in any form or by any means, electronic or mechanical, including photocopying, recording, or by any information storage and retrieval system, without permission in writing from the copyright owner.

This is a work of fiction. Names, characters, places and incidents either are the product of the author's imagination or are used fictitiously, and any resemblance to any actual persons, living or dead, events, or locales is entirely coincidental.

Any people depicted in stock imagery provided by Thinkstock are models, and such images are being used for illustrative purposes only.
Certain stock imagery © Thinkstock.

Print information available on the last page.

Rev. date: 11/04/2015

To order additional copies of this book, contact:
Xlibris
1-800-455-039
www.Xlibris.com.au
Orders@Xlibris.com.au
633485

Contents

Introduction ix
Acknowledgement xi

Part One
The Cultural Captivity of the church

1. CULTURE: GENERAL CONSIDERATIONS 3
   1.1. What is Culture? 3
   1.2. The Study of Culture 6
   1.3. Uncovering the Assumptions 12
   1.4. Missions and Culture 13
   1.5. Defining Christianity 15
   1.6. The Hermeneutics of Culture and the Culture of
        Hermeneutics 16
   1.7. Christ and Culture 18
   1.8. The Transformation of Culture 19

2. THE TREND OF THINKING AMONG
   OVERSEAS CHINESE CHURCHES 21
   2.1. The Overseas Chinese Churches 21
   2.2. The Chinese Understanding of God 23
   2.3. Bringing the Gospel to the Chinese 38
   2.4. Patterns of Chinese Theology 42

Part Two
Trinitarian Theology Defined and Denied

3. THE HEART OF CHRISTIANITY: THE TRINITY
   AND THE COVENANT 47
   3.1. The Triunity of the Godhead and the Covenantal
        Relationship 48
   3.2. Implications of the Covenant 57

4 THE TRIUNE GOD DEFINED AND DENIED..................66
   4.1 Early Church...67
   4.2. Nicea: The Grafting of the Trinity onto the Greek
      God or the God of Any Culture 69
   4.4 Post-Nicea..72
   4.6. Medieval Church...76
   4.7. Reformation 77
   4.8. Post-Reformation 79
   4.9. Federal Theology and Scholastic Calvinism 79
   4.10. The Age of Enlightenment...81
   4.11. The Indicatives of Grace Precede the Imperatives of Law......82
   4.12. Covenant, not Contract, Grace, not Law 83

5 AN EVALUATION OF THE CHINESE CHURCH
   IN THE LIGHT OF THE TRINITY 86
   5.1. A Recovery of the Trinitarian Faith......................................86
   5.2 A Recovery of Covenantal Relationship: Our
      Participation in God.. 90
   5.3. A Departure from Confucianism 94
   5.4. God's Sovereignty 97
   5.5. The Nature of Our Response..98
   5.6. Ethnocentricity 99
   5.7. Denial of the Trinity 100
   5.8 Conclusions..104

Part Three
The Transformation to a New Framework

6 A Theology of Blessing...107
   6.1 Introduction 107
   6.2. A Setting in Life..108
   6.3 The Chinese Preoccupation with Blessing 109
   6.4. Time and Space (A Receptacle or Relational Notion)............110
   6.5. Participation (κοινωνια)...113
   6.6. Our Life of Discovery..114

7 A THEOLOGY OF MINISTRY 117
   7.1. Introduction..117
   7.2. Derivation of the Term Ministry 118

7.3. How Is 'Ministry' Understood?	119
7.5. In Christ	125
7.6. Service in Christ	127
7.7. Justification of Our Ministry (Barrenness in Ministry)	128
7.8. Ministry as Response	130

8 A THEOLOGY OF RESPONSE 132
8.1. Introduction 132
8.2. Priesthood in the Buddhist Context 132
8.3. Jesus Christ: The Only Acceptable Response 133
8.4. Unitarian or Trinitarian 135
8.5. The Continuing High Priesthood of Jesus Christ ... 136
8.6. The Law and Our Response 138
8.7. Conclusion to the Theology of Ministry and of Response 139

9 COVENANT AS IT RELATES TO OUR CULTURE 140
9.1. The Culture of Narcissism 141
9.2. Worship: What We Are or What We Do? 145
9.3. Church Life: Pastor-Congregation Relationship 145
9.4. The Workplace 147
9.5. Family Relationships: Covenant or Contract? 148
9.6. The Fringes of Life (Euthanasia) 156
9.7. Ethics 165

10 CONCLUDING REMARKS 167
Bibliography 203

Introduction

The purpose of this dissertation is to show that the overseas Chinese churches have subordinated Christianity to their Chinese cultural heritage and that the recovery of the doctrine of the Trinity will lead the church out of her cultural captivity.

The overseas Chinese churches show the common traits of ethnocentricity, egocentricity, and isolation—features of the cultural heritage that powerfully shapes the Chinese mind. This heritage, coupled with her need to be assimilated in the country of her adoption, reinforces the tendency of the Chinese church to harmonise her culture with the newfound faith, an exercise in which the Chinese have been engaged for centuries. In so doing, Christianity has been subordinated to the Chinese culture. The history of Christianity is a history of the subordination of the triune God to the culture of the day, and the Chinese churches are no different.

Our theology needs to be grounded in the triunity of God. The triune God exists in covenant relationship and has made Himself known to us in covenant relationship. Unfortunately, the covenant was turned into a contract. The implications of this will be explored and used as the basis for a fresh understanding of the theology and practice of the Chinese church. Only through the adoption of this relational stance can the Chinese church see her way out of this cultural captivity.

The dissertation will be presented in three parts. The first part will deal with Christianity and culture in general and the Chinese understanding of god within her cultural framework.

The second part will state the dogma of the trinity and the covenant. God's self-disclosure as Father, Son, and Spirit is the central theme of the Christian faith. It is the 'root' doctrine from which all theology and practice is derived. The way in which the church in its two millennia of history has distorted this understanding according to the cultural norm will be reviewed briefly. The Chinese church fits into this pattern. This will lead us to conclude that her traits of ethnocentricity, egocentricity, and isolationism, in fact, correspond to the denial of the Father, Son, and Spirit.

The third part will deal with specific issues in theology and practice in order to highlight the theological deficiency. In particular, the theology of blessing and ministry will be presented and contrasted with the contractual cultural framework. The new framework of the triune communion with the Father in the Spirit through Jesus Christ will be presented as the basis on which the transformation can be achieved—the transformation that will liberate the Chinese church from her cultural captivity.

The goal of this paper is the shift of Chinese thinking from the humanistic and naturalistic framework rooted in her cultural heritage to see that the Christian faith cannot be planted on this basis and that the establishment of this triune faith is the work of the triune Godhead.

Acknowledgement

My interest in the topic came after I attended the Fuller Seminary Doctor of Ministry seminar conducted by Prof James Torrance on 'Theology of Worship' held in Melbourne in 1993. I wrote a paper titled 'A Personal Reflection on the Chinese Churches in the Light of the Trinity' as my postseminar project. I reflected on my experiences in a Chinese church and on my interactions with others in similar Chinese churches throughout Australia. I had difficulties with some of their practices but until then was not able to think through the issues involved in a coherent manner. The seminar enabled me to see clearly the core issues involved.

Two years prior to the seminar in Melbourne, in 1991, I was at the New Creation Teaching Ministry Pastors' School held in Adelaide. It was conducted by the late Rev Dr Geoffrey Bingham (principal) and others on the topic 'Trinitarian Theology: Human Unity and Relationships'. This opened up to me a new dimension in my thinking and laid the foundation for the resolution of my own difficulties. Dr Bingham has also stimulated and encouraged me to work through many other related theological issues and given me the opportunity to present some of them at his pastors' school in subsequent years.

Much of the work done here is a personal pilgrimage in trying to understand my heritage as a Chinese and to relate that to the situation in which I find myself, i.e. in trying to resolve the contradiction between Christianity and my culture. The primary problem is that we have subordinated the gospel to our culture, and this dissertation seeks to show that this is so. The heart of Christianity is the triune God and the way He has related with His creation in the covenant. This will be the fulcrum on which the evaluation of the Chinese church will be made.

As I read more on the issues involved, I realised the brevity of the project I wrote in 1993 and wanted to enlarge on that. The doctor of ministry dissertation presents the opportunity. I knew I had to do more work on the Chinese heritage to form a basis for the critique. Further work on the topic was presented to Dr Hoover Wong as an independent study on 'Christianity and the Chinese Culture'.

I also want to acknowledge the advice given to me by Dr Ching-Hwang Yen, associate professor in history at the University of Adelaide, in correcting my understanding of Confucianism and certain aspects of the Chinese culture. However, any remaining defects remain mine.

I want to express my thanks to those who have helped me to understand my cultural heritage and enabled me to see my glorious inheritance from the Father in the Spirit through Jesus Christ our Lord.

Part One

THE CULTURAL CAPTIVITY OF THE CHURCH

Part One, Chapter 1

CULTURE: GENERAL CONSIDERATIONS

This chapter will discuss the general issues of culture and point out that the church has mistaken culture for Christianity. As has happened in the missionary outreach, to embrace Christianity is to embrace Western culture.

1.1. What is Culture?

The word *culture* is derived from the Latin verb *colere*, which means 'to cultivate' or 'to care for', e.g. agriculture.

It is not easy to define culture. We can talk about the culture of a nation or of a community or of a church. It is the sum of how we conduct ourselves and is expressed in language, actions, or the arts. It is part of what we mean by being human. One may say that culture is what we do that give us meaning. The following are two attempts to define culture:

1. A set of common understandings for organising actions and language and other symbolic vehicles for expressing common understanding.[1]

---

[1] P Frost, *Organisational Culture* (Newbury Park, CA: Sage, 1985), 170–172.

2. 'Culture is religion made visible; it is religion actualized in the innumerable relations of daily life.'[2]

Perhaps a quote from Tevye, in *Fiddler on the Roof*, may help us here:

> Because of our traditions, we keep our sanity. . . . Tradition tells us how to sleep, how to work, how to wear clothes. . . . How did it get started? I don't know—it's a tradition. . . . Because of our traditions, everyone knows who he is and what God expects of him!

There is some truth is what Tevye said. Culture is what gives us meaning as we relate with the external world. The pattern of life we know, i.e. our culture allows us to express the values we hold. Therefore, as our values change, so will our culture. So while our culture shapes our lives, we, in turn, as our values change, will cause changes in our culture.

Niebuhr categorised several characteristics of culture[3] that will help us come to a more workable definition.

1. It is social. Culture is very much the way of life of the community. It contains within it symbols and forms that the whole community understands and feels comfortable with. These forms and symbols provide the meaning and security for the social existence of the community.
2. It is human achievement. There is evidence of human purposiveness in culture and, as Niebuhr exemplifies, 'a river is nature, a canal culture; a raw piece of quartz is nature, an arrowhead culture; a moan is natural, a word cultural'.[4] These accomplishments are the heritage of the community and require continued input for their maintenance.
3. It speaks of the values of humankind. The human achievements are designed for a purpose indicating the value system of the community. These achievements are important for those who create them, e.g. European art is not afraid to display the bodily forms whereas Chinese art tends to hide them and emphasises symmetry.

---

[2] J H Bavinck, *The Impact of Christianity on the Non-Christian World* (Grand Rapids: Eerdmans, 1948), 57.

[3] H R Niebuhr, *Christ and Culture* (New York, Harper and Row, 1951), 32–38.

[4] Ibid., 33.

4. It is for the good of humankind. In a general sense, this is so. What is considered good for humankind is dependent on the value system of the community, and as we will see later, this value system results directly from the concept of the transcendent, i.e. the community's idea of god.
5. It is concerned with the temporal and the material realisation of values. To put this in modern business language, it is the realisation of the goals of the community so that the community can see it in tangible forms.
6. It is concerned with the conservation of those values. If the achievement of culture strikes at the core value of the community, then it is not difficult to see that no effort is spared in the conservation of those values. Thus, we see that a culture reflects the community's value system governed by its concept of the transcendent.

It is difficult to define culture in a few words or sentences. Culture is the sum of all human activities by a community over long periods, imposed upon the environment so as to enable the human person to be 'at peace' with the self and the environment. The above characteristics pointed out by Niebuhr serve to highlight the issues involved in culture. Falling back onto one's culture is a useful way to 'justify' one's action if one is in need of justification. On the other hand, one would need to be very careful in confronting a culture as it will bring forth the wrath of the community. The questioning of one's culture indicates a transgression of the ideals and values that the community holds. A useful definition of culture is given by Kroeber and Kluckhohn:

> Culture consists of patterns, explicit and implicit, of and for behaviour acquired and transmitted by symbols, constituting the distinctive achievement of human groups, including their embodiments in artefacts; the essential core of culture consists of traditional (i.e. historically derived and selected) ideas and especially their attached values; culture systems may, on the one hand, be considered as products of action, on the other as conditioning elements of further action.[5]

---

[5] A Kroeber and C Kluckhohn, *Culture: A Critical Review of Concepts and Definitions* (New York: Vintage Books, 1952), 357, quoted in C H Kraft, *Christianity in Culture* (New York: Orbis, 1979), 46.

Though this is quite a lengthy statement, nonetheless, this gives a working definition of culture. The complexity of culture does not allow one to reduce it to a simplistic formula. The following section will expand on this concept in order to obtain a more comprehensive idea of culture and to see the way it captivates the human person and the society.

1.2. The Study of Culture

Culture is not an exact science whereby our analytical tools can provide us with assured results. Difficult though it may be, these are still useful analytical tools, which will enable us to study culture and to understand how it operates in our society. They render some objectivity to our understanding of culture. These tools[6] are the following:

1. Psychology and sociology—explain why a particular pattern of behaviour occurs. Though these disciplines are not exact sciences like physics or chemistry, nonetheless, they seek to give some understanding of the behavioural pattern of the person and society. It is easy for some sections of society, e.g. secular humanism, to take the results from these studies as the norm of society. We must not fall into this mistake.
2. Theology and ethics—judge how acceptable the pattern is. Theology must be the central axis around which all the other tools revolve. As an ancient dictum goes, 'Theology is the queen of sciences and philosophy its handmaiden'. The theology of the triune God revealed through the incarnation of Jesus Christ and made real to us by the Holy Spirit must form the starting point of our reflection.[7] Informed by the perfect humanity of Jesus Christ, we then evaluate the psychological and the sociological in an attempt to understand where humanity is at and where humanity ought to be.
3. Organisation development—change the pattern. This is not an easy process as most people are reluctant to change. Yet change does happen, and to the Christian mind, this only makes sense when one is aware that our God is working within history to bring about His eternal purpose. L Schaller, in his book *The Change*

---

[6] C Dudley, *Building Effective Ministry* (San Francisco: Harper and Row, 1983), 80.

[7] This is indeed to centre point of the dissertation and will be taken up in chapter 3, 'The Heart of Christianity: The Triune God and the Covenant'.

Agent,[8] acknowledges the difficulty of this process. He views change as a balance of forces operating at the particular situation. It requires all the tools mentioned as many of the situations in life are not two dimensional but multifactorial and require skills to balance the forces acting upon them. He cited a crisis as an opportunity for change. People are more ready to accept change in a crisis than at any other times. Another important factor in causing change is the level of trust a leader has to instill in the group he leads.

4. Ethnography and literary criticism—help in exploring the pattern and to understand its meaning among those who undertake it. This is not an easy undertaking as it is immensely difficult to unravel the assumptions of a culture in order to understand it.[9] This will be discussed in more detail below when we see the link between the underlying assumptions and the artefacts (external manifestations) of a culture.

Carl Dudley[10] presented the above when he was writing about culture in relation to the local church. All the above tools are necessary in arriving at a balanced picture of what the culture of any community is, whether it be the church or an organisation. If only the theological and ethical are used, then one becomes very judgemental without a compassionate understanding of how that situation has arisen. If only a sociological or psychological approach is used, then one will compromise the norm because what that community ought to be will become clouded. What is central is theological and ethical considerations. They give some standard by which culture can be interpreted. This is what our postmodern culture is lacking. Of course, this interpretation may be altered when there is an interaction between culture and hermeneutics. This will be discussed further later in this paper.

We can look at culture at four levels:[11]

1. Artefacts—these are the external manifestations of a culture. They are the easiest facets of a culture to be studied and this can be

---

[8] L Shaller, *The Change Agent* (Nashville: Abingdon Press, 1972).

[9] Some pointers as to how this process may proceed are given in the next section, '1.3. Uncovering the Assumptions'.

[10] C Dudley, *Building Effective Ministry*, 80.

[11] P Frost, *Organisational Culture*, 171–172.

done by observation. However, to stop here would mean that we miss the way these manifestations have developed. There is a relationship between the outward forms and the inner meanings. This relationship is well presented by P Hiebert in his article 'Form and Meaning in the Contextualisation of the Gospel'.[12] Some discussion of his configuration will be presented below.

2. Perspectives—this is the way the external world is viewed. The way the external world appears to us depends precisely on the way we view it, i.e. according to our perspectives. We then respond to this perceived external world and produce the artefacts, i.e. the cultural forms. For example, if one perceives the workers in a workplace to be unreliable, then one would develop a legal system of checks, e.g. the workers will need to clock in and out at the workplace.

3. Values—the values that one holds will determine what one's perspective is. Many Chinese communities put a high value on saving face, i.e. one should not embarrass the other or highlight the fault of the other in public. In this way, one's perspective of the external world would be to avoid facing the harsh realities and a culture of artificiality develops.

4. Assumptions—here we come to the very foundation of culture. These assumptions are shared by the community and are sometimes very difficult to uncover. This aspect of culture will be explored in more detail below.

What we see in a culture is only what is external, i.e. the expressions or the artefacts. What produced the artefacts are the perspectives with which one sees the world and people. These perspectives are determined by the values one holds; and this is ultimately dependent on the assumptions we hold regarding life, the world, and who God is.

P Hiebert's analysis of the relationship between the external forms and the underlying meaning has been referred to above. He pointed out that the external forms and the underlying meaning are not to be equated, as in positivism, or be separated, as in pragmatism. The former was employed by Western missions, and the introduction of Western tunes and ritual forms was thought to preserve Christian meanings.[13] Conversely, the divorce between forms and meaning will

---

[12] P Hiebert, 'Form and Meaning in the Contextualisation of the Gospel', *The Word among Us*, ed. D Gilliland (USA: Word Publishing, 1989), 101–120.

[13] This will be elaborated on in the section below: '1.4. Missions and Culture'.

only reinforce the dualism that is already so prevalent in our society. It will also reduce Christianity to a set of beliefs with no change in behaviour. The greatest danger in separating meaning from form, Hiebert contends,

> is the relativism and pragmatism this introduces. Relativism undermines our concern for the truth of the gospel. Pragmatism turns our attention from the cosmic history of creation-fall-redemption to solving the immediate problems of our everyday life.[14]

Yet there is a relationship between form and meaning. This is complex, and Hiebert presents four configurations[15] to enable us to see the relationship between them. We need to note that these are not absolute categories as they represent points in a spectrum of relationships. These are the following:

1. Meanings and forms arbitrarily linked. He cites the use of language and the way the usage of words can change with the passage of time.
2. Meanings and forms loosely linked. These are areas where the forms are most dependent on the perspectives of the community. He cites universal symbols such as colours and animals; natural symbols such as body forms and sexual union; and, finally, cultural symbols such as books, cars, and radios in today's technological society. The forms and meanings are linked on the basis of similarities and analogies and result from our common humanity on earth.
3. Meanings and forms tightly linked. These are symbols that provide the skeleton on which the rest of a culture hangs. They provide stability for a community. These are expressive symbols such as laughter, cry, groans, dance, and music. Next are the ritual symbols such as going to church and the sacraments. He cites Douglas who notes that 'one of the characteristics of modernity is the divorce of form and meaning'.[16]
4. Forms equated with meanings. Here, the forms and the meanings cannot be separated as to change one is to change the other. Firstly,

---

[14] P Hiebert, 'Form and Meaning in the Contextualization of the Gospel', 108.

[15] Ibid., 108–116.

[16] M Douglas, *Purity and Danger* (London: Routledge and Kegan Paul, 1966), chapter 3, quoted in P Hiebert, 'Form and Meaning in the Contextualization of the Gospel', 114.

the historical facts about the incarnation, the life, the death, and the resurrection of Jesus Christ cannot be altered without producing heresies. Secondly, performative symbols, such as the pronouncement of the 'husband and wife' in a marriage ceremony, must take the force of the words said. Lastly, boundary symbols such as fences and line marking on roads and sporting fields mean precisely that.

This may be illustrated with a diagram from Stott and Coote in *Down to Earth*:[17]

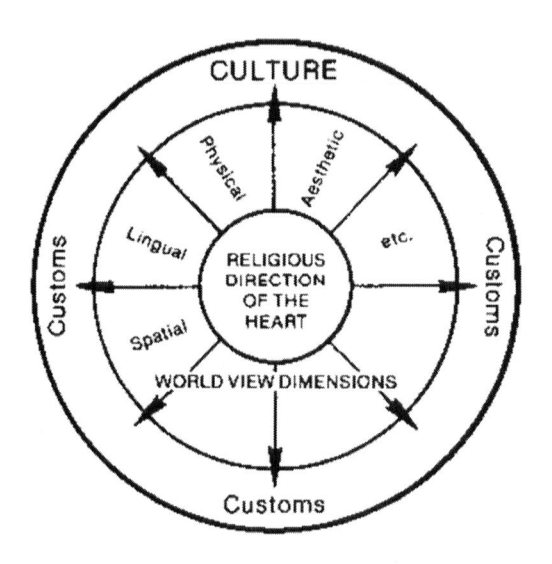

Figure 1. The Core Assumptions and Culture

The way we see the external world depends on these assumptions and in particular the core assumption or, as expressed in the figure above, the religious directions of the heart. These assumptions are not easy to define. Based on these assumptions, we construct a framework in our minds on which we insert the perception we receive. Through this framework, we see the external world and hold in our minds what we perceive to be reality. Kraft refers to this as a process of theory and model building on the part of the observer.[18] All our observations are subject to the grid that exists in our minds.

---

[17] Lausanne Consultation on Gospel and Culture, *Down to Earth*, eds. J Stott and R Coote (London: Hodder and Stoughton, 1981), 149.

[18] C H Kraft, *Christianity in Culture*, 28.

When we look at culture we, are only looking at the artefacts, i.e. what is external. There are values and assumptions that produce those artefacts. Any culture, i.e. the artefacts, may change depending on the basic assumptions that the community holds. As we probe into these underlying assumptions in sociological studies, various dimensions have been uncovered. Around these underlying assumptions, cultural paradigm form. These assumptions are:

1. Humanity's relationship to nature—at the organizational level, do the key members view the relationship of the organization to its environment as one of dominance, submission, harmonising, finding an appropriate niche, or what?
2. The nature of reality and truth—the linguistic and behavioural rules that define what is real and what is not, what is a 'fact', how truth is ultimately to be determined, and whether truth is 'revealed' or 'discovered'—basic concepts of time and space.
3. The nature of human nature—what does it mean to be 'human', and what attributes are considered intrinsic or ultimate? Is human nature good, evil, or neutral? Are human beings perfectible or not?
4. The nature of human activity—what is the 'right' thing for human beings to do on the basis of the above assumptions about reality, the environment, and human nature: to be active, passive, self-developmental, fatalistic, or what? What is work, and what is play?
5. The nature of human relationships—what is considered to be the 'right' way for people to relate to one another, to distribute power and love? Is life cooperative or competitive; individualistic, group collaborative, or communal; based on traditional lineal authority, law, charisma, or what?[19]

This list of assumptions is taken from the book by E Schein, *Organizational Culture and Leadership*. It deals with social and behavioural science and does not claim to be theological, yet it lists the very issues that relate to the heart of theology. While it would be of great interest to discuss each of these assumptions in the theological framework, it is not the purpose of this dissertation to do so. However, references will be made to these assumptions in the relevant sections of this dissertation. Some of

---

[19] E Schein, *Organisational Culture and Leadership* (San Francisco: Jossey-Bass, 1985), 85–111. I came across this while reading for the Fuller's Doctor of Ministry Seminar on 'Management and Leadership'. I have reproduced in full what is in tabular form in the book as the issues involved are summarised succinctly.

these assumptions will be cited in relation to the Chinese culture as they find expression in Confucianism, Taoism, and Buddhism.

It suffices just to comment briefly on some of the above assumptions at this stage as they have a bearing on the discussion of the Chinese concept of god. These assumptions are humanity's relationship to nature, the nature of reality and truth, and what it means to be human.

The Chinese have embraced a close relationship between humanity and nature as a result of the five elements theory that forms the basis of an early Chinese cosmology. It was believed that the five elements—wood, fire, water, metal, and earth—were the sources of everything. They succeeded one another in sequence and become mutually destructive of one another in rotation. This was later associated with yin-yang, two opposing yet complementary agents that explain all the phenomena of life. Thus, the Chinese have developed a naturalistic mind and tend to work from nature towards reality. Therefore, the Chinese mind tends to be materialistic, and their appreciation tends to be towards that which is visible.

The understanding of reality and truth finds its basis in the natural. This is seen in the teachings of Confucius. This reasoning from nature is discussed later in 'Section 2.3.1: Ancient Chinese Concepts of God' (terminology for *God* in the Chinese language).

It follows from the above that the Chinese understanding of what it is to be human is based on the naturalistic and materialistic notion. It does not speculate on the origin of the human person. There is little on the notion of creation or evolution in its culture. However, there is much on the mythological stories of the gods and their involvement with human affairs. There is a free intermingling between the gods and humans, but there is no hint of any union in the way they relate.

These assumptions raised here will be further discussed in the second chapter under the 'Section 2.3.: The Chinese Understanding of God'.

1.3. Uncovering the Assumptions

It is of interest here to explore briefly how one can uncover some of these cultural assumptions. As the process involved is complicated, I can only make reference to part of the methodology used. One should not assume that these cultural assumptions could be easily perceived as they are often very deeply ingrained into the minds of the community and often shared by the community. Furthermore, subjectivity on the part of the investigator can often lead to false inferences. In order to avoid this, it requires a close interaction with the group in order to experience the culture and from this to arrive at the values that the group holds. In the process, it is necessary that the investigator finds an 'insider' who is analytical and willing to disclose some of the 'intricacies' of the internal workings of the group. Mere observations on the part of the investigator are often misleading without some knowledge of the values held by the group. When sufficient information has been collected, the investigator needs to formulate a working hypothesis and then tests its predictive value. Only in this way can one build up a 'model' of the culture.

Sometimes an interview system may work, but this depends on the openness of those interviewed. This can be used in conjunction with the above in order to supplement the findings. However, what is most difficult to evaluate are the myths, legends, and stories held by the group as these are very powerful images in the development of a culture.[20] What is most difficult about this process is that the deepest-held assumptions may not even be evident to those within the community, i.e. the assumptions are held in subconscious and not verbalised.

1.4. Missions and Culture

When we look at these dimensions of thinking, i.e. the assumptions listed at the end of the previous section, we see that these are the issues that deal with reality and our understanding of God and man. These are the fundamental issues for us to engage. A culture will not change unless there is a change in these underlying assumptions. Writing on the issue of pluralism, D A Carson commented, 'Recognised or not, the doctrine of God lies at the heart of contemporary debates over pluralism.'[21] What we do so often is to address culture at the artefact level, i.e. we try to change the external manifestation of a culture. It appears that the missionary movement in the past has focused on changing this external artefact of culture rather than the core assumption.

In the tenth section of the Lausanne Covenant of 1974, the authors made this comment. 'Missions have all too frequently exported with the gospel an alien culture, and churches have sometimes been in bondage to culture rather than to Scripture.'[22] This was again brought up in a volume of Fuller's *Theology, News and Notes*.

---

[20] These issues are discussed in some detail in E. Schein, *Organizational Culture*, chap. 5, 112–136.

[21] D A Carson, 'Christian Witness in an Age of Pluralism', in *God and Culture*, eds. D A Carson and J D Woodbridge (Grand Rapids: Eerdmans, 1993), 46.

[22] C R Padilla, *The New Face of Evangelicalism* (London: SCM, 1982), 177.

The failure to differentiate between the gospel and Western culture has been one of the greatest weaknesses of Western Christian missions. Western missionaries too often have equated the gospel with their own cultural background.[23]

The authors of the above two quotations have put in strong words an indictment of our missionary movement. As one who heard the gospel first preached by the mission movement from the West, I can affirm that this is so. Vincent Donovan, a Catholic missionary, in his book *Christianity Rediscovered*,[24] speaks against the cultural and structural approach to missions. In a radical departure from accepted mission practice, he worked on the core assumptions and simply taught the Masai people what God is like and what Jesus Christ has come to do. In so doing, the core assumptions are changed, and he allowed the Masai people to work these assumptions into the artefacts of their culture.

He expressed the reason for his approach succinctly in this way.

> Because a missionary comes from another already existing church, *that* is the image of church he will have in mind, and if his job is to establish a church, *that* is the church he will establish. I think, rather, the missionary's job is to preach, not the church, but Christ. If he preaches Christ and the message of Christianity, the church may well result, may well appear, but it might not be the church he had in mind.[25]

There needs to be an openness regarding what may eventuate as result of our ministry. Whether we view our churches as organisations or communities, they should really be seen as cultures. The perceptions and experiences of any culture are expressed in what we term *myths*.[26] Dominant myth within a community goes back to the past and is not easily assessable to change. This is so because these 'symbols' are held as representation of reality in the minds of the people. Within the powerful symbols in a culture, people find

---

[23] G P Alexander, 'The Changing Hands of Leadership', *Diversity: Threat or Opportunity?* Fuller's Theology, Notes and News (Dec. 1993), 5.

[24] V. Donovan, *Christianity Rediscovered* (London: SCM, 1982).

[25] Ibid., 81.

[26] The term 'myth' is used in a technical sense. See P. Frost, *Organisational Culture*, 288.

the meaning of life.[27] Analysis of the culture is not easy as what is deepest in people's feelings is often not verbalised. There is no easy solution for the pastor. To understand, a particular culture, e.g. church culture, requires a patient and close interaction with the membership in an effort to learn from them so as to feel with them what their symbols of reality are.

It has been pointed out that much of the conflict between pastors and congregations is in the area of changes and decisions,[28] i.e. at the artefact level. This is to misunderstand the true nature of our ministry, which, as Vincent Donovan pointed out, is at the level of the assumptions and indeed the core assumption. Many of us in pastoral ministry are really tinkering at the periphery without making the changes that matter most. We have often missed the opportunities given to us as ministers of the gospel to minister the essentials of the gospel.

1.5. Defining Christianity

Because we are locked into our culture, we will see Christianity with cultural glasses, and the Christ that we have come to know may have been a product of our culture. The god of some of the Chinese may have been the god of Confucianism, the god of Taoism or the god of Buddhism, or a blend of the three. The god of Schleiermacher is the god of the aristocrat culture, and H Richard Niebuhr in his most expressive style describes this god of liberal theology thus: 'A god without wrath brought men without sin into a kingdom without judgement through the ministrations of a Christ without a cross'.[29]

We cannot approach the subject of Christianity and the Chinese culture without defining Christianity. Now Christianity cannot be defined by the Christians or by the community of the Christians as they do not exist as perfect entities. Christianity has to be defined by its very founder, i.e. by Christ Himself. The question 'Who is God?' must be answered in Trinitarian terms, that is, He is the 'God who exists in the Triunity of Father, Son and Holy Spirit'.[30] Christ can only be defined by the triunity

---

[27] Ibid., 234.

[28] R Croucher's article reprinted in *New Life* (30 June, 1994): 11.

[29] H R Niebuhr, *The Kingdom of God in America* (New York: Harper and Row, 1959), 193.

[30] This paper does not allow space to deal with this immense subject. The Triunity of the Godhead and the Covenant will be dealt with in a brief manner historically in the third chapter of this paper.

of the Godhead in which He exists[31] and that understanding comes from the revelation that Christ Himself brings. God can only be known through God Himself, and this is given to us in the revelation of the triunity of the Godhead. This will be discussed in more detail in chapter 3.

1.6. The Hermeneutics of Culture and the Culture of Hermeneutics

When we can interpret our own culture, we come to understand ourselves. When we confront a culture, we need to interpret that culture in terms of its core assumptions and not according to the 'invading' culture. This is not an easy process. More often, we judge it in terms of our own understanding and methodology. We may think of culture as a text that has come to us and we need to interpret it. We can look at culture sociologically, historically, and philosophically, as well as theologically.

The problem of hermeneutics can only be dealt with superficially here. There is no doubt that we bring to the Bible our presuppositions. Indeed, it was Bultmann who insisted that 'there cannot be any such thing as presuppositionless exegesis'.[32] I have mentioned above a few of the cultural gods that Christians have created.

As we interact with the text of scripture, the so-called hermeneutical circle is set up.[33] The deeper the appreciation of the text,[34] the more it informs us of our culture, and the richer the understanding of our culture, the greater our appreciation of the text; and so a deepening spiral is established. This is illustrated in the following diagram.[35]

---

[31] I apologise that this may sound preposterous to make the claim that one is able to define Christ. How could any creature seek to define the Creator? However, for the purpose of this paper, the Chinese mind needs some statement to start its thinking; and in the course of the paper, the response to the Creator will be emphasised.

[32] R Bultmann, *Existence and Faith* (New York: Meridian, 1960), 347.

[33] C R Padilla, 'Hermeneutics and Culture', *Down to Earth*, 75–76.

[34] Hermeneutics is often discussed in relation to the text of scripture, but in this context, I am using it to refer to the text of our culture, i.e. the artefacts of our culture.

[35] Ibid., 75.

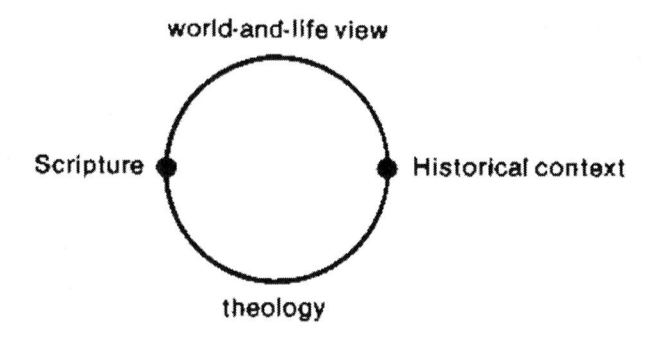

```
              world-and-life view

Scripture  ●              ●  Historical context

                 theology
```

Figure 2. The Hermeneutical Circle

The late bishop Lesslie Newbigin also made reference to the hermeneutical circle recognising that

> no one comes to the text with a completely vacant mind. Everyone comes with a pre-understanding: without this no understanding is possible. But the reader must also, in a sense, place a temporary moratorium on his judgement, allow the text to speak in its own way, and accept the possibility that the pre-understanding will be changed into a new understanding.[36]

However, he did not feel that the hermeneutical circle is adequate to explain the relationship between the gospel and culture.[37] It is not simply that one informs the other. The Enlightenment has resulted in modern historical and critical studies that have informed us about the biblical texts in ways that earlier traditions had not appreciated. These technical studies are likened to the fingering of the pianist. Yet music is produced not by concentration on the fingering but when the 'mind and soul are wrapped up in the glory of the music, completely forgetting the finger work'.[38] In this context, Bishop Newbigin sees the relationship between culture and gospel, i.e. the two are so intertwined and are expressed in the whole of Christian living. He quotes from Stuhlmacher, 'The biblical texts can be fully interpreted only from a dialogical situation defined by the venture of Christian existence as it is lived

---

[36] L Newbigin, *Foolishness to the Greeks* (Grand Rapids: Eerdmans, 1986), 51.

[37] Ibid., 53.

[38] Ibid., 57.

in the church.'[39] Only in the faith and obedience of active discipleship—which embraces the whole of life, both private and public—is faith nourished.[40]

1.7. Christ and Culture

Niebuhr's classic work on *Christ and Culture* remains a most useful framework for our thinking on this issue. His classification of the relationship between Christ and culture into five neat categories does not imply that these are separate entities; but rather, in many of the responses to define the relationship of Christ and culture, there are components of these five elements. In some responses, one of these may stand out more than others while in some responses there are several of these elements intertwined together.

The categories in Niebuhr's framework are the following:

1. Christ against culture
2. The Christ of culture
3. Christ above culture
4. Christ and culture in paradox
5. Christ, the transformer of culture

The antithesis between Christ and culture is set out in the first two responses. The first response is closely associated with asceticism and is best exemplified by Tertullian's classic question, 'What has Athens to do with Jerusalem?' It demands an either-or decision. The second response recognises Jesus's incarnation in the Jewish culture and that He expressed Himself within that culture. In its attempt to reconcile Christ and culture, it moves in the direction of an accommodation to the culture and eventually subordinates Christ to the culture. This has been mentioned above in reference to the god of Schleiermacher.

As a way to express the relationship between Christ and culture, Niebuhr sets out the following three responses of which the last response, where Christ is seen as the transformer of culture, best expresses the biblical viewpoint. The latter three propositions try to hold in tension something of the inevitability of culture in the expression of humankind and the claims of Jesus Christ upon them. The 'Christ above culture' motif acknowledges the cultural expression

---

[39] P Stuhlmacher, *Historical Criticism and Theological Interpretation of Scripture* (Philadelphia: Fortress, 1977), 89, quoted in L Newbigin, *Foolishness to the Greeks*, 57.

[40] L Newbigin, *Foolishness to the Greeks*, 58.

of humankind and tries to maintain that with a centredness in Christ. This will produce some degree of perfection in the cultural expression. A synthesis of the two is produced. The danger of this is that it tends to absolutise that which is relative and eventually drift towards the 'Christ of culture' motif. Holding that 'Christ and culture exist in paradox' keeps the tension between Christ and culture and acknowledges the authority of both. It maintains a dualism, and this is the position that Luther held. It sees a conflict between the two, and the life is then lived in great tension.

1.8. The Transformation of Culture

The culture of our day is pluralistic. However, our present pluralistic culture is not new. Pluralism existed in the early church, and how the early church dealt with it is well discussed in M Green's book, *Evangelism in the Early Church*.[41] We work in an open and tolerant society even when there is strong disagreement with our ideas.[42]

In such a pluralistic culture, more and more Christians are pushed against the wall, and we need to be able to trim off the peripheral and nonessential and stand on what makes Christianity distinctive. This very distinctive feature must reside within the nature of the God that we worship. In the book *God and Culture*, the author concludes the subsection on 'Christian Witness in an Age of Pluralism' with the question 'How then shall we know what God is like?' He then continues in the next two subsections to discuss the question of revelation in the Christian faith.[43] We cannot know God from our human categories of thought. God can only be known by God Himself and that communication from Him regarding His nature is what we refer to as revelation.

The question 'Who God is?' lies at the heart of our debate over pluralism. While we work through the culture of our day, Christianity needs to exert an influence to shape culture as well. We need to go back again and again to the revelation of the Trinitarian God to judge culture and not allow the present pluralism to chip away at our foundation and captivate us to the worship of a cultural god.

If this transformation is to take place, it must take place at the level of the assumptions and not at the artefactual level. This is the deepest level of

---

[41] M Green, *Evangelism in the Early Church* (Grand Rapids: Eerdmans, 1970), 13–47.

[42] D A Carson, 'Christian Witness in an Age of Pluralism', *God and Culture*, 31–66.

[43] Ibid., 49–60.

the human person, and the transformation that takes place is 'spiritual'.[44] This will lead to a change in the cultural pattern.

The transformation of culture is the transformation of the conceptual system of the culture,[45] i.e. a transformation of the core assumptions. As the human person is an integral whole, the core assumptions will work through to the artefactual level. Kraft further maintains that by the transformation of the 'core concepts as the people's understanding and commitment to God, such peripheral matters as polygamy and infanticide will be dealt with in due time, . . . under the leading of God'.[46]

Much has been written about contextualisation, and it has been popularly understood that this is the process whereby the gospel is put into the context of the cultural framework. In so doing, it will only serve to distort the gospel, making it subordinate to the culture. This has indeed happened. Covell corrects this understanding and makes the point that the aim of contextualisation is 'not so much to accommodate itself to a specific culture as to change the culture to conform to the demands of the gospel'.[47]

We will leave the general discussion of Christianity and culture here and will take up the point again in our critique of the Chinese culture after we have examined it in the next chapter.

Kraft also refers to the work of Nida, the absolute supracultural and our relative culture-bound expression:

> Biblical relativism is not a matter of inconsistency but a recognition of the different cultural factors, which influence standards and actions. While the Koran attempts to fix for all time the behavior of Muslims, the Bible clearly establishes the principle of relative relativism, which permits growth, adaptation, and freedom, under the Lordship of Jesus Christ. . . . The Christian position is not one of static conformance to dead rules, but of dynamic obedience to a living God.[48]

---

[44] As the discussion takes us into the Triune God, then it is the Spirit of God that works this transformation.

[45] C H Kraft, *Christianity in Culture*, 349.

[46] Ibid., 364.

[47] R Covell, *Confucius, The Buddha, and Christ* (New York: Orbis, 1986), 15.

[48] E Nida, *Customs and Cultures* (New York: Harper and Row, 1954), 52, quoted in C H Kraft, *Christianity in Culture*, 128.

Part One, Chapter 2

THE TREND OF THINKING AMONG OVERSEAS CHINESE CHURCHES

This chapter will discuss the impact of the Chinese culture upon the Chinese churches and how culture has ordered the churches' concept of god. Culture has been the framework on which Christianity is understood and practised by the Chinese. All cultures will do the same. The chapter will seek to engage some aspects of the Chinese cultural framework in order to understand it. This is done to identify the points of strength and weakness so that we have a model for our critique from which we can propose changes in the light of the gospel. These changes will be the subject of chapter 5.

2.1. The Overseas Chinese Churches

The migrant Chinese—and, for that matter, any migrant group—have tended to cluster together wherever they go. This has been the pattern of Chinese migrants worldwide. When the Chinese migrated to Southeast Asia, they formed clans and associations to preserve their ethnic identity. This has been pattern of other migrant groups, and the Chinese Christians are no different. In North America, where the Chinese migrated much earlier than in Australia, there are numerous independent Chinese churches all over the country. Most of them are small churches, managed by one or two dominant families. They are aloof from the mainstream churches and exist in isolation from them. The pattern in Australia in not much different.

In Dr C H Yen's study of the pattern of Chinese migration to Singapore and Malaya in the nineteenth and early part of this century, he made this observation regarding the structure and organisation of the Chinese clans:

> The formal structure of the clan organisation was a three-tier model: a standing committee, a management committee, and rank-and-file membership. The standing committee consisted of the clan head, or *tsu-chang*, . . . a deputy . . . an honorary secretary; an honorary treasurer, and an honorary auditor. These few top office-bearers were elected from among the members of the management committee, who were elected by the rank-and-file members.[49]

Now this three-tiered model of leadership finds parallels in many of the overseas Chinese churches, and it also explains why most of them are managed by one or two dominant families (the clan heads or *tsu-chang*)[50]. They are the ones who make most of the decisions to be executed by the management.

In the last eight or ten years, a large number of Chinese churches, mostly independent and so-called evangelical, have mushroomed in the Eastern States of Australia and, to a lesser extent, in Adelaide. During ACCOE I in 1985, all the Chinese churches were introduced during the conference as there were only about twenty. Today, about fourteen years later, it is a problem just trying to compile a mailing list to send material to all the Chinese churches. As soon as a list is compiled, it is out-of-date because another church has just sprung up.

There are some inherent problems within the Chinese churches in North America and Australia. These are mainly the two factors of ethnicity and self-sufficiency resulting in isolation from other churches and the mainline denominations. The two characteristics of ethnocentrism and self-sufficiency (egocentricism) are hallmarks of the Chinese over the centuries.[51] What is even more disturbing is their isolation from all around

---

[49] C. H. Yen, *A Social History of the Chinese in Singapore and Malaya 1800-1911* (Singapore: OUP, 1986), 79.

[50] In the Chinese churches, they are commonly called the elders or chairman (and/or executives) of the management committee.

[51] These traits will be discussed in chapter 5 of the paper.

them, even in relating to other Chinese churches. This is not a healthy state of affairs, and while justifiable in terms of sociology and certain sections of the church growth movement, this trend falls short of the biblical norm of 'all one in Christ'.

Before going further, we need to make an exception here for the Chinese-speaking churches as their medium of communication does not permit them to move freely outside their ethnic grouping. Despite this, they can still relate with other Chinese-speaking churches in an effort to express the relationship of the visible church. However, because of their sense of self-sufficiency, they have preferred to isolate themselves, reflecting their connectedness with years of tradition of Chinese culture rather than the transformation[52] that should have taken place as a result of their salvation in Jesus Christ.

2.2. The Chinese Understanding of God

This scope in this subsection is indeed very wide, and the treatment can only touch the surface of each of the issues raised. Our concern here is not so much to study all the influences upon the Chinese mind but, rather, to highlight the relevant issues that throw some light on the way the Chinese culture has impacted upon the church and subordinated the gospel.

This subsection will highlight the Chinese terminology for God and the Confucian influence. The other religious influences will be discussed insofar as they impact upon Confucianism, which is the dominant system of thinking in the Chinese mind.[53] The Confucianist influence will be illustrated from the text of the *Analect*.[54] Several influences upon the Chinese mind are discussed briefly below.

---

[52] This has been referred to in the relationship between church and culture in chapter 1.

[53] Other influences on Chinese thinking come mainly from Taoism and Buddhism.

[54] There are many English translations of the *Analects*. The quotations in this dissertation are taken from *The Analects of Confucius*, translation and notes by S. Leys (New York: W W Norton, 1997).

2.2.1. Ancient Chinese Concepts of God (Terminology for 'God' in the Chinese Language)

Chinese concepts of God are referred to by three terms: *shang-ti*, *tien*, and *shen*. They signify different aspects of God. *Shang-ti* refers to the Lord on high. Interestingly, the word *ti* means *emperor*, and *shang* means *above* or *on high*. The worship of shang-ti goes back to the Chinese emperor Shun who worshipped shang-ti in the twenty-third century BC by offering a sacrifice. Shang-ti was worshipped as a supreme ruler over the earth. Now whether shang-ti was a personal or impersonal god has been subjected to extensive debates among scholars. Mateo Ricci (1551–1611), a Jesuit missionary to China, favoured the use of this term, *shang-ti*, to refer to God. He equated shang-ti with the personal God Yahweh of the Bible,[55] and thus this term *shang-ti* has been retained in the Union Version of the Chinese Bible. This brings to the Chinese mind connotations of authoritarianism and oppression, which were inflicted upon the peasants by the emperors.

If this connotation of God is not erased from the Chinese mind and allowed to linger in the background, then it will undermine the Christian gospel. In other words, the gospel would only be grafted onto this concept of shang-ti, and the full significance of the message of grace would not be heard at all. It is not unusual for Christians to hold to the idea that Jesus Christ has come to save us from a judgemental and vengeful Father.

While Mateo Ricci might have thought of shang-ti as the personal God of the Bible, this association does not seem to have been communicated to the Chinese. This term has long been used for an impersonal god. Of course, the use of an expression can change in the course of time; but with the naturalistic mind-set of the Chinese, it would be difficult to alter that understanding as the use of the second term, *tien*, reinforces the correlation with an impersonal god.

The second term, *tien*,[56] refers to the heavens above, an idea that is remote from the minds of the people. The worship of tien (lit. heaven) also goes back to the same period, and it represents the impersonal deity from which are derived the moral standards of man. It is probably close to the Greek concept of Logos. The Roman Catholics preferred the term tien chu, meaning master of heaven, in referring to God. This is a more

---

[55] B. R Ro, 'Chinese Concepts of God and the God of the Bible', *God in Asian Context*, eds. B R Ro and C C Albrecht (Taiwan: ATA, 1988), 169.

[56] There is a sense of fatalism in the use of this term as the decree of *tien* is unavoidable.

neutral term and avoided the connotations of the other term *shang ti*. This was confirmed in a papal decree Ex illa die in 1715. The religion of tien chu is the term the Chinese use for 'Catholicism'. It leans to the idea of natural theology rather than of revelation.

The concept of tien is a powerful force in shaping culture. It is authoritative, and if it is the will of *tien*, then it is difficult for anyone to go against it. It transfers that ultimate authority to the one who invokes the name of tien. Furthermore, it gives a sense of fatalism as all is decreed and unchanging.

The third term, *shen*, is usually used for the spirits. It is a generic term and was not favoured by the early translators. However, this is the term favoured by the modern translation of the Chinese Bible to avoid the connotations of the other two terms. However, this has led to the development of folk religions as will be discussed below.

From this, it can be seen that Chinese thinking about deity has its roots in natural theology rather than from what is revealed. Ricci contributed significantly to this process as a Catholic steeped in natural theology. He leaned heavily in this direction, having found the compatible Chinese mind. This approach of naturalism is inherent in the thinking of Confucius (which we will see later) and Mencius.[57] The starting point in natural theology then is the natural created order, and from this, one presumes that the reasoning process will lead to the knowledge of the Creator.[58] It subordinates grace to nature as we shall see in chapter 4. While this process may lead one to conclude that there is a god, it will not disclose the love of the Father much less the incarnation of the Son and the indwelling of the Spirit.[59]

2.1.3. Confucianism

It is not the intention of this subsection to enter into a comprehensive discussion of Confucianism. Rather, it will highlight the areas in Confucianism that will enable us to see the way this system of philosophy has captivated the Chinese mind for more than two millennia and to see that its influences are still evident in the Chinese churches despite the preaching of the gospel.

---

[57] R R Covell, *Confucius, the Buddha, and Christ* (New York: Orbis, 1986), 46.

[58] Ibid., 97ff.

[59] The knowledge of the Triune God comes from revelation given in the scriptures.

Confucius (551?–478 BC) was a humanist and emphasised moral ethics and human relationships. His philosophy is contained in nine ancient works collected by his followers. These writings are divided into the five classics[60] and the four books.[61] His thoughts and saying were collected and compiled in the *Analects* by his disciples and their followers over some seventy-five years following his death. In the *Analects*, we encounter the real Confucius. Many Chinese do not regard Confucianism as a religion. There is no worship of god in Confucianism. Confucius merely taught that it is good to acknowledge god. This god is an impersonal god and is referred to as *tien* (see above). The basis of the philosophy of Confucius are the four virtues: sincerity, benevolence, filial piety, and propriety. These will be discussed briefly below.

The Chinese mind is oriented towards the practical. Whether this is innate or the result of the Confucianist influence is subject to debate. Confucius teaches the unity of knowledge and actions. In the *Analects*, we read, 'Zigong asked about the true gentleman. The Master said: "He preaches only what he practices"'(Analect 2:13).

---

[60] The five classics are *I Ching* (*Book of Changes*), *Shu Ching* (*Book of History*), *Shih Ching* (*Book of Poetry*), *Li Chi* (*Book of Rites*), and *Ch'un Ch'iu* (*Spring and Autumn Annals*). *I Ching* is one of the core works of the Confucian canon. It consists of texts built around eight trigrams of broken and unbroken lines, and these were developed into sixty-four hexagrams. It is a pseudoscience used by diviners. *Shu Ching* consists of documents purporting to record the words and deeds of ancient rulers to about 1000 BC. *Shu Ching* is an anthology of songs from the feudal states of early Chou, the first and one of the greatest works of Chinese literature. *Li Chi* was compiled about the second century BC and consists of materials of a philosophical nature. *Ch'un Ch'iu* chronicled the feudal of Lu for the years 722–484 BC and is attributed to Confucius himself. L G Thompson, *Chinese Religion: An Introduction* (California: Dickenson Publishing Company, 1975), 124.

[61] The 'four books' (Chinese, *Ssu Shu*) referred to here are the *Confucian Analects*, the *Book of Mencius*, the *Great Learning*, and the *Doctrine of the Mean*. The *Confucian Analects* comprises notes of the sayings and actions of Confucius. They are compiled by later generation of followers. The *Book of Mencius* was compiled under his supervision (390–305 BC). It consists of his conversations and gives an insight to his thoughts. The *Great Learning* is a compilation of the sayings for the structure of society and the development of the self. It is dated around the fourth century BC. The *Doctrine of the Mean* deals with the ambitions of the individual. It is traditionally ascribed to Tzu Ssu, grandson of Confucius. L G Thompson, *Chinese Religion: An Introduction*, 125.

At the heart of Confucianism, the principle of *li* is considered very important. It concerns etiquette and courtesy and forms the central point of his ethics. His ethical stance is more akin to what is discernible from natural theology. Because Confucianism is more a moral philosophy than a religion, emphasis is paid to what constitutes a right relationship between individuals and people. Filial piety expresses this relationship in the home and leads to the cultivation of respectful affection towards one's parents.

However, it should be noted that in these relationships, each remains within one's class distinction as Confucius taught,

> Duke Jing of Qi asked Confucius about government. Confucius replied: 'Let the lord be a lord, the subject be a subject; the father a father; the son a son.' The Duke said, 'Excellent! If indeed the lord is not a lord, the subject not a subject, the father not a father, the son not a son, I could be sure of nothing anymore—not even of my daily food.' (Analect 12:11)

By inference, the Chinese mind could very well conclude, 'Let God be God and man be man.' There is a lack of the sense of union in Confucianist thinking as it is rooted in naturalism. It tends to maintain the distinction between different classes. The Chinese understanding of relationship lies more in terms of harmony rather than union. Therefore, the communion that Christ came to achieve would be difficult for the Chinese mind to conceive. Because the Chinese mind is steeped in naturalism, it conceives of unity in terms of harmony. That is why the Chinese mind is able to hold the concept of harmony (balance) much better than the concept of union. In fact, 'the most deep-rooted desire of the Chinese people is for harmony'.[62]

Moltmann pointed out the excellence of the Chinese in achieving harmony when describing the Forbidden City in Beijing. He wrote:

> The layout reflects perfect harmony; everything matches: left and right, height and width, walls and roofs, foreground and background. . . . Here there is no history of style nor any break in style, but only the one, timeless, uniform harmony. . . . The basic notion of 'harmony' also dominates the old Chinese religion of the *I Ching*. The Chinese people accepted alien religions on the basis of this

---

[62] J Wu 'Chinese Legal and Political Philosophy', *The Chinese Mind*, ed. C. Moore (Honolulu: University of Hawaii Press, 1967), 227.

fundamental pattern. To make a very rough classification, it might be said that ancient Chinese Taoism is the religion of natural harmony; Confucianism is the religion of social harmony; and Buddhism, whether Amitabha or Zen, is the religion of inner spiritual harmony.[63]

We shall see the significance of this quest for harmony later in the way Buddhism was accepted into Chinese society.

As a foundation for the life of perfect goodness, Confucius insisted chiefly on the four virtues of sincerity, benevolence (*jen*), filial piety (*hsiao*), and propriety. As the Confucian system is mainly an ethical system, its underlying principle is that of *jen*, variously translated as 'love', 'goodness', 'humanity', and 'human-heartedness'. It is difficult to find the English equivalent for *jen*, but it may perhaps be best rendered as humanity. It speaks of an inner human capacity to do good or to be humane. *Jen* is a supreme virtue representing human qualities at their best. It is the foundational principle in all relationships. It is an extremely high state of being and rarely acknowledged of any human being by Confucius:

> The Master said: 'I have never seen a man who truly loved goodness and hated evil. Whoever truly loves goodness would put nothing above it; whoever truly hates evil would practice goodness in such a way that no evil could enter him. Has anyone ever devoted all his strength to goodness just for one day? No one ever has, and yet it is not for want of strength—there may be people who do not have even the small amount of strength it takes, but I have never seen any.' (Analect 4:6)

As the Confucianist system does not acknowledge a personal god, it assumes a fundamental innate goodness in the human person and challenges its followers to aspire towards it. This is the Chinese form of pelagianism. This is highlighted in the opening rhyme of the *Three Characters Classics*, which is a primer used as a text for children when they are learning to read. It consists of rhymes arranged in groups of three characters. The opening rhyme affirms that the innate nature of mankind is essentially good. It says,

---

[63] J Moltmann, *Creating a Just Future* (Philadelphia: Trinity Press International, 1989), 88–89.

Ren	zhi	chu,	xing	ben	shan
Humanity	from	beginning,	nature	origin	good

As the system of philosophy is based on nature and humanity, the sense of self and achievement are very powerful forces in the Chinese mind. This explains in part the high achievement of migrant Chinese (and other Asians) in Western societies.

Fundamental to all right relationships is that of filial piety[64] (*hsiao*), which involves the respect and taking care of one's parents. This is a well-known trait of the Chinese and has been the single most important factor binding Chinese societies over the millennia. If this is cultivated, then all other relationships will fall into place. This respect binds the son even after the father's death.

> The Master said: 'When the father is alive, watch the son's aspirations. When the father is dead, watch the son's actions. If three years later, the son has not veered from the father's way, he may be called a dutiful son indeed.' (Analect 1:11)

It can be seen that filial piety 'can lead to subservience, blind obedience and feudalistic oppression.'[65] A Chinese professor, Woon Swee Tin, describes Confucianism in these words: 'It is a closed system that puts excessively emphasis on filial piety, chastity, material achievement, loyalty to family and moderation to the point of insensitivity.'[66] Further quotations from the *Analects* are useful in showing that the Confucian teaching of filial piety, while honouring to one's parents, binds the individual to a system that is closed and insensitive. This is well illustrated in the few quotations below taken from the *Analects*:

> Lord Meng Yi asked about filial piety. The Master said: 'Never disobey.' As Fan Chi was driving him in his chariot, the Master told him: 'Meng Yi asked me about filial piety and I replied: 'Never disobey.' Fan Chi said: 'What does that mean?' The Master said: 'When your parents are

---

[64] The emphasis in this section is on filial piety as it is the leading Chinese moral principle.

[65] R Covell, *Confucius, The Buddha, and Christ*, 190.

[66] Quoted in G. Knight, *The New Israel*, International Theological Commentary, eds. G Knight and F Holmgren (Grand Rapids: Eerdmans, 1985), 57–58.

> alive, serve them according to the ritual. When they die, bury them according to the ritual, make sacrifices to them according to the ritual.' (Analect 2:5)
>
> Lord Meng Wu asked about filial piety. The Master said: 'The only time a dutiful son ever makes his parents worry is when he is sick' (Analect 2:6)
>
> Ziyou asked about filial piety. The Master said: 'Nowadays people think they are dutiful sons when they feed their parents. Yet they also feed their dogs and horses. Unless there is respect, where is the difference?' (Analect 2:7)
>
> Zixia asked about filial piety. The Master said: 'It is the attitude that matters. If young people merely offer their services when there is work to do, or let their elders drink and eat when there is wine and food, how could this ever pass as filial piety?' (Analect 2:8)

As a result of this emphasis on filial piety, a respect for the elders of the community is developed, though this attitude is gradually eroded in the more open societies that the overseas Chinese find themselves in today. Confucius considers that filial piety is the natural corollary of the fundamental virtue of *jen*. The filial is derived from *jen* (humanity). Once this is in place, then the fabric of society is stable and so is the government of the land, as Confucius goes on to explain:

> Master You said: 'A man who respects his parents and his elders would hardly be inclined to defy his superiors. A man who is not inclined to defy his superiors will never foment a rebellion. A gentleman works at the root. Once the root is secured, the Way [*tao*] unfolds. To respect parents and elders is the root of humanity [*jen*].' (Analect 1:2)[67]
>
> Someone said to Confucius: 'Master, why don't you join the government?' The Master said: 'In the Documents it is said: "Only cultivate filial piety and be kind to your brothers, and you will be contributing to the body politic."

---

[67] The brackets are mine in order to aid the non-Chinese reader.

This is also a form of political action; one need not necessarily join the government.' (Analect 2:21)

The ethical concept of filial piety has been pivotal in Chinese society over the millennia. It is claimed as the 'unchanging truth of heaven, the unfailing equity of earth, the [universal] practice of man'.[68] It has 'penetrated into every corner of Chinese life and society, permeating all the activities of the Chinese people'.[69] This is the ethical principle that has enabled the Chinese to maintain the fabric of their society over the centuries. It has preserved order within the society by maintaining the harmonious relationship from generation to generation.

The intellectual activities of the Sung dynasty (960–1279) gave rise to a new system of Confucian thought based on a mixture of Buddhist and Taoist elements; the new school of Confucianism was known as neo-Confucianism. The scholars who evolved this intellectual system were themselves well versed in the other two philosophies. Although primarily teachers of ethics, they were also interested in the theories of the universe and the origin of human nature.

2.2.3. Taoism

Taoism originated in China and was founded by Lao Tzu (604–531 BC). He searched for the 'Way',[70] i.e. the physical and moral laws of nature. The philosophical division of Taoism declined in about the AD fourth century when Buddhism took root in China. The religious division of Taoism borrowed many ideas and cults from Buddhism while the Buddhists took over Taoist terminology to express their philosophy. Thus, Buddhism and Taoism fused in the popular thinking.

The classics of Taoism are the compilations in the *Tao Te Ching* and the collections of parables in the *Chuang-Tzu*, both about the third century BC. It is not a rational philosophy like Confucianism. It is more interested in intuitive wisdom.

Whereas Confucianism urged the individual to conform to the standards of an ideal social system, Taoism maintained that the individual should ignore the dictates of society and seek only to conform with the underlying pattern of the universe, the *tao* ('way'), which can neither be

---

[68] *Book of Filial Piety*, VII. Quoted in Y W Hsieh, 'Filial Piety and Chinese Society', *The Chinese Mind*, 176.

[69] Y W Hsieh, 'Filial Piety and Chinese Society', *The Chinese Mind*, 174–175.

[70] '*Tao*' in Chinese.

described in words nor conceived in thought. To be in accord with *tao*, one has to 'do nothing' (*wu-wei*)—that is, nothing strained, artificial, or unnatural. Through spontaneous compliance with the impulses of one's own essential nature and by emptying oneself of all doctrines and knowledge, one achieves unity with the Tao and derives from it a mystical power (*Tô*).

2.2.4. Buddhism

Buddhism entered China in the AD first century from India and provided the doctrines of transmigration and salvation (Nirvana). It found ready acceptance in China and was very quickly assimilated into Chinese culture and history. This ready acceptance is probably because of the common trend of natural theology, which the Chinese mind and Buddhism shared.

Buddhism flourished during the period (AD 156–220) where there was social disintegration, political disunity, and culture chaos. In such a context of intense suffering, Buddhism spread.[71] Buddhism met the practical needs of the people during that time. It also provided 'new answers, many of them transcendental, in contrast to Confucian ideology, and was able in a flexible manner, easily adaptable to differing conditions in north and south, to provide answers that all levels of Chinese society were able to appropriate for their own needs'.[72]

Buddhism taught the four noble truths:

1. Life is full of suffering.
2. Most of that suffering, including the fear of that suffering, can be traced to 'desire', the mind's habit of seeing everything through the prism of the self and its well-being.
3. This craving can be transcended, leading to peace and eventually to an exalted state of full enlightenment called Nirvana.
4. That the means to do that lies in the eightfold path of proper views, resolve, speech, action, livelihood, effort, mindfulness, and concentration.

Buddhism is able to give a rational explanation and a hope for suffering, which makes it readily identifiable with the peasant community in China. For the majority of the peasants, suffering is their lot and the hope of a

---

[71] R Covell, *Confucius, The Buddha, and Christ*, 137.

[72] Ibid., 139.

better future continues to sustain them in their suffering. It is no wonder that the masses embraced Buddhism so readily.

Buddhism spread throughout the East, and as it separates from the mainstream, it developed characteristics of its own in each of its branches.

1. Theravada (Southeast Asia)—this branch remains closest to the original, concentrating on meditation-aided awareness. It regarded the Buddha as a great sage but not a deity.
2. Mahayana (China, Japan, and Korea)—it maintains the four noble truths and the practice of meditation. It regards the Buddha as divinity.
3. Zen—adopted by the Japanese samurai class.

It is interesting that Timothy Richards, a radical Baptist missionary, found great affinity between the Christian faith and two portions of the Buddhist scriptures: the *Lotus Scripture* and *The Awakening of Faith*. He saw the doctrine of immortality in the *Lotus Scriptures* and was also impressed by the teachings of light and love and the patient endurance of wrongs. He also saw the goddess Kwan Yin as parallel to the love and compassion of God.[73]

There are certainly similarities here. These similarities may be because of the common Mesopotamian origin.[74] Humanity is created in the image of God, and the similarities reflect this relationship. While this is to be acknowledged, it does not allow one to build upon this as the foundation because this approach does not acknowledge the uniqueness of Jesus as the Son of God and the only One who came from the bosom of the Father to reveal Him.

Buddhism made an impact in China. This is partly because of its ability to accommodate to the Chinese situation and partly because of the genius of the Chinese mind in constructing a harmony between Buddhism and Confucianism. That the Chinese mind is well skilled in this harmonisation has been mentioned above. The lack of an authority figure in Buddhism helps in its accommodation to Chinese life. The teaching of a life of suffering in its first noble truth gave meaning to the oppressed masses in China under the tyrannical rule of the emperors. Its rich imagery and captivating ritual offers sharp contrast to the dry

---

[73] Ibid., 125.

[74] Ibid., 127.

philosophical Confucianism. Furthermore, its promise of an afterlife fills in the gap that Confucianism left void.[75]

2.2.5. Folk Religion

In addition to the above, there developed many minor deities among the Chinese. These vary with the localities. Examples of these are Tu Ti Kung (the earth god, also considered as the god of wealth), Wang Yeh (king), Tien Hon (seafaring goddess), the kitchen god and ancestral spirits. These had developed from various localities at different times, and it is difficult to be precise as to their origins.

All these influences serve to accentuate the I-centred life and lead to a utilitarian and pragmatic outlook. The need to create idols to ensure one's happiness is very compelling in Chinese society. In fact, this way of thinking is so entrenched in the minds of many Chinese that to build a temple is a guaranteed way of making money.[76] This leads to the proliferation of deities and temples. This has continued to be a dominant theme in the thinking of many Chinese Christians, and they have come to the church with the same framework. This, in part, explains the rapid expansion of the churches in Asia as they teach the health and prosperity doctrines. These seeds of these teachings already have a well-prepared and receptive ground for germination.

2.2.6. Ethical Particularism

One of the characteristics of the Chinese culture is what is known as ethical particularism.[77] This is a useful concept in trying to characterise the way the Chinese relate. The term is derived from two characteristics of the Chinese culture: its particularism and ethical base. C B Tan presented this in an article in the book *The Word Among Us*, and I quote from his article:

> One of the characteristics of Chinese culture is usually described as particularistic, because, in contrast to the 'universalistic' love in the Christian tradition, no general

---

[75] Ibid., 140f.

[76] B R Ro, 'Chinese Concepts of God and the God of the Bible', 174.

[77] C B Tan, 'Ethical Particularism as a Chinese Contextual Issue', *The Word Among Us*, ed. D. Gilliland (USA: Word Publishing, 1989), 262–281. The historical development of ethical particularism and a biblical critique is discussed in this paper.

rule(s) applies in interpersonal in every case for everyone. Yet, at the same time, it is called *ethical* particularism because such a relationship is built on an ethical base.[78]

C B Tan traces this from the Shang dynasty (1750–1100 BC) when ancestral worship was practised. Through the deceased ancestors, the will of god could be ascertained. A characteristic of the feudal system in the Chou dynasty (1100–222 BC) was the blood relationship, and this family basis was extended to cover the whole sociopolitical structure. This is reinforced by the concept of *li*[79] in Chinese philosophy. *Li* is commonly translated to *propriety*. Relationship within the sociopolitical structure is then governed by *li*, which is specific (particular) for the way in which the parties are related. Confucius made use of *li* as the foundation of the social order and gave the concept of *li* an ethical base. So this 'cement' of the Chinese society regulated relations in terms of role, status, and position within a structured society.[80] C B Tan explained the way this is practised in Chinese society with this illustration, and I quote:

> At the time of spring and autumn, the duke of Lu, Chao Kung (541–510 BC), met with the duke of Chi, Ching Kung. Ching Kung greeted Chao Kung with the rite of *kow-tow*, but the latter returned the greeting only by making a bow with hands folded in front because, as the Lu officials later explained, a duke only performs the rite of *kow-tow* to the king.[81]

The concept of *li* is linked with the concepts of *jen* and *yi* (righteousness). *Jen* has been discussed above. *Yi*, the concept of righteousness in Chinese minds, is a relational concept rather than legal. In other words, what is right or wrong is not determined by an universal axiom but rather dependent on the relationship between the two parties. The way in which *yi* is expressed is dependent on *li* in that particular situation. As an example, the son will not expose his father and neither the father the son.

---

[78] Ibid., 263.

[79] This has been mentioned above on p. 35 in relation to Confucianism.

[80] Ibid., 265.

[81] Cheng-tung Wei, History of Chinese thought (Taipei: Ta Ling Press, 1974), vol. 1:41–43, quoted in C B Tan, 'Ethical Particularism as a Chinese Contextual Issue', 264.

> The Governor of She declared to Confucius: 'Among my people, there is a man of unbending integrity: when his father stole a sheep, he denounced him.' Confucius said: 'Among my people, men of integrity do things differently: a father covers up for his son, a son covers up for his father—and there is integrity in what they do.' (Analect 13:18)

Thus, the law *fa* 'is not the highest authority in the Chinese value system'.[82] It is coordinated, rather than subordinated, with another basic value: filial piety. *Li* is ultimately the external expressions of a capacity for 'humanity' (*jen*), and righteousness (*yi*) is intrinsic to the human organism as is his whole physical organisation.[83]

The way in which the three concepts relate to one another is best expressed in this quotation by Mencius:

> The substance of *jen* is to serve one's parents; the substance of *yi* is to obey one's older brother. The essence of wisdom is to know these two things and not to depart from them; the essence of *li* is to perform these two things according to ritual orders; the essence of music is to rejoice in these two things. When joy is found in them, (filial piety and fraternal affection) arises; if so, how can they be repressed? When they cannot be repressed, unconsciously one's feet will dance and one's hands will flutter.[84]

Much of the expressions in the Chinese culture are determined by the relationships. While this may appear on the surface to be close to the biblical emphasis, this relational interaction is hierarchical and utilitarian rather than covenantal.[85] C B Tan relates the image of a network of concentric ripples with a centre known as the self.[86] It is around this 'self' centre that relationship is built, and that is what makes it particularistic.

---

[82] C B Tan, 'Ethical Particularism as a Chinese Contextual Issue', 266.

[83] Ibid.

[84] *Mencius*, IV.A.27. Edited and translated by C Chai and W Chai (New Hyde Park: University Books, 1965), 157, quoted in C B Tan, 'Ethical Particularism as a Chinese Contextual Issue', 267.

[85] The Trinity and the covenant will be discussed in the next chapter.

[86] C B Tan, 'Ethical Particularism as a Chinese Contextual Issue', 269.

It is also ethical because it recognises the traditional values of *jen*, *li*, and *yi*; but it subordinates them to the self. We will see how this takes place as the Chinese mind fuses all these values into one single framework.

2.2.7. A Fusion

It is not possible to estimate the contribution of each of the above to the Chinese mind. Over the centuries, the excellence of the Chinese mind in achieving synthesis among various contrasting systems has integrated all of the above into its culture. The world view of the majority of Chinese is a mixture of Confucianism, Buddhism, and Taoism.[87] Presented here are traces of the trends of thinking in the classic systems of Confucianism, Buddhism, and Taoism, which are merged into a complex system and modified over time. In fact, this fusion is continuing to take place with the migration of the Chinese to the West. With the excellence of the Chinese mind in harmonising the various cultures and systems of thought as they have done over hundreds of years, the Chinese have merged the varying influences that they find themselves into a system that guarantees them a place in the new society.

Basically, the system revolves around the I-centred life.[88] The essential question asked is, 'How can this god or goddess help me?' With this pragmatic filter, the Chinese have developed a deeply entrenched framework that virtually excludes the *who* question so necessary in a theological mind. The importance of the *who* question will be brought out in the early part of the next chapter.

The chart below summarises much of the above discussion. This is taken from Dr B R Ro's article 'Chinese Concept of God and the God of the Bible' in the book *God in Asian Contexts*. The chart is an excellent summary on the traditional Chinese mind.

---

[87] Ibid., 262.

[88] B R Ro, 'Chinese Concepts of God and the God of the Bible', 177.

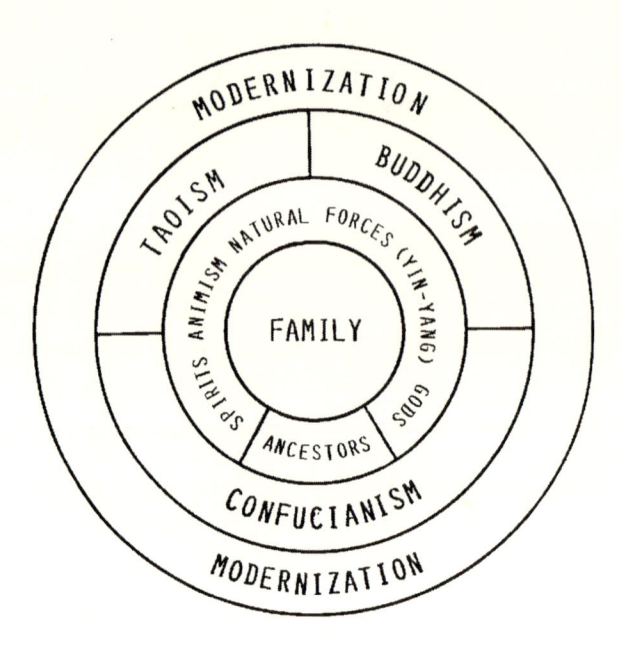

Figure 3. The Traditional Chinese mind. Chinese traditional beliefs in animistic spirits, natural forces of yin-yang, gods, ancestral spirits and religious practices of Buddhism, Taoism, folk religion, and Confucianism centre around the family. However, modernization today brings a tremendous challenge to the traditional Chinese culture.[89]

2.3. Bringing the Gospel to the Chinese

The early effort to bring the gospel to China was by the Syrian Nestorian Church, which entered China in the seventh century, and the Roman Catholic friars in the thirteenth century. There was little recorded of what was achieved during those times apart from a few manuscripts.

In the sixteenth century, Mateo Ricci, a Jesuit priest, presented to the Chinese people the gospel, which was largely reasoned from general revelation. He worked mainly within the framework of natural theology in order to make the gospel acceptable to the Chinese. This process of making the gospel acceptable to the local populace is termed the contextualisation of the gospel. It attempts to make the gospel understandable to the local

---

[89] Ibid., 166.

community and in itself is a laudable effort. However, in the process, the understanding of God was distorted because the Chinese, with their background of Confucianism, Buddhism, and Taoism, have tended to work around the premise of natural theology rather than on the specific revelation of the Bible.

Ricci equated God with the Chinese deity *shang-ti* and *tien* (see above). In his approach to the proclamation of the gospel, Ricci relied primarily on the faculty of reason.[90] He reasoned mainly from the letter to the Romans where Paul argued that what was created was known to the people and therefore they have no excuse (Romans 1:18–20). He made little reference to the special revelation in the Bible and his proclamation went forth without the Trinitarian God of the Bible.[91] It was an extreme case of the indigenisation of the gospel. He spared no effort to accommodate the gospel to the local civilisation.

Not until the missionary movement in the nineteenth century did the gospel reach the masses in some regions of China. The first Protestant missionary to reach China was Robert Morrison from the London Missionary Society. He arrived in Canton in 1807. The China Inland Mission (now the Overseas Missionary Fellowship), in the 1900s, made a concerted effort to present the gospel to the Chinese people. Several other missionary societies made inroads into China. This was also the period when many Western nations tried to dominate China in the name of trade as the Chinese imperial government was in a state of decline.

Many well-intentioned missionaries came to China on the coattails of the gunboats to proclaim the gospel. The Chinese perceived that it was a gospel of power. This perception is inevitable in the situation when the European missionaries were preaching the gospel and at the same time other Europeans were selling opium with gunboats anchored in the harbour. Unequal treaties were made with the Chinese, and it was a time of humiliation for the Chinese.[92] I quote from Covell:

> To ride the coattails of political power that provided an 'open door' to the Middle Kingdom helped to create attitudes that, although usually directed the official class, spilled over towards the general populace as well. Missionary activities were frequently characterized by a

---

[90] M Ricci, *The True Meaning of the Lord of Heaven*, ed. E J Malatesta (Taipei: Ricci Institute, 1985), 71.

[91] B R Ro, 'Chinese Concept of God and the God of the Bible', 180.

[92] R R Covell, *Confucius, the Buddha and Christ*, 82.

certain arrogance, an insistence on 'rights', and assumption of European superiority, an easy acquiescence in any action as long as it seemed to promote the progress of the gospel, a disdain for the need to adjust to Chinese culture, a satisfaction with mediocrity in carrying out their tasks, and a resignation to the alliance of the gospel with worldly power.[93]

This attitude of the missionaries in 'associating the cross with the flag stimulated adverse reactions from the target society'.[94] This was quite different from the earlier attempts by the Catholics and the Jesuits whose efforts 'were not accompanied by political clout'. They were unsupported by their governments and suffered for their activities.[95] From then until 1949, the gospel in China was proclaimed in the context of power.[96] The cross was obscured in such an attempt to proclaim the gospel.

In his paper to the Australian Chinese Conference on Evangelism, Dr Hoover Wong commented that because the gospel was associated with imperialism, it was never heard by the Chinese. I quote:

> Early American missionary endeavours met with limited success in China. Such efforts were approximate to and so identified with colonialisation and imperialism by foreign powers in the west. *The Gospel for its own sake was never heard.* In addition, the missionaries interpreted Chinese ways as 'low' and sought to raise personal and community standards to white, eurocentric values. One issue concerned ancestral worship. This meant rejecting one's own culture and world. Being a Christian meant forsaking one's past. *Again, the Gospel was never heard and evaluated on its own terms.* Missionaries laboured on with little reception and success.[97]

---

[93] Ibid., 83.

[94] Ibid., 84.

[95] Ibid., 83.

[96] Ibid.

[97] H Wong, 'Chinese Churches in America: An Historical Perspective'. Paper presented to the Third Australasian Chinese Conference On Evangelism, (Dec. 1995). Italics mine.

> Over the few centuries when the gospel has been preached to the Chinese, the God of the Bible has been understood in terms of the Chinese concept of god and heaven. The traditional term for God in Chinese, *shang-ti* (lit. the emperor from above), makes it difficult for the Chinese mind to grasp comprehensively the gracious Trinitarian God of the Bible. The association of the gospel with the imperialism of the West has reinforced this understanding. Many Chinese still conceive of their *shang-ti* as one demanding perfection from them before they are accepted.

Christianity has not been widely accepted by the populace as it has always been seen as a foreign religion in Asia. The anti-Christian force was gathering momentum while the missionaries continued with the preaching of the gospel and various social work. The Boxer Uprising and the expulsion of the missionaries demonstrated the extent of the anti-Christian sentiment in the nation. The Christian church was thrown into disarray, and large numbers of foreign missionaries were forced to leave the country. It was then left to the indigenous Christian leaders to defend the Christian faith.

The problem of the whole period of missionary outreach can best be summarised in the words of Dr W H Lam: 'The gospel consisted primarily in a western Christ presented to the humanistic and pragmatic Chinese mind.'[98]

This is precisely what Dr H Wong meant when he said that the 'gospel for its own sake was never heard' by the Chinese. It was a Western cultural Christ that was presented to a Chinese mind that has not been taught to accept revelation. We can see that the problem of bringing across the Trinitarian God of the Bible to the Chinese is not easy. The concepts of God and the supernatural are not alien to the Chinese mind, but because of their roots in natural theology, there are difficulties in accepting the revelation of the Trinitarian God as we shall see below. While some may try to come to grips with revelation, they may do so on the basis of Chinese mythology where the gods and humans intermingled.

In summarising the fundamental problems in the theological development in China, G H Anderson, in his book *Asian Voices in Christian Theology*, made these two observations:

1. Christianity has been largely a 'potted plant' in Asia. It was transported without being transplanted. It is still viewed by Asians as

---

[98] W H Lam, 'Patterns of Chinese Theology', *The Bible and Theology in Asian Contexts*, eds. B R Ro and R Eshenaur (Taiwan: ATA, 1984), 328.

a foreign importation and imposition. The challenge has been for the churches to relate themselves more fully to the soil of Asia to get down to the rice-roots level of Asian civilisation.

2. The second problem is that Christians have tended towards a ghetto mentality of nation building among themselves. The churches have been preoccupied with their own existence and organisation, and correspondingly, they have lagged behind in prophetic concern for the social relevance and outreach of the gospel into the mainstream task.[99]

2.4. Patterns of Chinese Theology

W H Lam summarised Chinese theological thinking into five categories.[100] These are the following:

a. Presence of classical precedents
b. Harmonisation of cultures
c. To fulfil, not to destroy
d. Cultural dualism
e. Christianity judges culture

This summary follows partly the classic work by Richard Niebuhr published in 1951.[101] The first category, presence of classical precedents, is particular to the Chinese as it accepts both the claims of Jesus Christ and the Chinese culture as valid expressions of what is true. So while trying to be obedient to the claims of Jesus Christ and being unable to deny the cultural bonds, the Chinese then produce something like an amalgam of the two without actually blending them together, i.e. 'Christianity and the Chinese culture will enrich each other.'[102] This is a common trend in Chinese thinking. Dr Lam cited an example of this in reference to the Holy Spirit being equated with the Confucianist jen. Since there is dimension of spirituality present in the jen, then it is appropriate to pray for jen to dwell in us.[103]

---

[99] G H Anderson, ed., *Asian Voices in Christian Theology* (Maryknoll, New York: Orbis, 1976), 5.

[100] W H Lam, 'Patterns of Chinese Theology', 327–342.

[101] H R Niebuhr, *Christ and Culture* (New York: Harper and Row, 1951).

[102] W H Lam, 'Patterns of Chinese Theology', 332.

[103] Ibid.

Of course, the next process will be for the Chinese then to display their excellence in the process of harmonisation (category b above), i.e. to take the best of both and form a composite system very much the way many Chinese have been able to fuse Confucianism and Buddhism together. In so doing, there has to be the subordination of Christianity to the Chinese culture as Dr Lam rightly points out: 'They saw Christianity not as the ultimate, absolute religion to substitute the time-honoured deposit of cultural excellence but as a colleague for mutual service.'[104] This will eventually lead to a cultural Christianity.

The next three patterns follow Niebuhr's categories. A core assumption of Chinese thinking is their heritage and the excellence of their culture. Most Chinese would find it difficult to depart from this. In the third category of the relationship between culture and Christianity, the thinking is still to preserve the cultural norm but at the same time allow the precepts of Christianity to bring about the perfection of the culture. While this may appear reasonable on the surface, in actual fact, it subordinates Christianity to the culture. Christianity only serves as an adjunct or a tool in the preservation and the perfection of the culture. Furthermore, as the basis of Confucianism is philosophical, then in order for Christianity to bring about fulfillment in the Chinese culture, Christianity has to be reduced to philosophical categories. In doing so, the personal nature of the triune Godhead would be reduced to mere impersonal forces. It would mean that the 'Word'[105] continues to be imprisoned within the bonds of Greek philosophical thought without ever becoming flesh (Jn. 1:14). The very foundation of Christianity is undermined in the process.

In the fourth category of 'cultural dualism', this parallels Niebuhr's category of 'Christ and culture in paradox'. It admits to the tension between Christ and culture and is reminiscent of the teaching of the missionary movement in the early twentieth century. Interestingly, Dr Lam cites Wang Ming-tao as a proponent of this system.[106] It leads to a system where Christianity is detached from the world and beats a monastic retreat.

The last category of Dr Lam's presentation, 'Christianity judges culture', is the same as the fifth category of Niebuhr's classification. The weaknesses of Confucian thought are pointed out in the light of the scriptural teaching of sin and the work of the incarnate Christ. The former has a starting point in man and nature while Christianity's starting point is in the self-revelation of God.

---

[104] Ibid.

[105] *Logos* in John 1.

[106] W H Lam, 'Patterns of Chinese Theology', 336.

The above patterns line up in a spectrum ranging from Christianity being subordinate to Chinese cultural thinking to Christianity judging culture. In my observation in Australia, the Chinese churches show the whole range of patterns given above. Most hold to some form of cultural practices and this none of us can avoid. If we accept the biblical records and the centrality of the cross for the redemption of the whole created order, then we need to accept that our culture, whatever it may be, has be to judged by that which has been revealed to us regarding the Godhead. This is the triune God Jesus Christ has come to reveal. The church through the ages has struggled with this revelation of the Trinitarian God, and to this topic, we shall now turn.

Part Two

TRINITARIAN THEOLOGY DEFINED AND DENIED

Part Two, Chapter 3

THE HEART OF CHRISTIANITY: THE TRINITY AND THE COVENANT

We have mentioned earlier that Christianity cannot be defined by the Christians or by the community of the Christians, as they do not exist as perfect entities. Christianity has to be defined by its very founder, i.e. by Christ Himself. The question 'Who God is?' must be answered in Trinitarian terms, that is, He is the 'God who exists in the triunity of Father, Son, and Holy Spirit'. This understanding comes from the revelation that Christ Himself brings. God can only be known through God Himself.

The theme of the Trinity is too immense a topic to be discussed here. I refer in particular to some of the recent writings on the subject.[107]

This chapter will state the dogma of the Trinity and the covenant as the root doctrine of the Christian faith and the starting point of theological reflection. It will then go on to point out the implications of the covenant relationship. This emphasises the priority of grace, underscores the mediation of Jesus Christ and therefore refocuses onto the Trinity and affirms the freedom and dignity of all humanity. This understanding will

---

[107] K Rahner, *The Trinity*; trans. J Donceel, (Great Britain: Burns & Oats, 1970). T F Torrance, *The Trinitarian Faith* (Edinburgh: T&T Clark, 1969). J Moltmann, *The Trinity and the Kingdom of God*, trans. M Kohl (London: SCM, 1981).

be applied to issues of theology and practice in the Chinese church in the subsequent chapters.

3.1. The Triunity of the Godhead and the Covenantal Relationship

When Christians refer to God, the term *God* is a shorthand term for Father, Son, and Holy Spirit. He is the triune God. In our Christian dogma of monotheism, we have suppressed this understanding of the triune God because we cannot hold in tension a triunity. We hold to a concept of an absolute monotheistic god. We see this to be a problem not only at Nicea[108] but also in much of Christian thinking today. If the essential nature of God is Trinitarian, then our lives and worship must of necessity be Trinitarian, and the nature of our church and ministry must also be Trinitarian. These issues will be taken up in the subsequent chapters of this dissertation.

The understanding of the triune God is not a figment of the imagination of the early church or a philosophical deduction from the Greek culture of the day. It was an experience that the Christians of the early church went through, and they understood that experience in Trinitarian terms.

There is little in the New Testament by way of direct reference to the doctrine of the Trinity. However, in many passages of the New Testament, the three-in-one Godhead is mentioned with reference to the Father, Son, and Holy Spirit.[109] This is so because of the following:

1. Jesus Christ had come in person to reveal God the Father (Jn. 1:18). His humanity is not foreign to His divinity.[110] The early Christians related to the human Jesus in a very real way as John the Apostle made it so clear in his gospel (Jn. 1:1–18) and letters (1 Jn. 1:1–4).
2. Following the ascension of our Lord Jesus Christ, the Holy Spirit was poured out at Pentecost and indwells the people of God as the advocate. The early Christians experienced the reality of the indwelling Spirit.

Out of these real experiences, the early Christians sought to express their understanding of God in Trinitarian terms—a unity of the three persons in the Godhead. The apostolic church was gripped by the revelation

---

[108] This will be mentioned in chapter 4 of the dissertation in relation to the subordination of Christianity to culture.

[109] 1 Cor. 12:4–6; 2 Cor. 13:14; Gal. 4:6; Eph. 1:17, 2:17, 4:4–7.

[110] See K Barth, *The Humanity of God* (USA: John Knox Press, 1960).

of the divine Trinitarian God and sought to express its understanding of God and salvation in terms of this foundational revelation. As L Hodgson rightly commented, 'Christianity was a trinitarian religion before it had a trinitarian theology.' What he means is as follows.

As a result of the revelation of the Father through the incarnation of Jesus Christ and the pouring out of the Holy Spirit on the Day of Pentecost, the early disciples were indwelt by the Holy Spirit who made the redemptive work of Christ a reality in their lives. This awakening by the Holy Spirit caused them to respond in ways that transformed the culture of the day. They realised that they had a new common humanity in Jesus Christ and they lived in that reality. This was manifested in their devotion 'to the apostles' teaching and fellowship, to the breaking of bread and the prayers' (Acts 2:42, NRSV). This was the *koinonia* (fellowship) of the early church, and 'all who believed were together and had all things in common' (Acts 2:44, NRSV). This became the essence of the new Trinitarian religion of the early church. The dogma of the Trinity was not developed till the fourth century at Nicea. That is not to say that the early church did not have a Trinitarian framework for its expressions. The way of life in the triune God was a reality in the early church long before the written dogma of the philosophers three hundred years later. That is why Paul could write to the Ephesians in this way: 'There is one body and one Spirit, just as you were called to the one hope of your calling, one Lord, one faith, one baptism, one God and Father of all, who is above all and through all and in all' (Eph. 4:4–6, NRSV). This is one example of the Trinitarian thought of the Apostles as they lived out their Trinitarian faith.

3.1.1. The Relevance of Trinitarian Theology

The term *Trinity* was first used by Theophilus of Antioch (ca. AD 170) when he referred to the first three days of creation. Tertullian first used this term *trinitas* with reference to the Godhead in his treatise against Praxeas around AD 213.

There have been many debates on the Godhead as theologians seek to understand what God is like, and this debate is still continuing in relation to the Trinity. In much of the theological effort of the Christian church, the focus has been on the *how* question. While it is important that there be a right and proper theological methodology in our approach to biblical studies, it is even more important to answer the *who* question: who is this God that we are approaching? So often when we start with the *how* question, we allow the problem to be the starting point, i.e. we start with an anthropology. Then Christ becomes the means of solving that problem. We must not work out the *who* from the *how*, but the *how* from the *who*.

Bonhoeffer pointed out that it is not the *how* question but the *who* question that needs to be asked first in theology. The *who* question leads us to Christology.

The question *who* has been asked in the Bible by various people. At the burning bush, Moses wanted to know who is this God that was sending him back to Egypt to deliver the people of Israel (Ex. 3:13). Jesus Christ wanted a response from His disciples as to who He was (Mark 8:27). When Paul was confounded on the Damascus Road by this light from the sky, he wanted to know who is this God that was confronting him (Acts 9:5). They had all started with the most important question: who.

Following Calvin's *Institutes*,[111] Karl Barth in his *Dogmatics*[112] places the *who* question right at the beginning. Far too often, we are only interested in what God does without first addressing the nature of His being. He argued thus:

> When we ask: Who is the self-revealing God? the bible answers in such a way that we have to reflect on the triunity of God. The two other questions: What does this God do and what does He effect? are also answered primarily, as we have seen, by new answers to the first question: Who is He?[113]

Instead of asking the *who* question, many are only concerned with irrelevant speculation as Barth remarked.

> And the doctrine of the Trinity itself is threatened by the same danger, the danger of irrelevant speculation, if we state it only at a later stage and do not give it the first word as that which gives us information on the concrete and decisive question: Who is God?[114]

---

[111] Calvin, *Institutes of the Christian Religion*, 2 volumes, ed. J T McNeill (Philadelphia: Westminster Press).

[112] K. Barth, *Church Dogmatics*, vol. 1.1. (Edinburgh: T&T Clark, 1975).

[113] Ibid., 303.

[114] Ibid., 301.

The doctrine of the Trinity is central to our understanding of revelation and worship and indeed to all areas of Christian life. Karl Barth continued,

> The doctrine of the Trinity is what basically distinguishes the Christian doctrine of God as Christian, and therefore what already distinguishes the Christian concept of revelation as Christian, in contrast to all other possible doctrines of God or concepts of revelation.[115]

In an earlier period, H Bavinck emphasised the importance of the doctrine of the triune God. He described it as the 'kernel of the Christian faith, the root of all dogmas'.

> With the confession of God's triunity stand or fall the whole of Christianity, the whole of special revelation. This is the kernel of the Christian faith, the root of all dogmas, the substance of the new covenant. . . . And precisely in proportion as this question is answered does Christian truth come either less or more into its own in all parts of Christian doctrine. In the doctrine of the Trinity beats the heart of the whole revelation of God for the redemption of mankind.[116]

We often find some proponents of Christian doctrine starting at some peripheral points other than from the root doctrine of the Trinity.[117] Our understanding of God must start from God Himself and not from the way we conceive of Him. God is known through God Himself.

However, for too long, the church has regarded the Trinity as mere academic curiosity. The church has little time to consider it. The doctrine of the Trinity was fought out in the early church and then lost in the Middle Ages. It was rediscovered at the Reformation and highlighted in the *Institutes* of Calvin. His followers turned it into academia and reverted to the piety of man. Adolf Harnack (1851–1930), a champion of liberal Christianity, taught that there is little to be gained from talking about the Trinity. Karl Barth and others in this century put the Trinity back onto

---

[115] Ibid.

[116] H Bavinck, *Gereformeede Dogmatiek*, vol. II, 4th ed., 1918, p. 346f., quoted in K Barth, *Church Dogmatics*, 1.1, 302.

[117] For example, the starting point in ecclesiology is often church order rather than the triunity of God.

the agenda of the church as the root doctrine of our faith. We need to peel back our formulations of the doctrines of the church to this root doctrine.

The doctrine of the Trinity—the triune God: the Father, Son, and Holy Spirit—is the very foundation for the understanding of our faith. The Father is the fountain of love and life. The Son is the Logos, the very expression of the Father and fulfils the Father's task of the redemption of His people. He is also our Great High Priest and today continues to intercede on our behalf in heaven. The Spirit is the Spirit of empowerment, who dwells within us, and His enabling power causes us to recognise God as the Father. So it is from God to God: what has come from God returns to Him. It is achieved by the Father's love, the Son's intercession, and the Spirit's empowerment through His redeemed creation. That is where we are involved in the whole picture of divine love.

The earthly life of Jesus Christ was lived in the triune relationship. It is unthinkable that this is not the case as the Father, Son, and Holy Spirit are one from eternity. This is shown to us in the baptism of Jesus Christ when the Father in heaven voiced His approval, 'You are my Son, the Beloved; with you I am well pleased,' and the Holy Spirit descended on Him (Mk. 1:10–11, NRSV). The farewell discourses by Jesus in John's gospel 14–16 highlighted the oneness of the Son and the Holy Spirit.[118] Jesus's union with the Father is brought out most passionately in His High Priestly prayer in John 17.

> [21]That they may all be one. As you, Father, are in me and I am in you, may they also be in us, so that the world may believe that you have sent me. [22]The glory that you have given me I have given them, so that they may be one, as we are one, [23]I in them and you in me, that they may become completely one, so that the world may know that you have sent me and have loved them even as you have loved me. (Jn. 17:21–23, NRSV)

The early church lived in this oneness achieved through the redemptive work of Jesus Christ who brings us into the communion that He has with His Father. This is made clear when Jesus prayed, 'May they also be in us' (Jn. 17:21). Paul expressed this oneness in no uncertain when he wrote to the Galatians, 'And it is no longer I who live, but it is Christ who lives in me. And the life I now live in the flesh I live by faith in the Son of God,

---

[118] The references of Jesus to the Spirit as the other Paraclete makes this oneness clear (Jn. 14:16, 26; 15:26; 16:7). John, in his first letter, makes the counter reference to Christ as the Paraclete (1 Jn. 2:1).

who loved me and gave himself for me' (Gal. 2:20). The way the early church community expressed this has been referred to in the previous section.

Therefore, this doctrine of the Trinity is not mere academic philosophy. It is relevant to our everyday living, to our worship, to our church life, to our marriage, and our workplace. We will work through some of these issues briefly in the later part of this dissertation. All our doctrinal formulations must derive from this: the Trinitarian Godhead as our root doctrine and source of inspiration, love, and rationality.

Our understanding of the Trinity will lead us to think in terms of the community of the Godhead, and this communion of the Trinity must then be the foundation of our community and indeed the church community. Take away the Trinity, as the liberal theologians have done, and we finish up with man at the centre and God becomes merely an object of our worship among our other objects.

There are two problems in Chinese thinking that have prevented them from thinking in Trinitarian terms:

1. They see God as merely a means to fulfilling their needs. Their experience of God becomes the fixed point, and God becomes the variable responding to their needs.
2. They see God as the absolute monarch. This is where their thinking about God starts, i.e. from an absolute monotheism and from here they try to graft on the Trinity. This will not take. This was the problem at Nicea as we will see later.

We have seen above that it is our core assumptions that determine our culture. One of the core assumptions is the way we conceive of God. As Christians, the way we think of our God determines the way we go about doing things that give meaning to our lives. Moltmann made this remark regarding the way our earthly political and religious orders are structured. 'The notion of a divine monarchy in heaven and on earth, for its part, generally provides the justification for earthly domination—religious, moral, patriarchal or political domination—and makes it a hierarchy, a "holy rule".[119]

When we think of God in His absolute unity, then we have monarchianism, i.e. one above all. We have used monarchianism as a model in political and church relationships and in government. That is why some of our churches have difficulty in adopting a plurality of presbyters. We have modelled our culture according to our core assumption of the

---

[119] J Moltmann, *The Trinity and the Kingdom of God*, 191–192.

Godhead. A doctrine of the Trinity must overcome this monarchianism.[120] However, that is not to say that there is egalitarianism in the Godhead. The Son and Holy Spirit are sent by the Father for the task of revelation and reconciliation. There is within the Godhead a superordination without subordination.

A culture will not change unless the core assumptions that people hold dear are changed. A core assumption is our concept of God, i.e. Who is He? The human person will always find meaning as an integral whole. At the NCTM[121] pastors' study on 'Christ Liberator of the Conscience'[122], it was pointed out that 'conscience is always incorporated within the framework of a particular anthropology. Hence, it is always indicative of a specific self-understanding of human existence.'[123] A person cannot deny that which his or her inner being holds to be true.

3.1.2 The Theology of the Covenant

The theme of the covenant is central to the Bible. This theme runs throughout the Old and New Testaments. The study is important to us today as we have discarded the covenant in favour of the contract or rather we have come to understand the covenant in terms of a contractual framework. The covenant is initiated and maintained by the sovereign grace of God. This has been debated and understood as a bilateral agreement between God and man. This understanding of the covenant has contributed to the contractual framework. Or rather, it is the contractual framework put in place by the philosophers of the Enlightenment that has contributed to this understanding of the covenant. This point will be elaborated in the next chapter.

The understanding of the covenant follows from the understanding of the triunity of God. It is because the Trinity has been neglected in the past that the covenant has come to be understood in the context of the contract. Herman Hanko expounded this well in his book *God's Everlasting Covenant of Grace*. In the opening two paragraphs of the first chapter of his book, he made this link between the triunity of God and the covenant.

---

[120] Ibid., 192.

[121] New Creation Teaching Ministry based in Adelaide.

[122] G Bingham, *Christ: Liberator of the Conscience*. Paper presented at the NCTM Pastors' Monday Study Group, Adelaide, 5 Sept 1994.

[123] H Thielicke, *Theological Ethics*, vol. 1 (Eerdmans, 1979), 314. Quoted in G Bingham, *Christ: Liberator of the Conscience*. Paper presented at the New Creation Teaching Ministry, Adelaide (5 Sept. 1994).

> God is a covenant God. The deepest ground for the covenant of grace must be found in the truth that God lives in a covenant life in Himself even apart from the creatures He has created.
>
> God is triune. That is, God is one in essence and three in person. This central and all-important doctrine of the church has stood as the immovable rock upon which all of the truth is based. And this trinity is the deepest reason why God is a covenant God and lives a covenant life within Himself. Without the reality of the trinity, the covenant would be impossible.[124]

And so it is in the covenant life of the triune God that we derive our understanding of the covenant. Further, as mankind is created in the image of God, so we are created to live in covenant relationship with the triune God and in covenant relationship with one another.

The word *covenant* in the Bible is used to describe the relationship between God and man. It is an everlasting covenant. We should note that the concept of an everlasting covenant lies within the relationship of the triune Godhead. The Trinitarian God, Father, Son, and Holy Spirit exist in eternity, giving to and receiving from one another in communion. They are distinct from one another, but they coinhere in a *perichoretic*[125] relationship. Man was created in God's image in that covenantal relationship.[126]

In our study of the covenant, we need to explore the general concept of covenant in the Bible and trace its development through the covenants with Noah, Abraham, Isaac and Jacob, David, and, finally, the excellence and glory of the new covenant. It must be emphasised that we are discussing the one eternal covenant of creation, and all these specific covenants in

---

[124] H Hanko, *God's Everlasting Covenant of Grace* (Grandville: Reformed Free Publishing, 1988), 7.

[125] See chapter 4.5 below.

[126] I recognise that the treatment of the biblical material in this section on 'The Theology of the Covenant' is brief as our concern here is more with its relationship to culture. For more detailed treatment on the subject of the covenant, see W J Dumbrell, *Covenant and Creation* (Great Britain: Paternoster, 1984) and G Bingham, *Love's Most Glorious Covenant* (Castle Hill, NSW: Redeemer Baptist Press, 1977).

the Bible must be considered as subsets or expressions of the one eternal covenant.[127]

The first mention of the covenant in the Bible is found in reference to Noah (Gen. 6:18 and 9:9ff). Yet it must not be assumed that the covenant began there. The triune God exists in covenantal relationship before the creation. It should be noted here that the reference to the covenant here is not 'to cut a covenant'[128] as is the usual way of expressing covenanting in the Old Testament. The term used in this context with Noah is 'to establish'[129] a covenant. In other words, the meaning here is to establish something that is already in existence. W Dumbrell argues this out well in his book *Covenant and Creation*.[130] What was in existence then was the covenant of creation. As we have pointed out earlier on, the triune God exists in covenantal relationship; and in the creation of humanity in His own image, humanity was created in covenantal relationship with the Creator. This allows us to speak of the 'One Eternal Covenant of Creation'; and in the working out of the implications of this One Eternal Covenant, the covenants with Noah, Abraham, Moses, and David are to be considered as subsets of this One Eternal Covenant. Of course, the culmination of all these is in the establishment of the new covenant through Jesus Christ.

The covenant is in no way a bilateral conditional transaction between God and humanity. In the covenant with Noah (Gen. 6–9), it was a universal covenant with the whole of creation. Noah was the silent partner, and it was God who transacted and committed to sustain His covenant. In the covenant with Abraham (Gen. 15), Abraham was put to sleep when God 'cut' His covenant. There is no hint of bilaterality in both events. We see this right through scriptures in the Mosaic (Exod. 19:3–8) and Davidic (2 Sam. 7:8–17) covenants. Finally, in the new covenant, it was transacted by the incarnation of the Second Person of the triune Godhead, Jesus Christ, an act that is totally of God and from God.

Covenant is a relational term. A contract is legal. The concept of covenant should undergird all our relationships. The concept of covenant is expounded from the Bible, yet its application is by no means restricted to

---

[127] G Bingham, *Christ: The Mediator of the Better Covenant I and II*. Paper presented at the New Creation Teaching Ministry Pastors' Study Group, Adelaide (17 Oct 1994 and 7 Nov 1994).

[128] The Hebrew term used is *karat berith* (Gen. 15:18), meaning to cut a covenant.

[129] A different Hebrew term is used here. *Heqim berith* (Gen. 6:18, 9:9) means to establish a covenant that is already in existence.

[130] W J Dumbrell, *Covenant and Creation* (Great Britain: Paternoster, 1984), 24–26.

the religious sphere. In fact, following the reformation, the recovery of the concept of the covenant influenced much of political theory up to today.[131] This will be take up at a later stage.

C H Dodd in his lectures on gospel and law, remarked that many theologians 'have protested against any construction of the Christian religion which, by introducing legal conceptions, seem to blur the splendour of the Gospel in the affirmation of the free and unconditioned grace of God to sinful men.'[132] Because this understanding of covenant has been understood in a legalistic framework, it distorts the whole approach to God and the scriptures. Unfortunately, this legalistic framework has been firmly entrenched in church thinking since the early centuries.[133]

3.2. Implications of the Covenant

We will now turn from the theological aspects to see what impact a theology of the Trinity and the covenant would make upon our culture, firstly in a general way and later in specific ways. I will seek to summarise some of the work of Prof James Torrance in this area.

We have shown that the triunity of the Godhead and the covenant relationship are foundational to our discussion. These are necessary areas in theology as we see something of the essential nature of the Christian faith, i.e. the Trinitarian God and the covenant with man. It is our understanding in these areas that will impact upon our relationship with others and thereby our culture, i.e. the things that we do that will give us meaning.

This line of study is necessary as we need to see the three levels or planes of persons in relationship. These three levels are:

1. within the triune Godhead as the eternal relation of the Father, the Son and the Holy Spirit;
2. between God and man as the free election by God that man should be his covenant partner;
3. between human persons as the basic form of humanity.[134]

---

[131] J Moltmann, 'Covenant or Leviathan? Political Theology for Modern Times', *Scottish Journal of Theology* 47 (1994): 19–41.

[132] C H Dodd, *Gospel and Law* (Cambridge, 1951), 65, quoted in J B Webster, 'Christology, Imitability and Ethics', *Scottish Journal of Theology*. 39 (1986): 311.

[133] This will be taken up in the next chapter.

[134] D K Miell, 'Barth on Persons in Relationship: A Case for Further Reflection?', *Scottish Journal of Theology* 42 (1989): 541–555.

There is a hierarchy of relationships here as the second and third levels are dependent on the first. All relationships have their basis in the relation of the triune Godhead as humankind is created in the image of God. As the relationship within the triune Godhead is covenantal, so the relation between God and mankind is spelt out in terms of the covenant. It then follows that all human relationship is covenantal.

We will move from here to the so-called horizontal axis, i.e. in our relationship with one another, and move more directly to the interaction between Christianity and culture. In doing this, we will consider the implications of the covenant and then see something of the humanist movement. We will conclude this chapter considering the way we understand the human person.

3.2.1. It Enables Us to Recover the Meaning of Grace

Grace was eminently demonstrated on the cross, and it gripped the hearts and minds of the people. The early church understood that. However, the meaning of grace was lost in the medieval church and recovered during the Reformation. Though we stand in the reformed tradition, legalism continually creeps into our thinking and interpretation of the Word and so transforms the grace of God into a system that we can manage within our legal framework. We are continually confronted with a 'covenant of works' and the priority of law. Our culture, whether it be East or West, is founded upon a legalistic contractual framework; and to this, we continually return. This must reflect something of our fallenness. If we were to reject the covenant of grace that flows from the relationship within the triune Godhead, then, inevitably, we must fall into the captivity of the legal framework.

Many of us today need to rediscover the meaning of grace. Covenant theology enables us to see that works and the law are subordinate to grace. Grace came first; then came the law to enable us to express our response to the grace of God. It gives us no occasion for boasting because who we are and what we are both are the results of the grace of God.

We cannot take grace and try to graft it into our egocentric and self-sufficient framework. We need to move over to a new framework or, as Matthew expresses it, 'put it into new wineskins' (Matt. 9:17). This new framework or wineskin requires that we take seriously the mediation of our Lord Jesus Christ and the Trinitarian Godhead.

3.2.2. It Underscores the Mediation of Jesus Christ

There is only one sacrifice that the Father accepts, and that is the perfect sacrifice of Jesus Christ. There is nothing that we can offer to a Holy God. We often pray that our praise and meditation may be acceptable to God. Our praises are only acceptable on the basis of what Jesus Christ has done for us. In other words, Jesus Christ gathers up all our weak and feeble worship and offers them to God on our behalf[135]—that is how our worship can be acceptable to God, not how righteous we may have been for we have not.

'For there is one God; there is also one mediator between God and humankind, Christ Jesus, himself human' (1 Tim. 2:15, NRSV). Because Jesus Christ is both God and human, this mediation is effected from God to humanity and from humanity to God. In other words, Jesus Christ mediates both revelation and reconciliation. John brought out the former in the prologue to his gospel. 'No one has ever seen God. It is God the only Son, who is close to the Father's heart, who has made him known' (Jn. 1:18, NRSV). Paul made it clear when he wrote to the Corinthians regarding the issue of the mediation of Christ in reconciliation 'that God was reconciling the world to himself in Christ, not counting men's sins against them. And he has committed to us the message of reconciliation' (2 Cor. 5:19).

In the discourse of Jesus recorded in John's gospel, He made clear the oneness He has with the Father. He was only doing what the Father has given to Him, and all who come to Him will be presented to the Father (Jn. 5:20–21, 6:37–40). Those around Him then did not understand what He was alluding to because their judgemental minds could only see that as a blasphemous statement. As Jesus came from the Father to reveal Him to us, so He wants to take us back to the Father through His vicarious humanity. For the latter to happen, we have to be part of Him. Jesus said precisely this in the context of giving us new life, i.e. reconciliation with God: 'Those who eat my flesh and drink my blood abide in me, and I in them. Just as the living Father sent me, and I live because of the Father, so whoever eats me will live because of me' (Jn. 6:56–57).

The writer to the Hebrews uses the motif of the high priesthood in the Old Testament to make his point relating to Christ's mediation. He sees Jesus as the Great High Priest, not after the earthly Aaronic order but after the order of Melchizedek (Heb. 5:6, 10, 20; 7:11, 15, 17), an order that is eternal, without beginning or end. In nothing short of divine revelation, he shows to us that this Great High Priest is not just offering an animal

---

[135] This is an expression that J Torrance was so fond of using in his class, and I cannot express it better in any other way.

sacrifice but has also become the sacrifice Himself. 'But when Christ had offered for all time a single sacrifice for sins, "he sat down at the right hand of God",' (Heb. 10:12, NRSV).

Jesus Christ is continuing to minister to us today, and that is the continuing mediation on our behalf before a righteous and holy God. Jesus Christ came as our High Priest and is continuing today as our High Priest, mediating between us and God. Jesus not only mediates the grace of God to us but also mediates our responses to the Father.

This mediation takes us away from our self-centredness and pride. It shows us that our response is acceptable insofar as it is through Jesus Christ. It enables us to acknowledge the responses of others as it is only through the mediation of Jesus Christ that theirs and ours are acceptable to the Father.

3.2.3. It Refocuses onto the Trinity

Not only has Jesus Christ mediated between us and God, the Holy Spirit is also our mediator. Romans made this clear. 'The Spirit Himself intercedes for us with groans that words cannot express' (8:26). So in our approach to God the Father, He has given us the Holy Spirit to enable us in our prayer and praise. These are then collected by Jesus Christ as our mediator and offered to God. We see here the priesthood of Jesus Christ and the priesthood of the Holy Spirit acting in different ways in our worship of the Father under the new covenant. Our worship to the Father is through Jesus Christ and in the Spirit.

We see that it is only through the new framework of the triune Godhead that we can move away from our legalistic culture to an appreciation of the covenant.

Just as the Father, Son, and Spirit exist in mutual love, fellowship, and interdependence, so too this is the model for our community. This brings us to the last implication, i.e. that of the freedom and dignity of all humanity.

3.2.4. It Reaffirms the Freedom and Dignity of All Humanity

Our triune God is one of grace and love, and the covenant that He has transacted for us is one of grace and love. This is a covenant with His creation and includes all people groups. When we worship this God, we express what He has done for us in terms of the relationship that has been re-established—a relationship with Him and with one another. It is the result of this restored relationship with one another that we can speak of freedom and dignity. By dignity, we do not mean the stiffness and air of a generation past. Reflecting on Christianity as the true humanism, J I Packer said, 'Our dignity is only realised as we love and serve God for Himself, and mankind for God's sake, according to the two great commands in which Christ said that all the law and the prophets are summed up.'[136]

Our affirmation of the dignity of all humanity has its basis on the work of Jesus for all humanity. The grace of the Father is towards all His creation. 'Show proper respect for everyone' (1 Peter 2:17).

J I Packer continues to elaborate on what it means in practical terms for us to confer dignity on our fellow beings:

> We would emphasise that the horizontal relationship of honouring God's image in others by seeking to give and secure to them respect, goodwill, help, protection, shelter, food, education, justice, and freedom of thought and religion—meaning liberty to differ from us without our neighbour-relationship to them being hereby endangered—is integral to the worship and obedience in which love to the Father and the Son finds expression.[137]

The reason for thinking in this way is that humanity is created in the image of God and has been given the capacity to relate with the Creator and with all in the created order. Above all, we have been given the gift of life so that we can give expression to that relationship. Therefore, to confer dignity upon our fellow humanity is the expression of our relatedness to the Creator.

We can only understand this on the basis of grace and covenantal relationship. When we worship a contract God, we think in terms of right and wrong, fairness and justice in an absolute sense. When we think in terms of a covenant God, we think in terms of relationships, relating to God through Jesus Christ and relating with one another. In our imperfect world, we are able to relate in a meaningful way only because we love and forgive, not that we are able to initiate these gracious gestures but that we have received it first from our Lord Jesus Christ. We are enabled to be gracious to one another because we are all under grace. We stand before God with nothing to boast of in ourselves but only of what Jesus Christ

---

[136] J I Packer and T Howard, *Christianity: The True Humanism* (England: Word Publishing, 1985), 154.

[137] Ibid., 156.

has achieved for us. We come together not because we are better than those who do not gather in this manner but because we have received of the free grace of God to appreciate the wonderful salvation that is being offered.

When we think in this way, we accord to our fellow beings irrespective of their background, ethnicity, religious or denominational background, and even their criminal background (if any), a dignity that is first given by God the creator who loves them and gave Jesus Christ for them and for us. We ought to think in terms of the one eternal creational covenant in our relationships. In that way, we learn to think of the other firstly as a fellow being having received the gift of life from the Father rather than in terms of some external characteristics such as colour, sex, or even their religious affiliation. Ray Anderson, writing for the Fuller's *Theology News and Notes* after the Los Angeles riots in 1992, has this to say when we refer to others in terms of their ethnicity.

> For the Korean American, the Asian American, the Mexican America, and the African American, the connecting issue is not 'American' but human. When one's ethnic identity only serves as the adjective and not the noun, there is already a loss of personhood at the human level.[138]

That is not to say that we cease to be Asian or African or whatever our ethnic origin may be, but rather our connectedness with one another is not because of our ethnic origin but because we have been given life by the same creator God and Father. To be in covenant means to be related as a core value of human existence. Our colour, race, and social status are only incidental to our human existence.

3.2.5. Christian or Secular Humanism

There are many others today, such as the secular humanist, who have the same approach to humanity but only in terms of asserting their human rights. It is unfortunate that the church had not been there in the early stages of this movement, though the movement indeed has its roots in Christianity. While our connectedness is on the basis of our common humanity, yet evangelical Christianity has chosen to ignore secular humanism.

---

[138] R Anderson, 'The Humanity of God and the Soul of a City', *Hope and Despair in the City of Angels*, Fuller's Theology, News and Notes (June, 1992): 15.

Secular humanism has its roots in Christianity but has developed along different lines since the days of the Reformation. With the Enlightenment, reason has been elevated to be the basic characteristic of what it is to be human. Thus, together with the development of the scientific method, secular humanism has gone a separate path from Christianity. The result of these developments is that secular humanism abandoned metaphysics and revealed religion and based its premise on the basic goodness of the human person.

The contribution of this movement to humanity is significant as it highlights the inhumanity that exists in our society. There is biblical support for the 'rights' movement, but we need to be careful that we do not interpret those references in the legalistic sense of the secular humanist because the language of 'rights' runs in opposition to the language of 'covenant'. How do two people relate when each stands on one's rights, especially when those rights may not be in congruity? The language of rights is judgement and conditionality. The language of covenant is forgiveness and unconditionality. To express forgiveness is to give up the insistence on one's rights. It is not enough for us to accord to our fellow beings their basic human rights. We need to go further than that. As the people of God who have tasted the grace of God, we need to call them our brothers and sisters.

God's one eternal covenant provides the framework for an appreciation of the dignity of humankind. Moreover, the issue of human right is grounded in the dignity of humankind. It is more desirable to talk of human dignity in terms of relations rather than human rights in terms of legality. Such an approach, on the basis of the covenantal relationship rather than rights and legality, will lead us to realise our creational status in God's image and to discover the reality of what God has bestowed upon us in our relationship because we are created for relationship.

3.2.6. The Trinity and the Human Person

Our discussion on Christianity and culture has taken us through a brief consideration of culture and the theology of the Trinity and covenant. We have stated simply that culture is the sum of how we conduct ourselves and this is expressed in language, actions or the arts. We have also noted that the doctrine of God lies at the heart of the contemporary debates of our pluralistic culture.[139] If that is so, then what we understand of the Godhead and what we mean by being human are central to the way our

---

[139] D A Carson and J D Woodbridge, eds., 'Christian Witness in an Age of Pluralism', in *God and Culture* (Grand Rapids: Eerdmans, 1993): 46.

culture develops. Christianity teaches that man is created in the image of God. We have criticised others for having created a god in their own image. May I be bold enough to say that we cannot help that. The way we think of God is the way we see humanity, and conversely, the way we think of humanity is the way we understand the nature of God.

We need to ask the question 'What is it to be human?' before we move on to consider specific issues in our culture. We can seek to understand the nature of being human through various methodologies, such as that of philosophy or science (biology and sociology). We know that biology is inadequate as a discipline to tell us what humanity is. Its inevitable conclusion is Darwin's *Origin of Species*. Sociology is a useful science in order to help us understand many of the issues relating to humankind, but its bold attempts to define humanity are really approaches from *below*. In other words, it makes observations of fallen humanity and then assumes that humankind possesses intrinsic goodness. That is the starting point of secular humanism. It is naturalistic and shows similar features to the Chinese mindset discussed in the previous chapter.

Since the secular humanist regards 'human persons as complete masters of their own affairs and destinies and deliberately excludes the transcendent from its philosophy',[140] it cannot legitimately claim to be able to see man in his essential nature, i.e. a humanity understood ontologically. A humanity understood ontologically can only be theological. It needs an approach from *above*.

Our understanding of what it is to be human must therefore flow from our understanding of the *imago Dei*. The supreme example of humanity is seen in the humanity of Jesus Christ. The concept of the imago Dei comes from a few passages in the Old Testament (Gen. 1:26f, 5:1, 9:6). The New Testament picks up this theme (Rom. 8:29; 2 Cor. 3:18; Eph. 4:24; Col. 3:10) and ultimately identifies Jesus Christ as the imago.[141]

Ray Anderson gives a succinct summary of the imago Dei as presented by three prominent Protestant theologians, Brunner, Berkouwer, and Barth:

> The emphasis has been on the unity of the 'imago' as the orientation of the person towards God as the source and determination of existence as a human being. . . . *The relational aspect of the 'imago' is primary.* Relation with

---

[140] R W Franklin and J M Shaw, *The Case for Christian Humanism* (Grand Rapids: Eerdmans, 1991), 5.

[141] 'He is the image of the invisible God, the firstborn of all creation' (Col. 1:15).

> God entails the intersubjectivity of relation with other persons as the content of the 'imago'. . . . The total person is affected by sin in such a way that no aspect of the human person continues to bear the 'imago' as a natural and positive orientation towards God. . . . The renewing grace of God is necessary for both a noetic and ontic restoration of relationship with God.[142]

Thus, the imago Dei is present in the specific and concrete encounter of human relationship. What is human is the ability to respond freely to the another being and in the relationship so developed discover what is self in the community of humanity. It finds its completeness in the 'other'.[143] Barth has this comment to make in his understanding of the imago Dei:

> Could anything be more obvious than to conclude from this clear indication that the image and likeness of the being created by God signified existence in confrontation, i.e. in this confrontation, juxtaposition and conjunction of man and man which is that of male and female.[144]

It is cohumanity in which we need to put our emphasis. Because the true orientation of humanity is towards the ontic restoration of relationship with God, humanity needs to seek the good of his fellow beings as the realisation of that restored relationship. Thus, the moral demand of humanity is firstly anthropological before it is ethical. The locus of the ethical is therefore found in the responsiveness of the essential nature of being human (anthropology), and this essential nature is hinged on the understanding of the imago Dei.

This understanding enables us firstly to see the internal relationships of the Godhead in honouring and serving one another—the perichoretic relationship. This is secondly applied to our human relationships and then worked out in our ethics.

---

[142] R Anderson, *On Being Human* (Grand Rapids: Eerdmans, 1982), 224. Italics mine.

[143] 'Male and female He created them' (Gen. 1:27).

[144] K Barth, *Church Dogmatics*, III/1, 195.

Part Two, Chapter 4

THE TRIUNE GOD DEFINED AND DENIED

The ideal of the previous chapter was not so in the history of the church. The purpose of this chapter is to present a fairly comprehensive, though brief, reflection of the understanding of the Trinity over the centuries. It presents the movement between culture and theology where theology is more often than not subordinated to culture. As the dissertation is to show how the doctrine of the Trinity releases us from the bondage of secular or cultural thinking, the historical aspects give vivid illustrations of the process over the centuries. We see the historical characters not as heroes or villains, saints, or heretics but as people struggling with their cultural bondage when they are confronted with the revelation of Jesus Christ and what this means to them. The point is really made in the controversy at Nicea where theology was subordinated to culture by Arius. Arius could not move out of the captivity of his Greek philosophical thought and heritage. Athanasius was able to move beyond his cultural heritage and refused to bow to culture. He stood solidly on the revelation of the incarnation of Jesus Christ, and from this, he did not waver. He stood his ground 'against the world'.

The doctrine of the Trinity was recovered by the Reformers whose stand was truly Athanasian. Subsequent to the Reformation, the church again subordinated theology to culture; and this was most evident in the understanding of the covenant, which was influenced by the philosophers of the social contract theory. The theory of social contract was then applied to our understanding of the covenant and indeed to most of scripture with quite disastrous result. In fact, many aspects of our understanding of the Christian faith today is still under the influence of the Enlightenment. J B Torrance's article on 'Interpreting the Word by the Light of Christ or the Light of Nature? Calvin, Calvinism and Barth'[145] deals with this issue.

This is presented in order that the reader may not think that the problem of cultural captivity in the church today is unique and new. In previous times many had wrestled with the same problem as we wrestle with today. It puts the discussion into a historical perspective.

This chapter will take a brief historical survey to look at a few key points in the history of the church. It will show the dominance of legalistic thinking and the way Trinitarian thought has been subordinated to the prevailing culture. This journey serves to show that philosophy has replaced the Trinitarian communion and the contractual framework has replaced the covenant.

4.1 Early Church

Legalism was rife in the early church. The Pharisaic movement comprised a very devout group of people, but unfortunately, they had enshrined into legislation the lessons learnt after the captivity. Jesus had to confront the Pharisees on numerous occasions to tell them that our living is by grace and not by law. The Pharisees did not accept what He said.

Paul had the same problem in the Galatian church. It was again legalism taking over the gospel of free grace. The people were returned to a bondage from which they were once freed.

4.1.1. Tertullian

In the AD second century, Tertullian, from Carthage in the Western Roman Empire, was the first of the Latin writers to gain prominence in the church. His contribution to theology is best remembered as giving us the word *Trinity* to describe the Godhead. He was also a rigorous apologist who went on the attack against the heretics of the church. However, his teachings suffered from one drawback. He had training in law, and he approached the issues of the church from that framework. The Latin vocabulary was rich in the legal and administrative fields, but it was limited in theology. Tertullian had to coin numerous theological terms to express

---

[145] J B Torrance, 'Interpreting the Word by the Light of Christ or the Light of Nature? Calvin, Calvinism and Barth', in R V Schnucker, ed., *Calviniana: Ideas and Influence of Jean Calvin*, Sixteenth Century Essays and Studies, X (Kirksville, MO: Sixteen Century Journal Publishers, 1988).

what was in Hebrew and Greek. Now, when the Greek word *metanoia*[146] (which means a turning around) had to be translated into Latin, it adopted a legal connotation, and this paved the way for the understanding of repentance in a legal sense. His teachings abounded with do's and don'ts, and there were severe penalties for not conforming. His teaching was quite clearly what Niebuhr termed *Christ against culture*, and eventually what developed was a form of 'cultural Christianity'.

The important unit in Roman law was the paterfamilias (the head of the family or household). This leads to the view that the law is the final authority. The rationale for this approach is that in the natural world and in human relationships, there are eternal principles inherent in the natural order. All are subjected to a common 'obligation'. Failure to fulfil this *obligatio* requires reparation either of offering compensation or enduring pain. Every offence carries an exact penalty. This can be mitigated by the bond of friendship. When applied to the gods, sacrifice is the answer.

Tertullian's starting point was the guilty man, and the questions of importance to him were 'How can I find acceptance and salvation?' and 'How are the benefits of Christ applied to me?'[147] From this, he worked towards the doctrine of the work and person of Christ. His approach was legalistic, and therefore, repentance and baptism became the *conditions* of grace. The sacrament of penance developed out of this, and this approach in the West laid the foundation for the early church to head straight into the legalism of the medieval church, and there it stayed until the Reformation.[148]

4.1.2. Irenaeus

The Eastern Church, being Greek dominated, was more philosophical in its approach to theology and more concerned with wrestling with the issues relating to the person of Jesus Christ rather than with the practical issues of the church. Their starting point was not how but who, i.e. 'Who is Jesus Christ?' Unfortunately, Western legalism dominated the church.

Irenaeus was the bishop of Lyons and Vienne and an important Christian theologian of the second century. He came from Asia Minor, and his teaching was based largely on the gospel and epistles of the Apostle John. This was because his teacher was Polycarp who in turn was taught by

---

[146] Translated as repentance.

[147] J B Torrance, Lecture Notes in Fuller's D. Min. course, *Theology and Ministry of Worship* (PM 706).

[148] Ibid.

the Apostle John. Irenaeus spoke to the church as a teacher and champion of the faith.

In his defence of the faith, Irenaeus confronted the gnostics with the *who* question and then proceeded to work out the implications of that answer. The early church fathers had no problem with the concept of the incarnation of God in man. Irenaeus made this clear in his writings (book 5, chapter 2) where he wrote, 'When Christ visited us in His grace, He did not come to what did not belong to Him.'

It was not difficult for Irenaeus to conceive of God coming in human form to make visible the perfect God in the person of Jesus Christ. Irenaeus's argument went something like this. Man was created in the image and likeness of God in the beginning, i.e. man belongs to God and shares something in common with the Creator. There is thus a connectedness between God and man. Only because God has now come in human form is He able to redeem fallen man. In this argument, Irenaeus underlines the incarnation as the basis for the atonement. Unless there is incarnation, i.e. God become man, there is no atonement for humankind.

Bromiley summarised Irenaeus's contribution in this way:

> Irenaeus . . . plunges into the heart and centre of theology. Tackling the main themes of <u>the unity of God and his purpose and work and the reality of the incarnation</u>, he develops the rationality and coherence of the biblical message with striking force and perspicacity.[149]

4.2. Nicea: The Grafting of the Trinity onto the Greek God or the God of Any Culture

So what has culture to do with theology? A great deal. We are all familiar with the Nicene Creed and have come to regard it as the foundational statement of our faith. We see the problem of Nicea to be a theological one, but it should also be seen as a cultural problem. Arian was not the villain of his age. He was genuine in wrestling with the concept of God and the deity of Christ. Arian presented his thesis with the assumption of God in Greek philosophical thought, i.e. he conceived of God in absolute oneness.

---

[149] G Bromiley, *Historical Theology: An Introduction* (Grand Rapids: Eerdmans, 1978), 26. Underline mine.

4.2.1. The Background to Nicea

In the early fourth century, there was a bishop of Alexandria named Alexander. He taught that the Son was eternally begotten of the Father and in every way equal to the Father. Because he so emphasised the oneness of the Son with the Father, he was accused of Sabellianism (or modalism, where there is no distinction between the Son and the Father). In Alexandria, there was also a very learned presbyter named Arius who taught differently. He subordinated the Son to the Father in his famous statement, 'There was a time when He was not', referring to the Son as the firstborn of all creation.

So the controversy engulfed the whole of Christendom and culminated at an ecumenical conference at Nicea. The dispute was over the words *omo-ousios* and *omoi-ousios*.

4.2.2. Theology Subordinated to Culture

Many of the theological differences in the early church, apart from the differences in terminology between the Hellenic east and the Latin west, stem from the fact that the Greeks tried to graft the incarnation onto a god whom they understood in terms of the Greek deity. This is the god of the philosophers, the first cause or the unmoved mover. This graft did not take. The controversy at Nicea over the term *omoi-ousios*, which Arian favoured, is an example of this problem. Arian's starting point was the absolute God onto whom he tried to fit the man Jesus Christ,[150] so his problem ran something like this. If he put Jesus Christ on the same standing as God, then God would no longer be absolute. To do otherwise would make Jesus Christ less than God. Athanasius pointed out that the incarnation[151] is the starting point in our understanding of God. He anchored his understanding of the incarnation firmly onto the redemptive work of God, and from this, he did not waver. Bromiley commented on the stand of Athanasius in these words:

> Athanasius undoubtedly put the incarnation at the centre of the gospel, yet not in the place of or at the expense

---

[150] J N D Kelly, *Early Christian Doctrines*, 5th ed., (London: Adam &Charles Black, 1977), 243.

[151] Athanasius, *The Incarnation of the Word*.

of the death and rising again, but rather in unbreakable relationship with them.[152]

The difference in the two approaches by Arian and Athanasius lies in their ability to go past their cultural heritage. Athanasius freed himself from his cultural heritage to interact with the reality of God while Arian was locked in by his Greek heritage.

The statement of faith from Nicea has remained the definitive statement for the doctrine of the Trinity up to today.[153] It has not attempted to speculate on how it is possible but merely to state the confession of the experience of the people of God. It is interesting that a modern-day theologian, T F Torrance, has taken a fresh look at the doctrine of the Trinity in his book *The Trinitarian Faith*, based on the work of Athanasius at Nicea.

4.3. The Incarnation as the Hermeneutical Centre

Why is a Christology important and central to the discussion of culture? If *the doctrine of God lies at the heart of contemporary debates over culture*,[154] and if this understanding of God is obtained from the revelation given in the Bible, then the supreme and final revelation of God in Jesus Christ must be central to our discussion of culture.

Calvin saw the only way to understand God is to place Christ at the centre of all things as He is truly God and truly man (Col. 1:15–18). He wrote the *Institutes* to help the people to understand the Bible. The only way to understand the Bible is to interpret it Christologically. In his commentary on John's gospel, he wrote, 'The Scriptures are to be read with the purpose of finding Christ there.'[155] The Bible is a book that enables us to appropriate the life-giving grace of God.[156] Calvin thought of the Bible as a mirror showing Christ. He saw the Lord's supper as the mirror God has given to us to see Christ, even more intimately than the Bible.

---

[152] G Bromiley, *Historical Theology: An Introduction* (Grand Rapids: Eerdmans, 1978), 80.

[153] The Nicea statement of faith has received only minor modifications in subsequent councils including that from Chalcedon in AD 451.

[154] D A Carson and J D Woodbridge, eds., 'Christian Witness in an Age of Pluralism', in *God and Culture* (Grand Rapids: Eerdmans, 1993), 46.

[155] Quoted in Calvin, *Institutes*, vol. I, lvi.

[156] Ibid.

The God that we worship is the triune God. It suffices to say at this juncture that our culture reflects our understanding of the God we worship. If this is so, then the way we conceive of God in His triunity is vital to the discussion on Christianity and culture.

4.4 Post-Nicea

It was not a smooth road after the Nicene settlement. Bishop Alexandria died in 328, and Athanasius succeeded him. Constantine died in 337. The empire was divided among his three sons: Constantine II, taking the West; Constans, Italy and North Africa; and Constantius, the East. Constantius was the strongest and eventually defeated his brothers and became sole ruler of the empire. Constantius was pro-Arian. It might be that he needed the Eastern bishops to support him in his war against the Persians. He coerced the Western bishops into supporting him against the Nicene Creed and was able to dispose Athanasius. After the death of Constantine, the Arians were in ascendancy. Athanasius was exiled five times. Athanasius stood firm on the ground that the Son is *omo-ousious* with the Father till the end, thus the expression, 'Athanasius against the world'. Athanasius died in 373.

4.4.1. Cappadocian Fathers

Three bishops from Cappadocia in the fourth century—Basil of Caesarea (~329–379), Gregory of Nyssa (~335–395), and Gregory of Nazianzus (~329–390)—refined the understanding of person and substance in the Trinitarian dogma. They developed the thinking of the triune Godhead as a community of persons. In their conception of the oneness and threeness of the Godhead, they approached this through the analogy of three different people having a common nature. This led to a charge of tritheism against them.

However, they insisted that the particularity of the three Persons of the Godhead did not destroy the unity of the divine life. Their understanding of *ousia* was cast in the internal relationship of the three Persons, the relationship being dynamic, mutually interpenetrating, unitary, and without opposition.[157] They continued the struggle for the orthodoxy of the Nicene faith and went beyond what Athanasius affirmed.

---

[157] T F Torrance, *The Trinitarian Faith* (Edinburgh: T&T Clark, 1988), 320.

4.4.2. Augustine and the Trinity

Augustine (AD 345–430) gave the Western world a more developed contribution in the understanding of the triune Godhead in his work *The Trinity*. While the Trinitarian dogma had been developed since the time of Tertullian, its fullest exposition was not until the time of Augustine. He developed the Trinitarian dogma as a category of individual persons as against the thinking of the Cappadocian fathers who developed the dogma as a community of persons.[158] The former understanding of the Trinity leads to the excesses of individualism in the West.

In opposition to Arianism, Augustine proclaimed that the Persons of the triune Godhead are of the same substance, i.e. omo-ousios. They are not to be thought of as three separate individuals, but there is a unity of the Persons. This concern lay behind his doctrine that the Holy Spirit proceeds from the Son as well as the Father—the 'double procession' that appears in the Western creeds. Up to this time, little had been said regarding the Holy Spirit as the heresies were mainly Christological.

Augustine used different images to describe the Trinity's mutual relation. It is, for instance, a relation like that of 'the lover, the beloved, and the love', which flows between them. The entire Trinity operates in the action of each Person just as an individual acts as a complete person in every act of memory, intelligence, and will. The significance of Augustine's contribution lies in the analogy he used not to prove the Trinity but to deepen our understanding of the one in three. Augustine's contribution henceforth dominates the Western doctrine of the Trinity.

4.4.3. Chalcedon

The confession of the Chalcedonian Settlement (AD 451) expresses without any ambiguity the consubstantiality between the Father and Son:

> In agreement, therefore, with the holy fathers, we all unanimously teach that we should confess that our Jesus Christ is one and the same Son, the same perfect in Godhead and the same perfect in manhood, **truly God and truly man**, the same of a rational soul and body, **consubstantial with the Father in Godhead, and the same consubstantial with us in manhood**, like us in all things except in sin; begotten from the Father before the

---

[158] J Moltmann, *The Trinity and the Kingdom of God*, trans. M Kohl (London: SCM, 1981), 1981.

ages as regards His Godhead, and in the last days, the same, because of us and because of our salvation begotten from the Virgin Mary, the *Theotokos*, as regards His manhood; one and the same Christ, Son, Lord, only-begotten, made known in two natures **without confusion, without change, without division, without separation,** the difference of the natures being by no means removed because of the union, but the property of each nature being preserved and coalescing in one *prosopon* and one *hupostasis*—not parted or divided into two *prosopa*, but one and the same Son, only-begotten, divine Word, the Lord Jesus Christ, as the prophets of old and Jesus Christ Himself have taught us about Him and the creed of our fathers has handed down.

This was the fourth and largest ecumenical council after Nicea. It re-established the Nicene Creed as orthodoxy. It affirmed Christ to be 'the same perfect in Godhead and the same perfect in manhood, **truly God and truly man**, the same of a rational soul and body, **consubstantial with the Father in Godhead, and the same consubstantial with us in manhood**, like us in all things except in sin; . . . made known in two natures **without confusion, without change, without division, without separation**'.

4.5. The Perichoresis

The persons of the Trinity are distinct from one another, and yet there is a oneness of substance. John of Damascus (AD ~652–750) expounded the idea of communion in terms of the interpenetration of the persons within the Godhead. He used the term *perichoresis*[159] to describe this relationship. He began with the Trinity and moved to the unity of the Godhead, which he expressed as the communion (koinonia). Each person of the Godhead indwells the other in eternal love to such an extent that they are one.

This interpenetration of the persons within the Godhead provides a dynamic approach to the understanding of the oneness and threeness of the Godhead as against the static understanding of trying to fit the three into one.

---

[159] The word is derived from the Greek *choreo*, meaning to dance. Hence, *perichoresis*, a dance around, one with the other.

We lack this insight into the interpenetration of the persons within our community. Where there is this interpenetration, this is often with the aim of control and manipulation, which leads to a loss of personhood.

Moltmann developed this idea of the interpenetration of the persons of the Godhead to avoid any idea of subordination within the Trinity. In his section on the 'Life of the Trinity', he concludes,

> Every divine Person exists in the light of the other and in the other. By virtue of the love they have for one another they ex-ist totally in the other: the Father ex-ists by virtue of his love, as himself entirely in the Son; the Son, by virtue of his self-surrender, ex-ists as himself totally in the Father; and so on.[160]

In this framework of our understanding of Trinitarian relationship, there is an implied freedom of the individual person. There is freedom in a community of men and women without supremacy and subjection. Yet at the same time, the men and women in the community retain their respective differentiation and are not enmeshed into an amorphous mass. Just as dignity is conferred, so is freedom conferred. Both are relational entities. I quote again from Moltmann:

> I am free and feel myself to be truly free when I am respected and recognized by others and when I for my part respect and recognize them. I become truly free when I open my life for other people and share with them, and when other people open their lives for me and share them with me. Then the other person is no longer the limitation of my freedom; he is an expansion of it.[161]

What is implied in this is that there is love within the relationship just as there is love in the Trinitarian relationship. In other words, it is a liberating love as the title of one book reads.[162]

Brueggemann engaged the metaphor of the 'dance' in relation to the covenant. He then used this concept to enhance the understanding of freedom. In a dance, the partners take each other seriously and are

---

[160] J Moltmann, *The Trinity and the Kingdom of God*, 173.

[161] Ibid., 216.

[162] G Bingham, *Liberating Love* (Blackwood, South Australia: New Creation Publication Inc., 1960).

together. They may respond in 'many postures, many locations, many varied relationships'; but within the covenantal relationship, they maintain 'fidelity with enormous freedom'.[163]

Thus, in this concept of the perichoresis, we are able to hold together the three in one and the covenantal relationship inherent within the triunity. To dwell only on the triunity without the covenant is an abstraction, and to dwell only on the covenantal relationship without the triunity of the Godhead would be to drift without an anchor. That is why the triunity and the covenant are so intrinsically linked together and the concept of the perichoresis so powerful in enabling us to think of it comprehensively. This perichoresis will lead us to think relationally and in terms of participation in the Godhead and with one another. This will be the basis in which we engaged some of the specific theological issues in section 2 of this dissertation.

4.6. Medieval Church

One of the great thinkers in the medieval church was St Anselm. His contribution to the church and theology is immense, and the influence of his thought is still being felt in the church today. His thesis on the doctrine of atonement has been a cornerstone in Christian thinking ever since. However, with his legal background, Anselm put his doctrine of atonement on a legal basis.

The real value of Anselm's theory establishes the objective character of the atonement and bases its necessity on the immutable nature of God, which makes it impossible that He should permit the violation of His honour to go unpunished. It deals with God first, and only secondarily with us, and a transaction that gives satisfaction to God. Thus, propitiation is the basis of reconciliation.[164] We can see that in Anselm's satisfaction theory, the basis of all succeeding study of the atonement had been laid. It ensures the approach to the atonement we call 'evangelical', that is, the approach from God's side.[165]

Anselm's theory bases the redemption exclusively on the death of Christ and denies the atoning significance of His life. It emphasises the substitutionary element but contains little on the participation on the

---

[163] W Brueggemann, *The Psalms and the Life of Faith* (Minneapolis: Fortress, 1995), 136–137.

[164] R A Finlayson, *The Story of Theology*, 2nd ed., (London: Tyndale Press, 1969), 41.

[165] Ibid.

merits of Christ. It represents the application of the merits of Christ to the sinner as a merely external transaction. There is no hint of the mystical union of Christ and believers.

Anselm's model (of the legal processes) of God's ordering of His world cannot be accepted to express the relations between God and man. He had taken the Roman model developed by Tertullian and applied it to explain the atonement. He appealed to reason and made little reference to the Bible. T F Torrance described Anselm's theory of the atonement as 'a severely juridical conception of atonement as an external penal transaction between God and sinful humanity'.[166] He again took up the point in his book *The Mediation of Christ* when he contrasted the difference between an intrinsic and extrinsic conception of atonement.[167] We can only gain a knowledge of things when they are disclosed in their internal relations and structures.[168] Thus, an extrinsic conception of the atonement will result in a detachment of Christ from the context of the covenant relationship with His chosen people.[169]

4.7. Reformation

The teaching on the covenant was recovered by Luther (1483–1546) and Calvin (1509–64). Both men identified the priority of grace in their teachings. Calvin developed the meaning of the covenant in II/10, 11 of his *Institutes*, setting out that there is only *one* covenant expressed in two different manners in the old and new periods.

We need to make two points about our discussion of the covenant:[170]

1. It is a covenant and not a contract. A contract is a mutual agreement, and the two parties bind themselves to an agreed set of conditions to ensure some future result. A covenant is not a contract. It is of grace and is initiated and maintained by the Lord. It is not conditional on our effort. It is all of grace. Grace precedes law as

---

[166] T F Torrance, 'Karl Barth and the Latin Heresy', *Scottish Journal of Theology* 39 (1986): 477.

[167] T F Torrance, *The Mediation of Christ* (Edinburgh: T & T Clark, 1992). 40–42.

[168] Ibid., 51.

[169] Ibid., 47.

[170] Calvin, *Institutes*, II/10/1–6.

Paul argues that the promise to Abraham came first and the law came 430 years later (Gal. 3:17).
2. There are not two covenants but one covenant expressed as two different forms, the old and the new, the shadow and the substance, the promise and the fulfilment. The grace of God is as much evident in the old as it is in the new.

When we refer to the old and the new covenant, we are not referring to two covenants but to the two expressions of the one covenant. The old covenant was external to the hearts and minds, demanding a compliance people did not have the ability to maintain. It is important to point out here that the law spells out the obligations of grace and *not* the conditions of grace.[171] In his epistle to the Romans and Galatians, Paul explained that the law could only bring about a sense of guilt and hopelessness. Indeed, our transgressions as made known by the law should make us aware of our need of grace.[172] It is the stubbornness of the human heart that denies this.

The writer to the Hebrews (8:6–15) contrasted the old and new covenants and made it clear that the new covenant through Jesus Christ would be internalised. He was quoting from Jeremiah 31:31 with reference to the promise of the new covenant. The new covenant would be internalised by a process that Jeremiah and his contemporaries did not know about. The writer to the Hebrews made it clear that the process of internalisation is through the mediation of Jesus Christ.[173]

At the last supper, Jesus announced that the new covenant would be written in blood, i.e. His very own blood, and the cup that they drank would then symbolise the new covenant brought in by His mediation (Lk. 22:20).

We do not assume that it is we ourselves who have transacted the new covenant by our decision and that we are now able to internalise the law ourselves. That is not so. We rely solely on the mediation of Jesus Christ to make it possible for us so that again no one may boast. As it has been pointed out above, Calvin has expounded *sola gratia* in terms of the doctrine of the vicarious humanity and sole priesthood of Christ (book

---

[171] J B Torrance, 'Covenant or Contract', *Scottish Journal of Theology* 23 (1970): 66.

[172] Ibid., 13.

[173] This topic has been discussed in the New Creation Teaching Ministry Pastors' Study Group, *Christ: The Mediator of the Better Covenant: I & II* (17 Oct 1994 and 7 Nov 1994).

2) and the doctrine of union with Christ through the participation in the Spirit (book 3).

Our Lord Jesus Christ is still our great High Priest today. While His earthly ministry has been completed, He is now 'at the right hand of the right hand of the throne' of God and continues to serve at 'the sanctuary set up by the Lord' interceding on our behalf (Heb. 8:1–6). This continuing high priesthood of Jesus Christ highlights the fact that while the victory has been won on the cross of Calvary, we are still living as it were in the shadow of that reality with Christ as our mediator and High Priest. This has implications for our interpersonal relationships and the worship of God.

4.8. Post-Reformation

After Calvin came several saints who veered away from the incarnational and Trinitarian approach to the understanding of God and emphasised piety from man's point of view. These are essentially theologies of works. St John of the Cross is an example of this trend.

St John of the Cross (1542–1591) was a Catholic mystical theologian and a Spanish Carmelite who went about barefooted. He came after the Reformation, was beatified, and made a saint in 1726 and a doctor of the cross in 1926. He wrote several books, among them *Ascent of Mt Carmel* and *The Dark Night of the Soul*. The latter book inspired a famous painting of the cross. In these two books, he showed the steps to be taken on the way to receive a vision of or union with God.[174]

The writings showed the typical piety of that age. It was thought that union with God is something one has to strive towards. It is not so. God has created us for union with Himself. That relation is internal to the triune Godhead. The question is not how we can attain to it, as these writers worked to demonstrate, but 'How can we participate in it?', i.e. in something that has already been accomplished. Jesus Christ came to draw us into it. We participate in His relation with God.[175]

4.9. Federal Theology and Scholastic Calvinism

After the Reformers, we see the inversion of grace and law. Natural theology and the light of reason dominated the thinking of that age. The

---

[174] A chart of the complexity of the steps required in given in the notes of the seminar on the 'Theology and Ministry of Worship'.

[175] This theme has been dealt with very clearly in Calvin, *Institutes* III/3–4.

law was regarded as the final authority and central to the covenant. Grace was given only to the elect of God. Grace was made subordinate to election and law. Among those who adopted this order are the Dutch Reformed Church in South Africa and the Southern Baptist in the United States. In fact, I may be permitted to add to this the overseas Chinese churches in Australasia, Europe, and North America.

Scholars who came after Calvin distorted his teaching, and soon there developed the school of federal theology (federal from *foedus*, meaning covenant). This school subordinated grace to law and made the grace of God conditional on the works of man. The thinking of the scholastic Calvinist was dominated by the Aristotelian method of logic and the conception of God as the absolutely omnipotent, omniscient, and immutable law giver.[176]

The reason for this trend is the development of the doctrine of 'double decree' by Calvin's successor, Theodore Beza, who made this the major premise of his system of theology.[177] Calvin had not taught this. Beza taught that Christ is the mediator not for all man but only for the elect. The inevitable result is a doctrine of 'limited atonement' because election is now made prior to grace.[178]

We have inherited from the scholastic Calvinist the phrase *covenant of works*. This is the first of a two-covenant scheme: the covenant of works with all creation and the covenant of grace with the elect. The phrase *covenant of works*—otherwise referred to as the covenant of nature, covenant of creation or covenant of law, as far as we know—was first used by Dudley Fenner, an English Puritan, in his publication, *Theolgia Sacra* in 1585.[179] This covenant of works was originally made with Adam. If he obeyed, he would live; and if he disobeyed, he would surely die. Adam was supposed to be able to discern the laws of nature by the light of reason. This set up a strictly legal relationship between God and Adam.

In the discussion on how this election relate to God's sovereignty and social ethic, J B Torrance traced the way this led to the grace-nature model and subsequently a covenant of works.[180] There was a return to the medieval view that *grace presupposes nature* and *grace perfects nature* in

---

[176] M Jinkins, 'Elements of Federal Theology in the Religious Thought of John Locke', *Evangelical Quarterly* 66:2 (1994): 123–141.

[177] J B Torrance, 'Interpreting the Word by the Light of Christ or the Light of Nature? Calvin, Calvinism and Barth', 259.

[178] Ibid.

[179] Ibid., 260.

[180] Ibid., 259–267.

contrast to the Reformation view that there is nothing prior to grace. So since God has by nature created mankind black and white, so grace does not destroy nature but conforms to nature and this justifies the segregation. It is a deeply dualistic approach so characteristic of our age too.

Theology after the Reformation had come full circle at this point. Law is again made prior to grace. It ought to be pointed out that this modification of Calvin's teaching was made by his successors. Calvin did not teach this.[181]

The federal theologians had great influence on the development of democratic governments and issues such as the divine rights of kings, etc. Unfortunately, the nature-grace model also advocated ethnic segregation and slavery.[182] In an article in the *Time* magazine[183] was a report that the Southern Baptist made a repentance at their convention of their stand on federal theology in the past 200 years.

4.10. The Age of Enlightenment

The concept of social contract was developed in the philosophy of politics and economics, in particular in the influential writings of Thomas Hobbes (1588–1679), in his *Leviathan* (1651). Hobbes made use of the social contract theory to justify the absolute power of the sovereign. The late sixteenth and seventeenth centuries saw the struggles for justice and liberty with the collapse of feudalism. Pacts and contracts were made to bind people to one another in an attempt to avoid conflict. Hobbes held that a person's duties are laid down by the state. If there is no government to enforce performance of the duties, then the 'duties' are not binding.

The events that led to formulations of this kind in Western Europe were the deposition of Mary, Queen of Scots, in 1567 and the massacre of the Huguenots[184] in 1572. Questions were raised as to how the rights of

---

[181] Space does not permit a discussion of the issues involved here, and I refer to the following article: J B Torrance, 'Interpreting the Word by the Light of Christ or the Light of Nature? Calvin, Calvinism and Barth', 255–268. This article traces the development of federal theology and the implications of this line of thinking in the social unrest of our day.

[182] Ibid.

[183] *Time Magazine* (3 July 1995): 41.

[184] They were French protestants of the sixteenth and seventeenth centuries and persecuted during the religious wars of the time.

both king and people can be safeguarded.[185] The answer was by 'covenant', by which they meant 'contract'. The covenant was understood in terms of the social contract theory developed by the philosophers of the day.

John Locke (1632–1704), known for his thesis on the social contract, came under the influence of scholastic Calvinism.[186] A movement was developing to reject the divine rights. There need to be checks and balances between the ruling class and the people. Scholastic Calvinism had taught the contractual framework based on natural theology and the light of reason. Locke saw God as the great lawmaker. His contemporary, John Milton (1608–1674), who had witnessed the civil war and the execution of Charles I (1600–1649), wrote, 'The crown sits on the constitution, not on the head of a man.' The law became supreme. Soon the law or a contractual relationship found its way into all avenues of life and dictated how humanity should relate to one another. It puts humanity again under a bondage that it should not have known.

4.11. The Indicatives of Grace Precede the Imperatives of Law

The covenant has been interpreted in terms of the law, and we have come to regard the law as supreme; and therefore, we seek our righteousness in terms of what the law demands. In a covenant relationship, the promise is prior to the law. The promise to Abraham made him the father of a great nation, not the law. M. Parsons, in his article 'Being Precedes Act: Indicatives and Imperative in Paul's Writing',[187] argues for the priority of grace over law in the pattern of Paul's letters. The indicative is not unrelated to the imperative, and neither should they be seen as one. An example of this relationship is seen in 1 Corinthians where Paul responded to the problems with a focus on Christ first of all and worked out the solutions from there. He responded to the divisions in the Philippian church with that majestic hymn in 2:1–11, focusing on the incarnation of Jesus Christ and the humility with which He adorns Himself.

He made this remark in his conclusion:

---

[185] J B Torrance, *Calviniana*, 261.

[186] M Jinkins, 'Federal Theology in the Religious Thought of John Locke', *The Evangelical Quarterly*, 66:2 (1994), 123–141. This article begins with the characteristics of federal theology and shows the influence of scholastic Calvinism in the writings of John Locke.

[187] M Parsons, 'Being Precedes Act: Indicatives and Imperative in Paul's Writing', *Evangelical Quarterly* LX, no. 2 (April 1988): 99–127.

> The indicatives speak of that which has been accomplished by God in and through Christ—but does not denote simply the divine element as opposed to the human activity in fulfilling the imperative. We have noted that Paul's ethical admonition is directed to, and is determined by, the present redemptive-historical situation. The new age that dawned with Christ's resurrection and the coming of the Holy Spirit determined that this should be so. The Spirit, himself, then, is the link between the indicative and the imperative of Christian reality and existence. He is at once an element of the former and a constituent part of the latter.[188]

He has given us a summary of the relationship between the indicatives and the imperatives. This is expressed in terms of the Trinity and enables us to see clearly the divine accomplishment in our 'being' and the divine assistance given to us by the Holy Spirit in the fulfilment of our 'acts'.

4.12. Covenant, not Contract, Grace, not Law

When we are in a covenantal relationship, we are in a relationship that is unconditional. The moment we introduce an 'if' into the relationship, we are introducing a conditional clause and that will turn it into a contract. As our relationship with one another develops, we come to know each other more and more. Knowing brings along with it problems. The more you know about a person, the more you see the idiosyncrasies, and the more difficult it is to accommodate to that. Closeness brings along an intensity of passion and also an intensity of demands.

Covenant relationship has its basis in grace and forgiveness, without which no relationship in our imperfect humanity can exist. The greater the expectation in that relationship, there will be a need for a greater degree of grace and forgiveness. So when God expects from us a perfect response, He provides the ultimate in grace and forgiveness, i.e. in giving to us His Son Jesus Christ, in whom God has provided the perfect response on our behalf. In responding to God's covenant, it is not our response that is perfect, but we come through the perfect covenant response of Jesus Christ. Only grace and forgiveness within the relationship will sustain and nurture it, thereby leading the participants into greater intimacy. Otherwise, its demands and conditionality will fragment the relationship; and we see so much of that today in families, society, and churches. It is so reassuring to

---

[188] Ibid., 127.

know in any relationship that when one stretches out a hand the other will take it and accept it unconditionally.

In a contractual framework, when there is a breach in the attached conditions, then one has to make recompense for that breach. That is our understanding from the natural law and the 'light of reason'. In other words, there is forgiveness, but it follows from repentance and whatever the recompense that is involved. This is falling into the error of making repentance prior to forgiveness, i.e. law prior to grace.

In book 3 of Calvin's *Institutes*, he differentiates between legal repentance and evangelical repentance.[189] Legal repentance, he pointed out, is when the sinner recognises the bondage of sin but is unable to escape from it. In evangelical repentance, the sinner recognises the bondage of sin, looks up to Christ, and sees the deliverance from that bondage. Calvin further pointed out that faith brings about that recognition of sin and therefore brings about the repentance. It is a response to the grace of God through Jesus Christ. This argument further emphasises the priority of forgiveness in relation to repentance.

In a covenantal relationship, forgiveness is built into the relationship. In other words, forgiveness precedes repentance. Did Paul not write, 'While we were yet sinners, Christ died for us' (Rom. 5:8)? In exasperation, Paul asked which came first, the promise or the law, to the Jews who took so much glory in their history.

J Torrance has argued that forgiveness is logically prior to repentance.[190] That has to be so in any relationship that is unconditional. If that is not so, then one would have to confess and repent of every sin committed during the day. Now what happens when the person forgets to confess one sin or wrong done? That one wrong will not be forgiven. That was the problem Martin Luther had when he spent each night contemplating on his sins during the day. One omission would mean that he remained a sinner.[191] If that is the scenario in a relationship, then what confidence have we in relating in a meaningful way without a continual sense of guilt?

One of humanity's basic needs is belonging. Our society has locked us into a conditional framework where we need to prove our worth before we can belong. This is based on the grace-nature model discussed above. The covenantal framework accepts us into the community (family of God) where grace is prior to law and forgiveness prior to repentance. Of course,

---

[189] Calvin, *Institutes*, III/3.

[190] J B Torrance, 'Covenant or Contract', 51–76.

[191] Calvin, *Institutes*, III/4/16. 'The enumeration of all sins is impossible'.

there will be some who will not accept this framework and continue to struggle to prove their own self-worth.

When we try to understand this covenantal relationship in a legalistic framework, then we have the continuing problem of our response. 'Shall we then continue in sin that grace may abound' (Rom. 6:1)? Or shall we repent so that God will forgive us? So we are back to either cheap grace or conditional grace.[192] Within the covenantal framework, our repentance is not the condition of grace but the response or obligation to grace.[193]

---

[192] J B Torrance, 'Covenant or Contract', 56.

[193] Ibid.

Part Two, Chapter 5

AN EVALUATION OF THE CHINESE CHURCH IN THE LIGHT OF THE TRINITY

The way in which the Chinese church has subordinated Christianity to its culture only conforms to the general pattern outlined in the previous chapter. The naturalistic Chinese mind would very readily adopt the grace-nature model mentioned in the previous chapter. This chapter will make a general evaluation of the Chinese church with a call to depart from Confucianism and to rediscover the Trinitarian faith. It will argue that Christianity with its basis in the Chinese cultural framework would, in fact, have denied the Trinity.

5.1. A Recovery of the Trinitarian Faith

While there is mention of shang-ti[194] in Chinese thinking, the idea of a personal god is still quite foreign to the Chinese mind. Many of the names of the gods are borrowed from Buddhism and others are from folklore pertaining to the local deities. To the naturalistic Chinese mind, the concept of god is mainly derived from nature. What is termed the Chinese religion is really Chinese philosophy at its foundation into which Buddhism and Taoism are blended in. In the Chinese classics referred to

---

[194] A term used to translate *God* and as mentioned before often equated with the personal God of the Bible.

before, and especially 'in the Four Books there is no story of creation, and no mention of heaven or hell'.[195]

> It is difficult for the naturalistic Chinese mind to comprehend a God who is personal and known only from His self-disclosure. There is no precedent to this concept in her millennia of history and philosophy. Just as the Chinese subordinated Buddhism and Taoism to its Confucianist base, they have also subordinated the self-disclosure of Yahweh to the same naturalistic base. In other words, the way the self-disclosure of Yahweh is understood in terms of the natural. Very often, the understanding of what God is like is reasoned from what is observed in nature.

This is not to say that one cannot work from nature. There are resemblances, and Jesus used many examples from nature in His parables on the Kingdom of God. Many have regarded these parables to have made clear the Kingdom of God and thus are able to argue from the natural to the spiritual. In the context of the Chinese naturalistic mind, this is precisely the misunderstanding. The parables are not wholly revelatory. There is a particular difficulty with what Jesus said regarding the parables in Mark.

> [9]And he said, 'Let anyone with ears to hear listen!' [10]When he was alone, those who were around him along with the twelve asked him about the parables. [11]And he said to them, 'To you has been given the secret of the kingdom of God, but for those outside, everything comes in parables; [12]in order that 'they may indeed look, but not perceive, and may indeed listen, but not understand; so that they may not turn again and be forgiven.' (Mk. 4:9–12, NRSV)

There is concealment in the parables, and at the same time they are meant to be revelatory. Many explanations have been given to clarify this apparent contradiction. Any explanation will have to hold in tension the concealment and revelation of the parables.

Our thinking starts from the natural phenomena. We observe the phenomenon and draw conclusions about what we have observed. Now this

---

[195] Y L Fung, *A Short History of Chinese Philosophy* (New York: MacMillan, 1948), 1.

is not an end in itself as the observation points to something beyond. For example, the natural phenomenon points to something beyond humankind as the psalmist exclaimed.

> ³When I look at your heavens, the work of your fingers, the moon and the stars that you have established; ⁴what are human beings that you are mindful of them, mortals that you care for them? (Ps. 8:3–4 NRSV)

In other words, the natural framework leads to another framework of thinking. This other framework is that of the triune Creator God. That is not to embrace the Platonic system. The natural is not just a shadow. The natural is an observed reality, but it points to something beyond itself.

When the parables are understood in their naturalistic framework, then the truth will be concealed. If through the parables one is able to move into another framework, then the secret is revealed. This is where the Chinese mind has difficulty. It wants to remain on the naturalistic framework and from this base moves towards the understanding of God, i.e. to understand God in terms of the naturalistic framework. In so doing, it will inevitably subordinate the triune God to the natural framework and this will be exemplified in the discussion below on the missionary outreach.

In the continuing debate on contextualisation in Asian theologies, Bruce Nicholls emphasised that 'we need to recover the central themes of dogmatic theology that are either neglected or misunderstood in Asia'.[196] He called for a recovery of the Trinitarian faith:

> God's self-disclosure as Father, Son and Holy Spirit needs to be constantly contextualised. Chalcedon faithfully expressed this knowledge in the midst of controversy in Greek and Roman cultures. In Asia, where the distinction and relationship of God's universal and His special revelation is not fully understood, where the Holy Spirit is often confused with Christ, the personal God lost in the impersonal principle and law separated from the Lawgiver, a recovery of the Trinitarian faith is urgently needed.[197]

---

[196] B J Nicholls, 'A Living Theology for Asian Churches', *The Bible and Theology in Asian Contexts*, ed. B R Ro and R Eshenaur (Taiwan: Asia Theological Association, 1984), 134.

[197] Ibid.

There needs to be a starting point in our theological thinking. This point is none other than the Trinitarian God as made known to us by revelation. So often, as in Nicea, the starting point is the god that we conceive of through our culture or philosophy, and onto this god, we try to graft the Trinitarian God. This was precisely the process taken by the missionaries to China. Covell commented, 'The process, then, for many missionaries to state the gospel in Chinese was first to establish the reality of the spiritual world within the Chinese intellectual framework and then teach the truths of the Bible.'[198]

In proceeding this way, the truth of the triunity of God will inevitably become subordinated to the Chinese naturalistic intellectual framework, and this framework will be the starting point of all theological thinking from then on. The triune God will be contorted into this framework, which is deeply rooted in Confucianism.

W A P Martin's *Tiandao Suyuan*[199] approached the apologetics from firstly natural theology, then evidences of Christianity, and finally revealed theology. Even in his section on revealed theology, he dealt with the attributes of God from a philosophical standpoint.[200] He should have started with the revelation in Jesus Christ and the triunity of God rather than trying to graft this onto natural or philosophical theology.

It may be unkind to criticise the methodology taken by the missionaries. Their intention was sincere as they had been brought up in their days with, and taught precisely, this approach. The Bible colleges in their days and many colleges even today taught firstly the concept of God and the attributes in a module termed *philosophy of religion*. At a later stage, the doctrine of the Trinity is brought in and subordinated to the god of philosophy as in Nicea. That is why for a long time in the nineteenth and twentieth centuries, the church did not have much to say about the Trinity.[201]

The Chinese churches are guilty of this as well. They start with the god of natural theology, the heavens (tien), and onto this god they tried to graft the Trinitarian God of the Bible. The Chinese churches need to consider seriously the fifth pattern of thinking proposed by Dr Lam above, i.e. to allow Christianity to judge our culture. By this is meant that the Trinitarian understanding is used to evaluate culture and not the reverse.

---

[198] R R Covell, *Confucius, the Buddha and Christ* (New York: Orbis, 1986), 98.

[199] The title means 'Evidences of Christianity'. It was written by him in 1854. It was used extensively by missionaries and in theological colleges. Ibid., 99.

[200] Ibid., 100.

[201] Personal communication from Prof J Torrance.

As many missionaries in those days were brought up in the pietist movement of the West, they naturally brought this emphasis to the Chinese, and this fitted perfectly with the piety of the Chinese. Again Christianity was subordinated to the culture of the day. In his assessment of the missionary outreach in China, Covell made mention of the pietism inherent in much of the thinking among Chinese Christians and in particular in the writings of Watchman Nee.[202] This pietistic brand of Christianity continues to be practised among the Chinese churches today.[203]

In the translator's preface to Ricci's *Tianzhu Shiyi*,[204] it was pointed out that 'in the later Ming and early Qing dynasties most Chinese scholars were materialists and either would not be able to comprehend anything Ricci might say about the Trinity or would reject it and him as foolish'.[205] It has been difficult for the Chinese churches today, with the way the Chinese mind has been influenced by Confucianism and its history of being evangelised by a grafting of the triune God onto the Chinese culture, to truly come to terms with the revelation of the Incarnation as the starting point of theology.

The gospel in many cross-cultural approaches has been presented from a cultural or anthropological perspective. This accentuates the dualism already existing in our society. What is needed is a unitary approach that starts from the triune God, and each culture then works through the core assumption of the culture in the light of this understanding. It calls for a participatory approach as this triune God has addressed His created humanity in the one eternal covenant of creation, which has been consummated through the Incarnate Lord Jesus Christ. The acknowledgement of the triunity of God requires us to relate to God in the way He has expressed His grace and mercy to us in His gracious covenant.

5.2 A Recovery of Covenantal Relationship: Our Participation in God

The gracious covenant of God sets the foundation for the relationship with God and indeed all human relationship. This is best summarised in chart 1 on the next page.

---

[202] Covell, *Confucius, the Buddha and Christ*, 195–201.

[203] Refer to chart in section 5.2 below.

[204] The title means 'The True Idea of God'. It was prepared in 1601 and used to present the gospel message to non-Christians. Covell, *Confucius, the Buddha and Christ*, 45.

[205] Ibid., 49.

To be in covenantal relationship with is to share in what He has given so graciously. This is the participatory approach and will be used in further discussion in the next section of this paper. It is enough at this stage to state the model and what it means to be in communion with the triune God and to give the scriptural basis for this.

DIVINE INITIATIVE
↑

HYPER-CALVINISM	PARTICIPATION *(IN THE SPIRIT THROUGH CHRIST TO THE FATHER)*
APATHY	PIETISM

→ → → HUMAN RESPONSE

Chart 1. Our Participation in God[206]

The ministry of Jesus Christ is to take us into the communion He has with His Father. This, He expressed very clearly in His High Priestly prayer.

> That they may all be one. As you, Father, are in me and I am in you, may they also be in us, so that the world may believe that you have sent me. (Jn. 17:21, NRSV)

---

[206] The arrows on the horizontal axis indicate the varying degree of the human response. On the vertical axis, there is no varying degree of the divine initiative which is perfect and sovereign. So the 'apathy' is solely the result of human indifference. It is not to be assumed otherwise.

To be in communion with Christ is to participate in Christ. This is expressed well by Paul in his teaching on the Lord's Supper (communion).

> The cup of blessing that we bless, is it not a sharing [koinonia] in the blood of Christ? The bread that we break, is it not a sharing [koinonia] in the body of Christ? (1 Cor. 10:16, NRSV)

To be 'in the Spirit' is a participation or sharing (koinonia) in the Spirit (2 Cor. 13:13; Phil. 2:1).

> The grace of the Lord Jesus Christ, the love of God, and the communion [koinonia] of the Holy Spirit be with all of you. (2 Cor. 13:13, NRSV)

> If then there is any encouragement in Christ, any consolation from love, any sharing [koinonia] in the Spirit, any compassion and sympathy, (Phil. 2:1, NRSV)

Before proceeding further, it is useful to refer to some assertions by C H Kraft in relation to God and culture.[207]

1. Human beings are totally immersed in culture.
2. God exists totally free of culture (except as He chooses to submit to cultural limitations).
3. God uses human culture as the milieu within which He interacts with human beings.

God relates with His people in their culture, and this is what He did in His call to various people such as Moses and Abraham. He called to them from within their culture and expressed this call as the covenant, a term that also expresses the relationship within the triune Godhead. Though He is the transcendent God, 'yet he has freely chosen to employ human culture and at major points to limit himself to the capacities of culture in his interaction with people'.[208] Within the one eternal covenant of creation, He expressed to them the details of the covenant in their cultural form. To Abraham, it was in terms of nationhood and descendants. To David, it was the essence of the throne. To the prophets Jeremiah and Ezekiel, it

---

[207] C Kraft, *Christianity in Culture* (New York: Orbis, 1979), 170.

[208] Ibid., 115.

was in terms of the stony hearts of the people and the implementation of a new covenant. In Jesus Christ and within the milieu of Jewish culture, the supreme and final revelation of the new covenant was declared in His vicarious humanity.

If 'culture is the milieu in which all encounters with or between human beings take place',[209] then the covenant must be the foundation of all human relationship. 'The Christian dynamic is in the venturesomeness of participating with God in the transformation of contemporary cultural forms to serve more adequately as vehicles for God's interaction with human beings.'[210]

The early church met and practised as a predominantly Jewish community using Jewish models and thought forms. As the church moved out of Judea and into Asia Minor, changes were made to their understanding and practice set out in Acts 15. Today, 2000 years later, the church of the West has dominated much of Christian thinking in terms of the models and thought forms from the period of the Enlightenment. As the gospel moves out to the Asian, African, and South American countries, the gospel needs to be embraced by these communities and expressed in their models and thought forms. The believers in these cultures cannot do otherwise. The Western world has much to learn from these communities as they reflect theologically on the ancient apostolic truth.

Newbigin has this to say regarding the monocultural understanding of the truth of scripture. He cited the Lordship of Jesus Christ as an example.

> That is to say that the full answer to the question 'Who is Jesus Christ?' can only be given when the fullness of humankind has been gathered into the confession of his name. When any one, standing within any of the cultures of mankind, says: 'Jesus is Lord', the meaning which is given by the word 'Lord' is shaped by, and therefore limited by, the culture in which he speaks. The full content of the word 'Lord', the full meaning of the Lordship of Jesus Christ, can only be that which it will have when every tongue shall call him Lord.[211]

---

[209] Ibid., 113.

[210] Ibid., 382.

[211] L. Newbigin, 'Christ and the Cultures', in *Scottish Journal of Theology* 30 (1977): 10.

In Ephesians 1:11, Paul made mention of 'all thing in heaven and earth together under one head, even Christ'. This is a difficult thought to grasp. Our conception is limited by our experience and understanding. It is not until all the redeemed from every nation, tribe, people, and language (Rev. 7:9) are gathered before Jesus Christ on the throne on that day of the Lord that we have the full understanding of what this means. We can only understand this in part with our limitation in space and time. This theme of participation will be taken up again in the discussion in the next section.

5.3. A Departure from Confucianism

Confucianism is very much a part of Chinese society and thinking. It is very deeply entrenched as it provides much of the needed stability in Chinese families and communities. Its influence is still retained to a significant extent among Chinese who have migrated to the West for generations. 'In Paris or San Francisco or Singapore, Chinese are still Chinese even after generations of sojourn. They seem all but unalterable.'[212] This very strong bond with the Chinese Confucianist heritage, though, having some merits of its own, presents problems in the way the gospel is understood. One example of this is seen in the conflict with the new generation of Chinese who have grown up in the west.

In Australia and America, this new generation is loosely referred to as the Australian- (or American-) born Chinese, the so-called ABC (American- or Australian-born Chinese). The older generation of pastors and elders still cling to the Confucian concept of filial piety, which retains the class distinction between senior and junior. In the concept of the filial in Confucianism, while there is reverence of the son for the father, the son and the father could not conceive of a oneness within that relationship. They will always remain father and son in their distinctive ways, and their relationship does not allow them to get any closer.[213]

The church continues to uphold this Confucian concept of the filial while trying to teach oneness of the church to the younger generation. The young people have rightly questioned where the locus of this oneness lies. They very quickly see this as a demand for submission and respect to the older generation in the Confucian context. While the younger rightly serves the older, it is difficult in Confucianism for the older to conceive of service to the younger except in a symbolic way from his high pedestal. This hierarchical relationship makes the concept of Christ's incarnation

---

[212] H G Creel, *Chinese Thought* (London: University Paperbacks, 1954), 17.

[213] This has been discussed in chapter 2.3.2.

foreign to the Chinese mind. While they may embrace the concept, they have understood this in an extrinsic manner.[214]

Now when one approaches the problem starting with the Trinitarian God, then the emphasis becomes very different. The relationship within the Godhead is described as a perichoresis,[215] i.e. an interpenetration of one another. When this occurs, there is not a fading of the distinctiveness of the individual but a oneness resulting from the receiving and giving to one other. There is a kind of circulatory movement within the relationship. While the father and son remain distinctively father and son, there is also a union in the relationship where the lives and acts of the father and son will be indistinguishable as one. This oneness and distinctiveness must not be separated or confused. When there is an interpenetration of one another within the relationship, there is a mutuality to be experienced. The Chinese church needs to return to the Trinity to understand what perichoresis is and then to express that in the horizontal relationship with one another.

Many have too often seized upon one aspect of the cultural emphasis and then interpreted Christianity on the basis of that. One example of this is the relational in Chinese culture. While it is said that the Chinese culture emphasises the relational, and indeed this is so, the relationship has become an ideological base in Confucianism. In the quotation below regarding the filial, Confucius has subordinated righteousness to the relational. He was unable to hold the two concepts together without separation and without confusion.

> The Duke of Sheh told Confucius: 'In my land, there are Righteous men. If a father steals a sheep, the son will testify against him.'
>
> Confucius said, 'The Righteous men in my land are different from this. The father conceals the wrongs of his son, and the son conceals the wrongs of his father. This is Righteousness!' (Analect 13:18)

In the wisdom of the triune God, He has not confused or separated the relationship with His people and the righteousness of His Person. Through

---

[214] Refer to the discussion on Anselm's theory of atonement in section 2, 4.6.

[215] John of Damascus (~AD 652–750) expounded the idea of communion in terms of the interpenetration of the persons within the Godhead. He used the term *perichoresis* to describe this relationship.

the incarnation of Jesus Christ and His vicarious humanity, through His mediation and the High Priesthood, and through His sacrificial death on the cross and subsequent resurrection and exaltation, the Father God has effected the reconciliation of mankind, i.e. restored the relational, and without having to subordinate His righteousness. He secured the reconciliation with fallen humanity in His own Person.[216]

There are many other notions in Confucianism that makes it difficult to come to terms with the Christian concepts of revelation and reconciliation. In fact, this notion of divine positive revelation is absent from the Chinese texts. Confucius also held the traditional view that all men are born good. Of anything, like original sin, there is not a trace in his teaching. Nor is there any notion of divine grace to strengthen the will and enlighten the mind in the struggle with evil. So to make oneself as good as possible was with him the main business of life.

Robert Morrison noted that Confucianism as practised in his times

> did not know God, only the material heaven; it espoused the five virtues, but had no knowledge of sin. He maintained, as did many others in subsequent years, that 'the doctrine and knowledge given by God through Jesus was needed to complete the inadequacy of Confucianism'.[217]

Many in today's Chinese churches have held to a Confucian framework and subordinated the understanding of the triune God to this framework. In so doing, Chinese Christianity has in effect rebuild the Chinese culture for its own sake rather than building up the people of God for whom Christ came.

In his analysis of the influence of Confucianism upon the Chinese, Dr H Wong, in his address to the Third Australian Chinese Conference on Evangelism 1995, made this remark.

> Confucian thinking, organized and formalized over 5,000 years ago, has been passed down as a single package to the Chinese people in the main. It has condition *ethnocentricism* in that China is seen as 'the middle kingdom'. It has encouraged *egocentricism* in that the single reference point

---

[216] 'He saw that there was no one, and was appalled that there was no one to intervene; so his own arm brought him victory, and his righteousness upheld him' (Isa. 59:16, NRSV).

[217] Covell, *Confucius, the Buddha and Christ*, 96.

for Chinese life resides in the family. It has also led to conservatism (satisfaction) in that the Chinese hold to the three verities of life, namely, the unit of community (family), the unity of authority (father) and the unit of harmony (hierarchical compliance). These verities of truth have been historically unquestioned, unchallenged; they have been absorbed and assimilated into Chinese world view and thinking. As a result, the Chinese have been a monolithic, consensus and conforming brand of people. Obviously, as one moves out from the cultural core . . . there are modifying degrees of what it means to be Chinese.[218]

In the comment above, Dr H Wong identified two characteristics: ethnocentricism and egocentricism, inherent within the Chinese culture. To this, I want to include a third characteristic of the Chinese culture, namely, isolationism, which must inevitably follow from the above two. This triad will be discussed below as characteristics that are inconsistent with the profession of the Trinitarian faith.

5.4. God's Sovereignty

If we are to take the triunity of God and His covenantal relationship seriously, then we need to rethink the issue of the sovereignty of God. The covenant is not a bilateral covenant where both God and man are equal partners or where the covenant requires the cooperation of humanity for its fulfilment. That the covenant is initiated and sustained by God is clear. The role of humanity in the covenant is not as an equal partner but to respond to a reconciliation offered so graciously and effected through the vicarious humanity of Jesus Christ.

So it is in this area of the sovereignty of God that the naturalistic Chinese mind has a problem. The Chinese are a pragmatic people. The end result is important to them, and they seek to determine that result in a way that does not pay attention to the means. Therefore, there developed a manipulative tendency that, in fact, does not acknowledge the true sovereignty of God.

Now, if again one were to start with the Trinitarian God and one acknowledges the continuing high priesthood of our Lord Jesus Christ

---

[218] Introduction to the paper on 'Cultural Issues in the Chinese Church' given by Dr H Wong at the Third Australian Chinese Conference on Evangelism held in Adelaide (Dec 1995). Italics mine.

and our participation in the Holy Spirit, one would take a very different stance. One would leave the end result undetermined and pay attention to the process, giving consideration to the people involved. The relationship becomes the central issue, i.e. attention is paid to the *who* question and not merely to the *how* question. One is able to take this approach knowing that it is the Holy Spirit that works within the hearts of His people.

There needs to be openness in the expression of the Christian faith if the Lordship of Jesus Christ is to be acknowledged. Therefore, the self-centredness of the Chinese culture makes it difficult for the Chinese to come to grips with the call of Jesus to faith in Him. The response to this call requires that there is now another centre for one's life, i.e. a centre outside of oneself. This centre is now in Christ, and as Lord and King, His Kingdom is an eschatological concept requiring us to embrace it in faith. In the materialistic Chinese minds, there is a need to see the result of this faith in the here and now. As a result, lip service is paid to His Lordship and devices are engineered to deceive ourselves into thinking that our faith has been rewarded. There needs to be openness to the future from a centre outside of ourselves if we are to truly acknowledge the sovereignty of God. The doctrine of the triunity of God underlines this sovereignty as we approach the Father in the Spirit through Jesus Christ.

5.5. The Nature of Our Response

The Chinese have always been a people with a strong sense of personal achievement. Their history of government by oppressive rulers and a religion steeped in natural theology have made them a very self-reliant people. As such, they have understood response in a legalistic manner. So when the Chinese embraced Christianity, they have understood response as a condition of grace. If they fulfil these obligations, then God will be gracious to them.

However, this is not so. We have mentioned briefly the covenant that expresses the relationship between God and man in terms of God's grace and sovereignty. The grace of God is shown to us in the covenant in a unilateral manner and is not conditional on our response. The commands of God are the obligations of grace and not the condition of grace.

God's dealing with us in reconciliation is based on His covenant with humanity. The covenants that we have in scripture must be seen as expressions of the one eternal covenant covering the whole of mankind. This is the covenant of creation—the primary covenant. Expressions of this primary covenant are seen in its particularity in history.[219] The covenant expresses the inner structure of the relation between God and man.

So our response, when understood in a Trinitarian manner, would have been effected by the Spirit dwelling in us, causing us to respond in ways that give us meaning in terms of our culture. This response to the Father would then be through the efficacious work of Jesus Christ as our mediator. The topic will be discussed in more detail in the next section in the chapter titled 'A Theology of Response'.

5.6. Ethnocentricity

The Chinese in general are an ethnocentric group of people. China is termed the 'Middle[220] Kingdom'. Their terminology of foreigners as 'foreign devils' (literal translation) belies their sense of racial superiority. This is often carried over to the church scene, and that is why most Chinese churches are so ethnically exclusive. Chinese Christians have to think of others in terms of their humanity and as fellow creatures of God. They need to rediscover the meaning and implications of covenant theology.

The root of this ethnocentricity lies in the naturalistic outlook of the Chinese. As has been pointed out previously, the concept of law in the Chinese mind derives from nature and does not occupy the same supreme position as is the case in the West.[221] The concept of law in the Chinese understanding lacked the Western assumption of an outside 'lawgiver'.[222] This naturalistic outlook coupled with the Confucianist dictum of 'filial piety' has made the Chinese an introspective race.

> Someone said to Confucius: 'Master, why don't you join the government?' The Master said: 'In the Documents it is said: 'Only cultivate filial piety and be kind to your brothers, and you will be contributing to the body politic.' This is also a form of political action; one need not necessarily join the government.' (Analect 2:21)

---

[219] The Noahic, Abrahamic, Mosaic, Davidic and new covenants are expressions of the primary covenant.

[220] *Middle* meaning *the centre*. The term implies that China is the centre of the world (nations).

[221] See chapters 2.3.6 and 4.10.

[222] L G Thompson, *Chinese Religion: An Introduction* (California: Dickenson Publishing Company, 1975), 3.

This introspection is brought to its logical extreme in the family. While the nuclear family has its basis in the Edenic injunction (Gen. 2:24), the Chinese family does not see the need to leave, i.e. for the man, and continues in an extended family under one roof. However, for the woman who marries, her relationship with her family of origin becomes minimal and often denied. She now 'belongs' to her husband's family. Her family of origin is then termed 'the outside family'.

It appears that in the Chinese system of thinking, there is difficulty in conceiving of 'the other' and even greater difficulty in conceiving of 'union with the other'. It may be able to harmonise and hold things in balance, but that is from a framework imposed onto the other. A union that takes place without confusion and without separation would seem to be totally foreign to the Chinese mind.

Being unable to embrace what is unknown in the 'other', the introspective Chinese mind retreats into the secure enclave of ethnocentricity from which it seeks to impose itself onto the 'other'.

5.7. Denial of the Trinity

As discussed above, the Chinese churches have a tendency to emphasise their ethnocentricism and self-sufficiency (egocentricism) with the result of increasing isolation. This tendency is in effect a denial of the Trinity.

5.7.1. Ethnocentricism: A Denial of God the Father as the Creator God

The ethnocentricity of the Chinese has been referred to above in section 5.6. Reference has also been made to the ethnic associations of the overseas migrant Chinese in new lands.[223] The tendency to cluster together is not unnatural to any migrant groups, and the Chinese are no different. It gives them a sense of security knowing that they can rely on one another as they adapt to the new culture. However, when these cultural associations become well established and tend towards self-sufficient communities, then the need to adapt to the new culture will not appear too pressing. The migrants then settle into the old culture they know well. Chinese communities outside of China tend to follow this trend, for example in the larger communities in San Francisco, Los Angeles, Vancouver, and Sydney. However, even in smaller communities as I found myself three decades ago in the small mining town of Broken Hill in New South Wales, Australia, with just three Chinese families, we developed quite an exclusive community among ourselves.

---

[223] See section 2.2, 'The Overseas Chinese Churches'.

Many Chinese churches outside of China have restricted their mission and outreach exclusively to the Chinese. This was brought home to me in the First Australian Chinese Conference on Evangelism in 1985. This has been referred to above in some detail.[224] In the Chinese churches, where there is an undue emphasis or exclusiveness as regards to ethnicity, this is to disregard the whole of humanity which God the Father has created. In doing so, they have denied God the Father as the Creator God. His grace is expressed towards the whole of His creation. In the covenant with Abraham, the blessings of God are to flow to the whole world and to all people (Gen. 12:1–3). In the servant songs of Isaiah, the task of the servant is to bring his teaching to all peoples (Is. 42:1–4, 49:1–7). The gospel of salvation is indeed given to the world (Jn. 3:16). We are called to be witnesses to the 'ends of the earth' (Acts 1:8).

God's covenant with humanity is the one eternal covenant of creation, though we see subsets of this in various epochs of history. Its intention is vividly described in the book of Revelation where we see the picture of 'a great multitude that no one could count, from every nation, from all tribes and peoples and languages, standing before the throne and before the Lamb, robed in white, with palm branches in their hands. They cried out in a loud voice, saying, 'Salvation belongs to our God who is seated on the throne, and to the Lamb!' (Rev. 7:9).

As we have seen above, a covenant theology implies that we acknowledge all of humanity and accord to them a dignity that befits the creation of God. Not to acknowledge this is not to acknowledge the creator God. The overseas Chinese churches cannot continue to disregard the communities that they find themselves in. The outlook and the thrust of their mission must be to all people and not merely restricted to a single ethnocentric community in which they feel comfortable and secure culturally.

5.7.2. Self-sufficiency (Egocentricism): A Denial of the Priesthood of Christ

The Chinese has been a very self-reliant race. This may perhaps be because of the centuries of oppression by the emperors. Living under those conditions, the people have no choice but to rely on themselves and whatever they could find for themselves. Welfare assistance was quite unknown in those days and even in many Asian countries today. They have to be resourceful and fall back on whatever they can come up with themselves. This is well exemplified in their cooking styles where every bit of the vegetable or animal is used and not wasted. Even the leftovers

---

[224] See section 2.1, 'A Personal Reflection'.

are given a new treatment in the well-known *chop suey*. This cultural heritage is passed on from generation to generation up till today. So they have developed this trait of self-sufficiency as a result of the adverse circumstances in their long history.

So this form of thinking is very much ingrained into the minds of the Chinese people. Thus, it becomes very difficult for the Chinese to stand back to allow something to happen. There is this deep urge within to ensure that the goal is achieved. Unfortunately, this attitude is read back into the scriptures, and coupled with pietism, the Chinese churches forged ahead to create a religion where God has become the adjunct and facilitator for their goals.

For the Chinese churches to think that they are self-sufficient is to deny the priesthood of our Lord Jesus Christ. We have seen a little of the difficulty that the Chinese have in relation to God's sovereignty and in the response to His covenant of love. This is in part the result of a contractual approach to the covenant of God where the response to the covenant is understood as conditional to the grace of the covenant. So this conditional understanding fits in well with the pietism of the Chinese. It starts with a centre in the self and works towards God. This is the exact reversal of the gospel of Jesus Christ who, as the Great High Priest, is the mediator of all that is between God and humanity. He initiated the covenant and sustained it by His own hand (Isa. 59:16). Jesus Christ mediates to us the revelation of God and at the same time also mediates our response to the Father. This mediation will be discussed further in the chapter on 'A Theology of Response'.[225]

The naturalistic mind of the Chinese wants to impose its structure onto the end point so as to be to have control over it. It lacks an eschatology in its whole philosophy. It cannot have one as it does not have a point outside of itself. Thus, the Chinese mind thinks in terms of the cycle of nature; and if it were to start with the principles of the past, then it must at some stage in the future return to the point where it had started.

It would be so easy starting from this egocentricity to develop a whole doctrine of works based on our innate ability. That creation moves to an end point bringing about our glorious liberation (Rom. 8:21) is the work of the Father, Son, and Spirit. This does not have a place in Chinese philosophy at all because of its egocentricity. The all-sufficient work of Christ on the cross has put all our works to shame. There is only one sacrifice that God accepts, and that is the sacrifice of Jesus Christ. All of humanity stands beneath the cross in order to have our offerings accepted by God through Jesus Christ. The all-sufficient work of Christ precludes

---

[225] See chapter 8, 'A Theology of Response'.

any sense of our own sufficiency. Therefore, the sense of self-sufficiency in the Chinese mind is a denial of the all-sufficiency of the work of Christ.

5.7.3. Isolationism: A Denial of Our Participation in the Spirit

The Chinese have been isolationist and protectionist in their development. China had chosen to isolate herself over centuries trying to preserve the purity of her race and the secrets of her skills. Trade secrets are kept within families and handed from parents to children and even then only in a restricted fashion. That China has been unknown to the outside world until the twentieth century testifies to the fact of her isolation. This isolation, so much a part of the Chinese culture, reinforces the ethnocentricity and egocentricity of the Chinese. This is not to imply that these traits are exclusive to the Chinese race but that these are the traits of any isolated community.

It has already been pointed out above that many of the Chinese churches exist in isolation from the rest of the Christian community. This goes even for those churches that are Chinese speaking. Perhaps this is a general statement regarding the whole of Christendom. Paul referred to the one body in the Spirit when he wrote, 'There is one body and one Spirit, just as you were called to the one hope of your calling' (Eph. 4:4).

For the Chinese churches to be inward looking and isolated from the rest of Christendom is to deny the oneness of God's people in the Holy Spirit. The event on the Day of Pentecost where 'Jews from every nation under heaven living in Jerusalem' (Acts 2:5) heard the gospel in their own tongue was indeed a remarkable one. It set the stage for the fulfilment of the promise to Abraham where through him the blessing will go out to the whole world. This event at Pentecost prefigures the vision of John in Revelation where 'a great multitude that no one could count, from every nation, from all tribes and peoples and languages, standing before the throne and before the Lamb' (Rev. 7:9). This is the great day of the eschaton, and the church should live in that reality.

The Holy Spirit creates faith in us making us conscious of the merits of Christ. This participation in the Holy Spirit makes worship real to us. All of God's people in their worship participate through the Spirit in the Son's communion with the Father. So as we worship, we are joining with all God's people in this participation. Our isolation results from our sense of self-sufficiency, and this is to deny the Holy Spirit. This does not reflect the Trinitarian God that we claim to worship.

5.8 Conclusions

The God that we worship is not one conceived from philosophy as the gnostics did. He is not the god known from natural revelation as the gods of Greek or Chinese mythology. The God that we worship is given to us by special revelation, i.e. biblical revelation, made known to us by the prophets and by Jesus Christ Himself. It is a reasonable faith.

The God that we worship is one who is incarnate in our midst in the person of Jesus Christ. God has created humankind in His own image, and there should be no difficulty in coming to grips with the biblical teaching that God made Jesus Christ a man in His own perfect image. 'He came to that which was His own', as John records for us (Jn. 1:11). He became flesh and remained one with the Father. God who inhabits in our midst brings to us the most intimate relationship expressed by the God of grace.

Part Three

THE TRANSFORMATION TO A NEW FRAMEWORK

So far, the discussion has taken us in the first section from a general consideration of culture and how at the core of it is the understanding of who God is. We have also looked at some aspects of the Chinese culture and the Chinese understanding of god. These assumptions, which have been carved into the Chinese culture over thousands of years, are very much ingrained in the Chinese mind. In the second section, a brief survey of the church's history with regards to its understanding of God was undertaken, and this shows that throughout history the church has oftentimes deviated towards the non-Trinitarian and contractual path, contrary to our understanding of the Trinity and the covenant. Finally, we made a bold evaluation of the Chinese church, and, like the rest of Christendom, ask that she may rediscover the Trinitarian God and reform her cultural core.

There has been no specific aspect of theology discussed in part two. However, in this third part, we will take up in particular two aspects of theology that are foundational to Christian thinking, i.e. a theology of blessing and a theology of ministry. These two aspects represent what God has given to us and how are to respond to God. The treatment is indeed Trinitarian, as it must be. We will see that the understanding of these two aspects of theology has often been non-Trinitarian and contractual. A Trinitarian understanding in these two areas must therefore consider seriously the relational and therefore the participatory nature of blessing and ministry. Some implications of a covenant theology will be spelt out, and this section will conclude with a brief summation of a few topical aspects of our culture that need transforming. The new framework of the triune communion with the Father in the Spirit through Jesus Christ will be presented as the basis on which the transformation can be achieved—the transformation that will liberate the Chinese church from her cultural captivity.

Part Three, Chapter 6

A THEOLOGY OF BLESSING

6.1 Introduction

What God gives is mostly thought of in terms of what is tangible. This is certainly so in the Chinese mind. The Chinese would often go to the Buddhist temple and seek 'blessing' for the self and for the family. These are usually sought in terms of the material. In response, there is usually a promise by the person to repay the gods for whatever will be given. The receiving and giving are conceived of in contractual terms. As I have been involved in the ministry in the Chinese churches, on many occasions people have come to me, telling me that one day God will repay me for what I have done. I shuddered at the thought of it. These people have appreciated what I have done and expressed their appreciation in terms of their contractual framework. They do not know otherwise.

In a paper given to the pastors' study group in February 1996, G Bingham wrote, 'The difficulty here is that many believers consider God's gifts—and giving—to be *contractual*.'[226] This is certainly not the case when the theology of blessing is seen from the Trinitarian and covenantal point of view.

The apostle Peter has expressed the generosity of God's giving succinctly in his letter when he wrote in 2 Peter 1:3–4:

---

[226] G Bingham, *The Giving of God: God the Giver*, paper presented at the New Creation Teaching Ministry Pastors' Study Group (5 Feb 1996).

³His divine power has given us **everything we need for life and godliness** through our knowledge of him who called us by his own glory and goodness. ⁴Through these he has given us his very great and precious promises, so that through them you may **participate in the divine nature** and escape the corruption in the world caused by evil desires. (Emphasis mine)

This is indeed the summary of this chapter. All that we need for life and godliness, i.e. in being human and in being able to relate to the Creator God, has already been given to us so that we may 'participate in the divine nature', i.e. in the perichoretic life of the Trinity. In calling us to Himself, God has given us everything we will ever need. He has not withheld some things that we may need as if they are optional extras or on a conditional basis like a good behaviour bond. Peter did not suggest in any way that God's giving is conditional on our response.

6.2. A Setting in Life

Some years ago, I was chairing a meeting, and one of the topics for discussion is the disbursement of some money that we have. A few proposals were made, and when it came to decision time, questions were raised as to the needs of the respective people and organisations. We knew the needs of some of them but not the others. The committee thought it unfair to decide when the financial situations were not known. I raised the point that we do not need to know and we do not give just because they were needy. Need is not the primary reason for our giving. I further pointed out that we should give out of what our hearts feel, i.e. we give as a result of our relationship with the respective people and organisation according to what the Lord has put in our hearts to do. We do not need to obtain a copy of other people's financial statement before we give. One response from the group was that I could be furthering the interest of the rich. I replied that it would then be the responsibility of that person in that situation to act responsibly before God. In the democratic setup that we have, I was outvoted and defeated.

6.3 The Chinese Preoccupation with Blessing

We have mentioned above that 'the most deep-rooted desire of the Chinese people is for harmony'.[227] This follows from their naturalistic mind as pointed out by Husutzu, a Chinese sage who lived around the third century BC.

> The stars make their rounds; the sun and moon alternatively shine; the four seasons succeed one another; the *Yin* and *Yang* go through their great mutations; wind and rain are widely distributed; all things acquire their harmony and have their lives.[228]

Though it has not been mentioned until now, the concept of yin and yang was developed in Chinese thought even before the time of Confucius. It is basic to the understanding of the cosmos. Nature was seen through a pair of opposing yet complementary forces, such as light and darkness, heat and cold, male and female, and so on. Each is opposite to the other, yet each complements and replaces the other.

The concept of yin-yang has its origin in the occultist.[229] One of the groups of occult arts is known as feng shui,[230] which is gaining increasing popularity in the Western world. The basis of feng shui lies in the concept that mankind is the product of the universe. Hence, in order to control one's destiny, then one must reorientate one's affairs, eg. one's house, business, etc., with these forces of nature, i.e. the wind and water. In practice, it implies the proper positioning of the house with regards to its direction, as well as the positioning of the doors and windows to take advantage of the prevailing forces in order that prosperity may prevail for the one involved. It is not a science or even a pseudoscience. It is really a form of divination with its basis in the occult.

---

[227] J Wu, 'Chinese Legal and Political Philosophy', *The Chinese Mind*, ed. C. Moore (Honolulu: University of Hawaii Press, 1967), 227.

[228] H H Dubs, trans., *The Works of Hsuntzu* (London: Probasthain, 1928), ch. 17, quoted in Y L Fung, *A Short History of Chinese Philosophy* (New York: MacMillan, 1948), 144.

[229] Y L Fung, *History of Chinese Philosophy*, 129.

[230] Literally meaning wind and water. Usually referred to as geomancy in Western writings.

With this concept of nature and life so deeply carved into its conscience, it is no wonder that the Chinese has for centuries been preoccupied with prosperity. Why not when one has the means to make it happen!

6.4. Time and Space (A Receptacle or Relational Notion)

A problem in our thinking as fallen creatures is that we need to possess and control. This has been given some impetus in Christian thinking from what was considered as the creational mandate.[231] This domination applies only to the nonhuman world, and the privilege is exercised by Man as the representative of God in His creation and in ruling over them as God would.[232] It is a responsibility exercised by Man. It is not a mandate applicable to the realm of human relationships.

Unfortunately, this way of thinking has become the way we relate with others as God's people and the way we consider the blessings of God. The blessings become something that we can possess and control, and then use what we have for the 'self-fulfilment of our lives'. So we have come to understand them as something that we need to ask for so as to have them in our possession. We come to God like an empty vessel waiting to be filled with His blessing. We see God's blessings as something that we need to appropriate for ourselves and then we can use these blessings for ourselves or in an altruistic sense for others or in the service of God. In this utilitarian framework, we happily apply Matthew 6:33[233] in seeking the kingdom so that 'all these things' can be given to us as well.

We cannot help thinking in this way because we have been created in time and space. We need some assistance when we look at the blessings of God from this side of creation as the hymn by H F Lyte (1793–1847) goes:

> Angels, help us to adore Him!
> Ye behold Him face to face;
> Sun and moon, bow down before Him;
> *Dwellers all in time and space.*
> Praise Him! Praise Him!

---

[231] Then God said, 'Let us make man in our image, in our likeness, and let them **rule** over the fish of the sea and the birds of the air, over the livestock, over all the earth, and over all the creatures that move along the ground' (Gen. 1:26).

[232] G von Rad, *Genesis*, Old Testament Library (London: SCM, 1961), 60.

[233] But seek first his kingdom and his righteousness, and all these things will be given to you as well (Matt. 6:33).

Praise the everlasting King.

However, God is before time. He is the creator of time. To Him, all time is present. His presence fills the universe that He has created. God has created us in time and space yet remains the infinite Creator God in relation to His creatures.

The problem of understanding God in our finite sphere of space and time is dealt with in the book *Space, Time and Incarnation*[234] by T F Torrance. He showed the development of the 'receptacle' notion of space in Hellenic philosophy and the way it has become incorporated into modern Protestant theology. In the decisive and formative period of the church, this receptacle idea was rejected by the church fathers at Nicea. However, it was reintroduced by the Medievals in the West, and this has led to a deistic dualism that is now so ingrained in the fabric of Western thought.[235]

The other conception of space and time is the 'relational notion'. This takes seriously the principle of the creation ex nihilo and the transcendence of God. In this notion, the 'spatial, temporal and conceptual relations were inseparable'.[236] There is an absolute priority of God over all space and time. God stands in a transcendent and creative, not a spatial and temporal, relation to the creaturely world.[237] This relational notion was very much a part of the patristic concept of space and time during the Nicene crisis of the early church. This framework forms the background to Torrance's book *The Trinitarian Faith*. He wrote:

> Athanasius drew a clear distinction between the absolute being of God and the existence of the world wholly dependent on his creative Word and Will, and thereby disentangled for the Church the twisted lines of thought between the ontological and cosmological dimensions in the Origenist and Arian ideas about God, Christ and the world.[238]

This notion provides the underlying framework for us when we come to see the blessings of God and indeed much of our theology.

---

[234] T F Torrance, *Space, Time and Incarnation*, (Edinburgh: T&T Clark, 1969).
[235] Ibid., vi–vii.
[236] Ibid., 58ff.
[237] Ibid., 60.
[238] T F Torrance, *The Trinitarian Faith* (Edinburgh: T & T Clark, 1988), 97.

I want to refer to another excellent article by Roger Newell[239] who used these two differing ways of conceiving of space and time to critique our understanding of the atonement. He developed two models from the above: the 'subject-centred appropriation' model and the 'object-centred participation' model.

In the subject-centred appropriation model, the individual by his moralistic effort and/or sacrifice seeks to appropriate the victory of Christ to himself. This is based on the receptacle notion. This is best marketed by evangelicals in their preaching 'Let go and let God'.[240] This has worked for many, and they have testimonies to go with that. But to those who struggled with this, an incredible degree of guilt is piled on them for their lack of faith. They are 'thrown back on themselves' as Prof James Torrance used to say.

This approach can only reinforce the contractual outlook by the individual. He is forced to believe that the more he tries or the more he gives up, the more blessings he will receive. This will only lead to an entrenchment of the narcissistic self and much weariness.

In turning us away from focusing on our narcissistic selves, we need to think in terms of the object-participation model. It takes us away from the focus on 'my conversion' and 'my victory'.[241] Newell continues,

> Participation in Christ rather than appropriation of Christ for my benefit repentantly redirects our focus to knowing and loving God for his sake, thereby reflecting the quality of God's own love for us. A theology of participation integrates our faith and our works as a grateful response to the initiating faithfulness of God and makes discipleship an ongoing and natural development of faith.[242]

In the incarnation of Jesus Christ, He has brought to humanity the fullness of the Godhead, and we have been given to participate in that fullness (Col. 2:9–10).[243]

---

[239] R Newell, 'Participation and Atonement', *Christ in our Place*, eds. T A Hart and D P Thimell (Great Britain: Paternoster, 1989), 92–101.

[240] Ibid., 95.

[241] Ibid., 96.

[242] Ibid.

[243] For in Christ all the fullness of the Deity lives in bodily form,[10] and you have been given fullness in Christ, who is the head over every power and authority (Col. 2:9).

6.5. Participation (κοινωνια)

Participation is a basic understanding of the New Testament church. The early church gathered together, and they were conversant with the idea of participation. The concept of participation is put succinctly by St Thomas Aquinas this way:

> To participate is, as it were, to take part in something. And so, when something receives in some particular way, that which belongs to another in a general way, he is said to participate in that thing.[244]

The word *koinonia* is often used in relation to the sharing of wealth or property in the early church (Acts 2:42). It is variously translated 'fellowship', 'participation', 'sharing', or 'partnership' in the New International Version of the Bible. Paul used this term to refer to the sharing in the life of Christ and the Spirit.

> The cup of blessing that we bless, is it not a sharing [koinonia] in the blood of Christ? The bread that we break, is it not a sharing [koinonia] in the body of Christ? (1 Cor. 10:16, NRSV)

> If then there is any encouragement in Christ, any consolation from love, any sharing [koinonia] in the Spirit, any compassion and sympathy, (Phil. 2:1, NRSV)

'In the Greek and Hellenic world, the word *koinonia* was a term which meant the evident, unbroken fellowship between the gods and men.'[245] The concept was then applied to the bond between men. From this usage philosophers developed the communal ideal.[246] While the New Testament used the term in relation to the fellowship within the new found

---

[244] St Thomas, quoted in N D O'Donoghue, 'Creation and Participation', *Creation, Christ and Culture*, ed. R McKinney (Edinburgh: T&T Clark, 1976), 137.

[245] J Schattenmann, 'Koinonia', *The New International Dictionary of New Testament Theology*, vol. 1, ed. C Brown (Grand Rapids: Zondervan, 1967), 639 ff.

[246] Ibid.

community of Christ,[247] the primary usage of this term in not secular but religious. Paul's usage in 1 Corinthians 10:16 underlines the primary meaning of koinonia, a sharing in the divine life. This sharing in the divine life is made possible for us by the taking up of our human nature by Jesus Christ (Rom. 8:3).[248]

In our understanding of salvation, we delight in the sin offering of God's Son as something transacted outside of our lives and on our behalf, and we do not take seriously Jesus's vicarious humanity, which is the perfect response to God on our behalf. Our participation in the divine life is our participation in the vicarious humanity of our Lord Jesus Christ. Our participation has its basis on the filial relationship of Jesus Christ to His Father. This is well summarised by J Torrance: 'The Son of God has participated in our humanity, that through the Spirit we might participate in his Sonship and communion with the Father.'[249]

6.6. Our Life of Discovery

While we reject the receptacle notion, in our Christian growth, we experience the blessings of God in increasing measure. We stand on this side of creation, and we see 'all these things' (Mt. 6:33) that will be given to us. We cannot help embracing the receptacle notion. Yet Paul talked about 'the full measure of the blessing of Christ' (Rom. 15:29)[250]. Paul seemed to present the blessings of God as an 'all or none' phenomenon, yet we experience that in an increasing measure. To reconcile this, we need to bring in the concept of 'discovery'.

We note first of all that the blessings of God are *in Christ,* and God has blessed us with 'every spiritual blessing'.

> Praise be to the God and Father of our Lord Jesus Christ, who has blessed us in the heavenly realms with every spiritual blessing **in Christ**. (Eph. 1:3)

---

[247] For example, 'They devoted themselves to the apostles' teaching and to the fellowship [koinonia], to the breaking of bread and to prayer' (Acts 2:42).

[248] 'For what the law was powerless to do in that it was weakened by the sinful nature, God did by sending his own Son in the likeness of sinful man to be a sin offering. And so he condemned sin in sinful man' (Rom. 8:3).

[249] J B Torrance, 'The Contribution of McLeod Campbell to Scottish Theology', *Scottish Journal of Theology* 26 (1973): 310.

[250] 'I know that when I come to you, I will come in the full measure of the blessing of Christ' (Rom. 15:29).

In our scientific world, when a new discovery is made or a new principle enunciated, it is not that there is something new that is given to our world that was not there before. Those scientific principles are all there since the beginning of time. It is our lack of instrumentation that precludes our knowledge of such things. Sometimes we are ignorant of the scientific principle because we have come to the physical world with the wrong questions and the wrong assumptions. Such is the case when we put a thermometer in the mouth hoping to get an answer on the pulse rate or blood pressure. We will not. When we interact with reality, we learn to ask the right questions and then change the assumptions that we hold.

So it is with the blessings of God. They have been given to us in grace and without reservation. The reason that God's blessings appear to us in increasing measure is that we have been using the wrong 'instrumentation' in our quest. That which we seek to know must determine the methods by which we come to know it. On the matter of God's blessing, we come to discover it by our participation in the divine life of God. Our contractual outlook precludes us from entering into the fullness of God's blessing. Not until we enter into the koinonia in the Spirit through Jesus Christ and to the Father do we discover the fullness of God's blessing.

When we hold to the receptacle notion, we will come to see God's blessings in a linear fashion, i.e. we come to Him to obtain His blessing as an optional extra conditional on our obedience. This is an approach based on the contractual framework. We impose our experience of the world in which we live onto our gracious heavenly Father. God's blessing is not something that is added on. It is all in Christ as Paul can so confidently talk of the *fullness* in Christ (Col. 2:9–10).[251]

The basis of Paul's confidence, expressed in those two words 'I know' in Romans 15:29, is not founded on his deductive objectivity. It is also not the result of his sense perception or verification, principles that we so often use. It is the result of the interaction or indwelling between the knower and the known. It is based on his *participation* in the life of Christ. His confidence in the blessings of Christ flows out of that participation.

We must now reject positively the receptacle notion, which does not adequately reflect the created world in which we live and the Creator God who resides outside of our time and space and yet has entered our world in the person of Jesus Christ. In Jesus Christ dwells the fullness of the Godhead bodily (Col. 2:9) and all that God desires to give to us is found in Him. This is the blessing of the covenant relationship that is mediated in Christ.

---

[251] 'For in Christ all the fullness of the Deity lives in bodily form,[10] and you have been given fullness in Christ, who is the head over every power and authority' (Col. 2:9).

This is not merely a neat theological exercise but has relevance for us in the practical outworking of our lives. We are so often called to seek self-fulfilment and resort to all the props that will enable us to create our own reality in life. We have sometimes been conditioned to think that God merely gives us life and then we are left to our own to make it all work out. This is the rationale of our technological society. We need to go back to the covenant of creation to see that we have been given life when we did not ask for it, and we have been given the fullness of the blessings in Jesus Christ when we did not ask for them and indeed did not even know that we need them. Our gracious heavenly Father has provided for all these things for us so that 'Solomon in all his glory was not arrayed like one of these' (Matt. 6:29 ASV).

The 'givenness' of life is a basic supposition of our humanity. We did not choose it or ask for it, and we must accept that givenness with gratitude. We do not have absolute control over it, and we must share this life with the rest of humanity as we live out our particular life in its limited way. In this participation with the rest of humanity, we discover the reality of life and living.

In our new creation in Christ, we see the givenness of a new humanity. We did not ask for it but have been drawn into it by God's rich grace. We do not have absolute control over the new life as the Holy Spirit leads us to call 'Abba, Father'. It is as we participate in the new Man, Jesus Christ, that we come to discover the reality of the rich blessings in Him.

It is only appropriate to conclude this chapter with a quote from Hans-Martin Barth writing in *Fulfilment*, where he commented on this obsession with self-fulfilment:

> The success of our life is not in question, but is **already fulfilled, already assured, in advance of ourselves.** . . . We do not have to realize ourselves, create our own reality and increase it, heighten it and intensify it.[252]

---

[252] Hans-Martin Barth: *Fulfilment* (London, 1980), 47, quoted in A Torrance, 'The Self-Relation, Narcissism and the Gospel of Grace', *Scottish Journal of Theology* 40 (1987), 509. Emphasis mine.

Part Three, Chapter 7

A THEOLOGY OF MINISTRY

This chapter will show how the Chinese church has based its understanding of ministry on the cultural model, i.e. works being prior to grace. The Trinitarian perspective will reverse this order.

7.1. Introduction

In the understanding of ministry, the Chinese church has taken the model from the missionaries of the West, i.e. that of the priestly intermediary. In fact, there is no other model. The focus is on the minister, and he serves on behalf of the church. In many ways, this is not dissimilar to the priestly intermediary in the Buddhist temple. There are many parallels. The people gather regularly or on special occasions. They seek the intermediary of the priest to secure for them the blessings from their god or gods. When their request is realised, then there is the thanksgiving offered to the god. Much of this pattern is present in many quarters even in modern day Protestant evangelicalism.

So for the Chinese mind to conceive of ministry there is no urgent need to transform the pattern which they already know from their cultural norms. All they simply need to do is to graft the missionary model onto what they already know. As I have already pointed out in the previous chapter, this service will then result in the god 'repaying' the individual for the services rendered as in a contractual relationship. This is putting the matter rather crudely, but the truth of the matter is that there is no concept of union[253] or participation in the triune God but only a contractual relationship. These comments are made with reference to the prevailing culture of many Chinese churches. I know that many of my Chinese friends hold true to the understanding of ministry that I will be putting forth in this chapter.

If ministry is understood as a calling, then the church as the called out people of God must fulfil its calling to minister. So often, ministry is thought of in terms of the group of special people called the 'ministers'. What has happened is that our church orders have become the foundation of our ecclesiology. In a letter sent to the participants of New Creation Teaching Ministry Pastors' School in 1997, G Bingham wrote, 'There is no ecclesiology which is authentic without the pateriological, Christological and pneumatological, soteriological, eschatological foundations.'[254] While the comment relates to ecclesiology, it applies equally to ministry as the church is called to minister. Though this chapter does not deal with these great doctrines of the church in any detail, it will weave together sufficient threads in each of these areas to enable us to see that it is the ministry of God that is the determinant of the church.

R Anderson, in his paper on 'The Theology of Ministry', argues that 'ministry precedes and produces theology'.[255] By 'ministry', he refers to that which 'is determined and set forth by God's own ministry of revelation and reconciliation in the world'. The task of theology is the reflection of this ministry as set forth by God. Theology does not stand on its own and determines ministry. And so Anderson continues, 'To say that all ministry is God's ministry is to suggest that ministry precedes and determines the Church.'[256] This paper will explore these assertions and in turn examines our concept of ministry.

7.2. Derivation of the Term Ministry

We can get an idea of the way the word *ministry* is used in the New Testament by looking at the ideas involved in the various words used:

---

[253] This lack of the concept of union has been discussed in section 1, subsection 2.3.2 of this paper.

[254] G Bingham, personal communications (1 May 1997) to participants of the New Creation Teaching Ministry Pastors' School.

[255] R Anderson, 'A Theology of Ministry', *Theological Foundations for Ministry*, ed. R Anderson (Grand Rapids: Eerdmans, 1979), 7.

[256] Ibid.

1. *diakonia*, derived from the verb, *diakoneo*, to serve or wait at table or care for household needs.[257] It is generally used for service (see Acts 1:17; Acts 1:25; Acts 21:19; Rom. 11:13; Rom. 12:7, 2; Cor. 3:3; 2 Cor. 3:7; 2 Cor. 3:8, 2; Cor. 3:9, 2; Cor. 4:1, 2 Cor. 5:18, 2 Cor. 6:3, 2 Tim. 4:5, 2 Tim. 4:11).
2. *logos*, as in ministry of the word (see Acts 6:2, Acts 6:4).
3. *energeo*, to be active or to be at work[258] (see Gal. 2:8).
4. *leitourgia*, public function as priest used in the cultic-sacred sense (see Heb. 8:6, 9:6). Thus, *leitourgos*, a minister or worshipper of God (see Rom. 13:6, 15:16, Phil. 2:25, Heb. 1:7, 8:2).
5. *latreia*, ministration of God, i.e. worship (divine) service (see Jn. 16:2, Rom. 9:4, Rom. 12:1, Heb. 9:1, Heb. 9:6.)
6. *nomizo*, to do by law (usage), i.e. to accustom (pass. be usual); by extension to deem or regard: suppose, think, be wont ('work' in NRSV) (see Lk. 3:23).

Ministry is often seen as a response of love to God and this is rightly so. However, we see here a usage that refers to ministry as an expression of the obedience to the command of God. This usage with reference to Jesus Christ should not surprise us as He has repeatedly told us that He does what the Father has commanded Him to (Jn. 5:30).

Several ideas are included in the words used in the New Testament for what we refer to as the 'ministry'. These are the services that we render, in the things that we do for others whether they be spontaneous or legislated (as in *nomizo* [Lk. 3:23]). It is also used in the context of worship in the temple.

7.3. How Is 'Ministry' Understood?

The way we see ministry is essential to the understanding of the church. We call the pastor the minister and his ministry expresses the way the church understands its own existence. The nature of ministry is the nature of the church. The minister par excellence, the leiturgos, is Jesus Christ Himself (Heb. 8:1–2 NRSV).

> ¹Now the main point in what we are saying is this: we have such a high priest, one who is seated at the right hand

---

[257] K Hess, 'Diakoneo', *New International Dictionary of New Testament Theology*, vol. 3, ed. C Brown (Grand Rapids: Zondervan, 1971), 545.

[258] Ibid., 1147.

of the throne of the Majesty in the heavens, ²a minister [leitourgos] in the sanctuary and the true tent that the Lord, and not any mortal, has set up.

Jesus Christ is the minister in the true sanctuary that the Lord has set up. He ministers to the Father on our behalf. All ministry is the ministry of the Father. God demonstrated His love to us in sending His Son that we might have life through Him (1 Jn. 4:9). The Son does not act on His own accord but carries out the will of the Father (John 5:17, 19, 30; 6:38). The Son's ministry is that of revelation (Jn. 1:18) and reconciliation (2 Cor. 5:17–19) in response to the will of the Father. The Holy Spirit as the other Paraclete continues the ministry of the Son (Jn. 14:26, 15:26, 16:7, 16:13–15; Rom. 8:9–15). Thus, we see that ministry is that of the Father and carried out in a specific manner by the Son and the Holy Spirit. On this Trinitarian basis, we reflect on ministry theologically. Out of this ministry of the Trinitarian Godhead, we have the church—the called-out people of God, the *ekklesia*. Thus, the primary control on ecclesiology is the tripersonal community of God.[259]

Christ's primary ministry is to the Father for the sake of the world, not to the world for the sake of the Father.[260] Christ ministers out of the Trinitarian relationship within the Godhead. Needs, therefore, do not determine the nature of Christ's ministry but the purpose of the Father. Jesus said, 'For I have come down from heaven, not to do my own will, but the will of him who sent me' (Jn. 6:38 NRSV).

So the church is given to continue this ministry of Jesus in the Holy Spirit. However, the church cannot continue the ministry of Christ and runs its own agenda. As the called-out people of God, the church must act only in accordance with the will of the Father just as Christ did only what the Father has told Him. When the church goes on with an agenda of her own, then she has removed from herself the very foundation of her constitution, i.e. Jesus her Lord.

As mentioned in the last chapter, that which we seek to know must determine the means or methods by which we come to know it. We cannot impose a methodology that is inappropriate upon that which we seek to know. If the church is indeed the ekklesia, i.e. the called-out people of God, then it is the calling of God that brings the church into being. The nature of this calling and indeed God's ministry in gathering together

---

[259] C Gunton, 'The Church on Earth: The Roots of Community', *On Being the Church*, eds. C Gunton and D Hardy (Edinburgh: T&T Clark, 1989), 77.

[260] R Anderson, 'A Theology of Ministry', 8.

this people must determine the way we come to know the church and its ministry. This may seem too obvious to mention, but it is not what most of our congregations conceive of as the 'church'. Without this calling, then there is no church. This calling of God to constitute His church is achieved through the incarnation of the Son and the indwelling of the Holy Spirit in His people. The Word was made flesh so that through His humanity, Jesus Christ made that perfect response to God on our behalf even as He continues to intercede for us as our Great High Priest in heaven. Without that awakening by the Spirit within us, there is no recognition on our part of God as the Father. So to know the church and its ministry, we must start with the ministry of the Father, Son, and Holy Spirit.

Jesus Christ mediates both revelation and reconciliation. His incarnation made manifest His solidarity with human flesh. Through His vicarious humanity He reveals the relations within the Trinitarian Godhead. Through His humanity, He made the response to God on our behalf. His response becomes our response when in our sin and weakness we are incapable of responding.

While we emphasise the substitutionary element in the sacrifice of Christ, we pay little attention to the participation in the merits of Christ. Our understanding of redemption rests almost solely on the application of the merits of Christ to the sinner merely as an external transaction.[261] There is no hint of the union of Christ and believers. Thus, an extrinsic conception of the atonement will result in a detachment of Christ from the context of the covenant relationship with His chosen people.[262] This inevitably results in the conception of the church as an institution and ministry solely in terms of our human effort.

In chapter 1.4, reference has already been made to Vincent Donovan's book, *Christianity Rediscovered* where he speaks against the institutional structure of mission and the human determination of the church:

> Because a missionary comes from another already existing church, *that* is the image of church he will have in mind, and if his job is to establish a church, *that* is the church

---

[261] T F Torrance described Anselm's theory of the atonement as 'a severely juridical conception of atonement as an external penal transaction between God and sinful humanity, as in the teaching of St Anselm'. He again took up the point in his book *The Mediation of Christ* (Edinburgh: T&T Clark, 1992) when he contrasted the difference between an intrinsic and extrinsic conception of atonement.

[262] T F Torrance, *The Mediation of Christ*, 47.

he will establish. I think, rather, the missionary's job is to preach, not the church, but Christ. If he preaches Christ and the message of Christianity, the church may well result, may well appear, but it might not be the church he had in mind.[263]

The church that results then is the determination of the ministry of the Godhead and not the institutional offshoot as prescribed by the parent church.

7.4. Revelation and Reconciliation

Many of the great doctrines that form the very foundation of the church are only mentioned in passing in this chapter. It is necessary to see revelation and reconciliation as the ministry of the Trinity and, in fact, to see all biblical doctrines from the viewpoint of the Trinity.

That which we seek to know must determine the means of the knowing. The knowledge of God must come from God Himself, and that is by revelation, firstly through the prophets and finally in the supreme expression, through His Son Jesus Christ (Heb. 1:1–4). This knowledge—which comes through the Word, Jesus Christ—is made real to us through the awakening by the indwelling Holy Spirit.

Through His vicarious humanity and His crucifixion at Calvary, Jesus Christ as our Great High Priest offered Himself for our reconciliation. 'In Christ God was reconciling the world to Himself.'

> [17]So if anyone is in Christ, there is a new creation: everything old has passed away; see, everything has become new! [18]All this is from God, who reconciled us to himself through Christ, **and has given us the ministry of reconciliation;** [19]that is, in Christ God was reconciling the world to himself, not counting their trespasses against them, **and entrusting the message of reconciliation to us.** (2 Cor. 5:17–19 NRSV)

There is a parallelism in vv. 18–19 as Paul seeks to clarify what he said. We may set this out in a tabular form like this:

---

[263] V Donovan, *Christianity Rediscovered* (London: SCM, 1982), 81.

18	All this is from God, who reconciled us to himself through Christ	and has given us the ministry of reconciliation
19	in Christ God was reconciling the world to himself, not counting their trespasses against them	and entrusting the message of reconciliation to us

The very act of reconciling the world was what Jesus accomplished through His life and sacrifice. God reconciled us through Jesus Christ and has given us the ministry of reconciliation. That is not to mean that the ministry of reconciliation becomes ours. There is a parallelism in verses 17–18 where Paul made his point in verse 17 and reiterated the contents in verse 18 and clarified that we are entrusted with the message of reconciliation. Our ministry of reconciliation is the proclamation of the message of reconciliation. This proclamation is not to be taken merely as a vocal exercise but involves the expression of the whole of our lives as individuals, in the family, and in the community of our churches and society. The reconciling is the work of God the Father through Jesus by the awakening of the Holy Spirit. Thus, our ministry of reconciliation is to participate in what Jesus Christ has accomplished, and our specific task is then the proclamation of that message.

The ministry of reconciliation is the ministry of God achieved through Jesus Christ. The church is called into this ministry by the mercy and grace of God (2 Cor. 4:1). The church is entrusted with this ministry and called to participate in this ministry, not to own or possess it. The church is given this ministry of reconciliation by the mercy of God. 'Therefore, since it is by God's mercy that we are engaged in this ministry, we do not lose heart' (2 Cor. 4:1 NRSV).

The church's ministry is to continue the ministry of reconciliation achieved through Jesus Christ, i.e. the proclamation of the message for the restoration and healing of the fractured relationship in our communities through the salvific work of Jesus Christ.

It is also a ministry in the Spirit. While we proclaim the message of reconciliation, it is the Spirit that causes the change within a person. We must not be deceived into thinking that it is our words that achieved the result. The 'other Paraclete' will declare the things of Christ to us in fulfilment of the Father's will.

> [13]When the Spirit of truth comes, he will guide you into all the truth; for he will not speak on his own, but will speak whatever he hears, and he will declare to you the things that are to come. [14]He will glorify me, because he

will take what is mine and declare it to you. ¹⁵All that the Father has is mine. For this reason I said that he will take what is mine and declare it to you. (Jn. 16:13–15 NRSV)

While in Christ we have redemption through His blood, it is by the awakening of the Spirit within us that we have this recognition.

> ¹⁴For all who are led by the Spirit of God are children of God. **¹⁵For you did not receive a spirit of slavery to fall back into fear, but you have received a spirit of adoption. When we cry, 'Abba! Father!' ¹⁶it is that very Spirit bearing witness with our spirit that we are children of God,** ¹⁷and if children, then heirs, heirs of God and joint heirs with Christ—if, in fact, we suffer with him so that we may also be glorified with him. (Rom. 8:14–17)

It is not to be conceived as an either/or ministry but a ministry where the primary determinant is the Father's will and we are all participants in that one ministry, i.e. we participate in the Father's ministry in the Spirit through Jesus Christ. All ministries must have their basis in the ministry of the Trinity.

This ministry of reconciliation requires a change in the direction in one's life. It is not merely subscribing to a creed or changing a particular life style or culture. It involves a change in the underlying values and assumptions that we hold. It is a radical change at the deepest level—a change only accessible to the Spirit. We cannot engage the world's assumption and hope that it will lead to that change. I include here a rather lengthy quotation by Prof T F Torrance when he writes about theological education today.

> We cannot convince others by formal argument, for so long as we argue within their framework, we can never induce them to abandon it. *'Formal operations relying on one framework of interpretation cannot demonstrate a proposition to persons who rely on another framework.'* That applies to theological communications as much as scientific controversy, and yet this is precisely the erroneous line taken so often by apologetics, whether by the theologian or the preacher. Whenever we take that line we are simply reducing ourselves to be servants of public opinion or popular ideas of science and religion, and in that event

we have nothing at all to offer to people which they do not already know or cannot tell to themselves much better than we. Moreover by taking this line we eliminate from theological knowledge its real meaning, for we deprive it of its proper message. That is why theological statements inevitably appear meaningless and impossibly paradoxical if we claim for them validity within a frame of reference which is the correlate of ordinary observable and empirically verifiable experience.[264]

It has to be noticed from Jesus's encounter with His opponents that He never answers their questions on their terms of reference. Jesus always points them away from their human framework to the spiritual framework.
Prof Torrance continues,

> The problem is deeper than that, for we are accustomed to *live* in our frames of reference; we and they belong together. Thus to cross from one frame of reference to another involves an act of radical self-denial on the one hand and the radical reconciliation to the new frame of reference on the other hand. This is another way of stating that theological communication and understanding always involve a movement of *reconciliation*.[265]

7.5. In Christ

The church continues the ministry of Christ on earth. Thus, Christ's ministry determines the nature and content of the church's ministry. As the called-out people of God, redeemed by Christ's precious blood, we are united with Him. The expression 'in Christ' is a recurring theme in the New Testament epistles. In fact, if this expression is taken out of the New Testament writings, there would not be much left for our contemplation as G Bingham concludes, 'In fact "in", "with", and "through" in relation to

---

[264] T F Torrance, *Theology in Reconstruction* (Eugene, OR: Wipf and Stock Publishers, 1996), 27–29. (Italics mine).

[265] Ibid.

Christ and his people are so frequent that not much doctrine of faith and practice of life would be left if they were withdrawn.'[266]

This is nowhere more beautifully expressed than in the opening chapter of the letter to the Ephesians:

> Eph 1:1 ..... faithful *in* Christ Jesus: ...3 .... blessed us *in* Christ with every spiritual blessing in the heavenly places, 4 ..... chose us *in* Christ ......5 .... adoption as his children through Jesus Christ, ...6 ....glorious grace ..... bestowed on us *in* the Beloved. 7 *In* him we have redemption through his blood, ...9 .... according to his good pleasure that he set forth *in* Christ, 11 *In* Christ we have also obtained an inheritance, ...13 *In* him you also, when you had heard the word of truth, and had believed *in* him, ...15 I have heard of your faith *in* the Lord Jesus 20 God put this power to work *in* Christ .... 22 ...... the church 23 which is his body, the fullness of him who fills all *in* all.

This is the charter of the church. God has 'blessed us in Christ' (v. 3), 'chosen us in Christ' (v. 4), 'adopted us through Christ' (v. 5), 'glorious grace . . . bestowed on us in Christ' (v. 6), 'redemption in Christ' (v. 7), and faith in Christ as a result of the hearing of the word of truth in Christ (v. 13). All these are made possible as a result of the power of God working in Christ (v. 15); the fullness of Him fills all and in all (v. 23). There is nothing apart from what God has wrought in Christ Jesus, the church being specifically mentioned here because she is the body of Christ, the continuing earthly expression of the humanity of Christ.

And so Paul could say, 'He is the source of your life in Christ Jesus, who became for us wisdom from God, and righteousness and sanctification and redemption' (1 Cor. 1:30 NRSV).

If God is the source of our life in Christ, then it must mean that there is no source of life (redeemed) outside of Christ.[267] And so Paul says, 'and it is no longer I who live, but it is Christ who lives in me. And the life I now live in the flesh I live by faith in the Son of God, who loved me and gave himself for me' (Gal. 2:20 NRSV).

---

[266] G Bingham, *The Everlasting Presence* (Blackwood, South Australia: New Creation Publication Inc., 1990), 75. The book expounds the faith union in Christ especially in the chapter 'The Apostolic Abiding'.

[267] Ibid., 77ff.

We need to start with who we are in Christ. The 'indicative' precedes the 'imperative'. What we do must results from what we are, and the way we express ourselves in ministry will tell clearly what the foundation of our ministry is. The ministry of the church continues the ministry of Christ and is the heart's grateful response to Christ.

7.6. Service in Christ

In his article on 'Service in Christ', T F Torrance pointed out that service is the response of love and also of obedience.[268] If we say that service is the response to the love of God, then the relationship with God that developed out of the experience of that love must be the determinant of the service. In other words, service is relational and not outcome determined, i.e. it is an expression of the relationship with Christ and it cannot be rendered in isolation from Christ.[269] It is an essential part of the relationship and sometimes regarded as a response to a command. Service is not an end in itself as if it has to be rendered in order to gain acceptance or favour with God. Furthermore, the service rendered cannot stand on its own outside of the relationship with God. Service does not have a driving force of its own. Service for service's sake finally results in boredom and despair.

Yet it is not a servitude but a freedom, a movement of love. It is not even a service of love for love's sake.[270] God commands a service of love and gives the love that empowers for the service.[271] The servant does not assume authority for the service nor is he responsible for the result of that service. He looks for no reward in rendering that service.

> I love I love the master
> I will not go out free.[272]

This is only possible because of the incarnation of Jesus Christ who has taken our humanity on Himself. He dealt with sin from within the depth

---

[268] T F Torrance, 'Service in Jesus Christ', *Theological Foundations for Ministry*, ed. R Anderson, 714f.

[269] Ibid.

[270] Ibid., 715.

[271] Augustine: 'Give what Thou commandest, and command what Thou wilt.'

[272] F R Havergal, *Redemption Hymnal* (Great Britain: Victory Press, 1951), no. 542.

of human existence. In Him and in His mercy lies the creative ground and source of such diakonia.

7.7. Justification of Our Ministry (Barrenness in Ministry)

So often in ministry, we seek justification in terms of what is achieved. We seek the outcome to justify our ministry. Abraham fell into the same trap. All ministry is God's ministry. We are called to participate in that ministry. When we fail to realise our calling, then we seek justification in terms of what is achieved. Our calling is a participation, not a proprietorship.

We are all familiar with the story of the birth of Isaac. There is a tendency to think of blessing as related to achievement and success, i.e. blessing has been equated with approval of what we are doing, and failure or barrenness means the curse of God and therefore disapproval of what we are doing.

It was related to me that when Christian workers confront difficult problems in their ministry, they almost always ask, 'What more can I do to make things better?' So they work even harder and get involved in more areas, and the more they get involved, the more problems they get themselves into. Instead, they should be sitting back and take a long hard look at what they are doing and what are they doing that for.[273]

Many interpreters have taken the stories of Abraham and make a comparison between faith and works. They say that Ishmael represents human works and Isaac represents faith in God. To a degree that is so, but when faith in God is understood as doing nothing on the part of Abraham and Sarah, then that is a wrong interpretation of God's purpose. I suppose we imagine Abraham and Sarah sleeping in their own tents every night, simply gazing at the stars in the sky, waiting for a son to appear. No, Abraham and Sarah needed to embrace each other in their mutual love as husband and wife. As they expressed the gift of their sexual relationship to each other, God worked within that relationship. It is not an argument between faith and work but a participation in the purpose of God.

We might make a visual representation of what has been discussed like this:

---

[273] This was related to me by Dr Robert Redman, former director of the D. Min. program at Fuller Theological Seminary.

MAN	↔	**DIVINE POSSIBILITY**	↔	**PROMISE**
		Vision		*Participation*
MAN	↔	**HUMAN POSSIBILITY**	↔	**COUNTERFEIT**
		Vision (tunnelled)		*Self-reliance*

So in barrenness, we need to sit back and take a hard look at our humanity and ask ourselves these questions.

- What are we created for?
- What is our relationship with God and with one another?
- What is God's purpose in our midst, and how have we envisioned that?

It is only as we understand the purpose of the divine that we in our humanity can participate with what He has ordained.

God has created us for relationships—with Him and with one another. This relationship is the outworking of His covenants, and that is what we refer to as covenantal relationship. God has chosen to work through human relationship as He exists in relationship. He is to be known in His relationship. The problem that Abraham and Sarah faced regarding their posterity is an issue of the husband-wife relationship between Abraham and Sarah. They have allowed the outcome, i.e. the son of promise, to determine the way they relate. Rather, their relationship with each other is the primary issue. God has chosen to work through the relationship between Abraham and Sarah, i.e. through a family and then through a community and later through a nation. Following the coming of Christ, God has chosen to work through the church. We may depict the way in which vision and participation are played out in both situations in this way.

	ABRAHAM and SARAH	**CHURCH**
VISION	→ PROMISE	→ KNOWING GOD'S PURPOSE
PARTICIPATION	→ FAMILY RELATIONSHIP	→ CHURCH RELATIONSHIP

Every church will have gone through many a barren time. Each time, we need to come back and look at God's purpose for the church. We need also to look at the relationships within the church.

What was Abraham and Sarah supposed to do while waiting for Isaac to come along? They should not be engineering all the other relationships to achieve an imitation of the fulfilment which God has planned for them. They were firstly to live in hope and secondly to maintain and deepen the relationship they have with each other. So it is with the church. While we go through periods of barrenness, which no doubt any church will in its life cycle, we need firstly to have a vision of what we may become. That is our hope. Secondly, we need to maintain and deepen our relationship with each other within the church so that we can meaningfully participate in the activity of God. The last thing we want to do in a time of barrenness is to engineer imitation outcomes and in the process sever our relationships.

Yet this is precisely what we do when we get into a barren patch in our lives. Because of Hagar, the relationship between Abraham and Sarah was put under a strain. If we understand that God has called us into covenantal relationship with Him and with one another, then that relationship is primary because God's purpose is to work through that relationship. Even though the situation may look impossible as in the case with Abraham and Sarah, we need to live in hope and with the vision that that will be so.

So we need to know what God has called us to and to keep that vision alive in the relationship within the church so that one day we will see its fulfilment. All these do not mean that there is a restriction in our ministry. Rather, there is a freedom of the church as it bases its ministry on the knowledge of who God is and what He seeks to fulfil. There is a freedom when we recognise our role as participants in God's ministry. We are confident of its fulfilment as God brings about His desired outcome in His time.

7.8. Ministry as Response

He ministered the things of God to man and the things of man to God.
—Athanasius

The covenant has been discussed in chapter 3 of this dissertation, 'The Heart of Christianity: The Trinity and the Covenant'. This is an important issue, and the whole of scripture cannot be understood outside of the context of the covenant. God's dealing with us in reconciliation is based on His covenant of love with humanity. The covenants that we have in scripture must be seen as expressions of the one eternal covenant covering the whole of mankind. This is the covenant of creation—the primary covenant. Expressions of this primary covenant are seen in its particularity in history.[274] The covenant expresses the inner structure of the relationship between God and man. That God's one eternal covenant with humanity is unilateral and unconditional must be affirmed at all times. Much of the difficulty in holding to the unilaterality and unconditionality of God's covenant is the difficulty in seeing our response within the covenant provisions and not outside of it. In other words, if we see the covenant response as outside of the provisions of the covenant, then we must maintain a bilaterality, and we are then left to our own initiative in maintaining the covenant. This is precisely the problem with Abraham and Sarah as we discussed in the above section.

The way we understand 'ministry' as response will be dealt with in the next chapter.

---

[274] The Noahic, Abrahamic, Mosaic, Davidic, and new covenants are expressions of the one eternal covenant of creation.

Part Three, Chapter 8

A THEOLOGY OF RESPONSE

8.1. Introduction

The discussion on 'A Theology of Response' could and should really be included in the chapter on 'A Theology of Ministry'. I have put them into two separate chapters to accommodate the Chinese mind, which sees ministry as performed by a select category of Christians. What I hope to achieve is that we comprehend the theology of response in the light of the Trinity and then go back to see ministry in a new light.

This chapter will show that the Chinese understanding of response is based on the Buddhist model of priesthood. The chapter will highlight the fact that indeed the whole of our lives is a response. This will focus on Christ as the response on our behalf. His continuing high priesthood will be discussed. Our response is the response to His response.

8.2. Priesthood in the Buddhist Context

Many Chinese Christians have come to understand the term *priest* in their cultural context. They have worked from concepts in their culture to the Bible. What is commonly understood is that the priest is a kind of an intermediary between the worshipper and the divine. The Bible uses the term in that sense as well but with a very different connotation.

In the West, the term *priest* means a special person who is able to communicate with the divine and thus use the position to facilitate a correspondence for the worshipper. The priest is endowed with a special skill in the performance of the cultic duties. In this pattern, there is very little difference between the understanding of West and the East as the basis of that understanding is contractual, utilitarian, and unitarian, i.e. it is primarily some kind of an agreement between the worshipper and the god, the priest being the intermediary. Because of these similarities, Hans Kung remarked that China is part and parcel of the single 'religious history of humankind'.[275]

However, the understanding of the function of the priest in the Chinese context takes on a more colourful meaning. The gods are able to enter into persons with this special cultic function, albeit only temporarily, and then depart. In that period of time, these persons are in a state of trance and quite beside themselves, being endowed with supernatural powers and knowledge. In that state, they can call on the gods and transmit messages to the worshippers. They are even able to bring back the spirit of the dead. After a time, the gods then leave these persons, and they become their normal selves again.

On the surface, this may appear to be similar to the Old Testament description of the priesthood. Yet there are some significant differences. Necromancy is condemned in the scriptures (1 Sam. 28:1–20). While there may be the indwelling of the Spirit of God onto various ones at certain epochs of time, these are not at the whims of the individual but at the express will of Yahweh. The purpose is to proclaim the will of God to His people (Heb. 1:1–2). This pertains to the Aaronic priesthood. With the incarnation of Jesus Christ, a new order of priesthood was announced. This is the order of Melchizedek.[276] The incarnate Jesus embodies our humanity and at once is both God and representative mankind. He is our priest and indeed the Great High Priest mediating our response on our behalf. In this context, we understand the New Testament priesthood.

8.3. Jesus Christ: The Only Acceptable Response

God is the initiator of the covenant, and as we have noted, this covenant expresses the movement of God towards man; and in so doing, there is a reciprocal movement from man towards God. This is the response from man. In a relationship, there is a two-way movement. We have placed great emphasis on the revelation of God that Jesus Christ brings to us as well as His mediation for our salvation and this is rightly so. We must not trade

---

[275] H Kung and J Ching, *Christianity and Chinese Religions* (London: SCM, 1989), 36.

[276] 'And he says in another place, "You are a priest forever, in the order of Melchizedek" (Heb. 5:6).

this for anything less. However, when we come to make a response to God, we consider it to be our own response. This way of thinking happens not only within the Chinese culture but also in most cultures. This reflects the fallen state of humankind in rebellion against God. Humankind will always want to build its own Tower of Babel. We make that response in our own name and on the basis of our achievement. We seem to ignore the mediation of Jesus Christ in our response to God.

Mediation is an important aspect in the approach to God in the Bible. The responses in the Old Testament were mediated by the priests in the temple. Saul sought to offer a sacrifice without this mediation, and he was reprimanded (1 Sam. 13:6–14). He was not the person ordained to offer such sacrifices. The priests were to officiate in such a ceremony on behalf of the person making the offering. Yet the offering of the sacrifice was not the primary consideration. Many prophets had made references to the wayward heart of Israel who thought that in making the sacrifice in the temple, God would be propitiated when there was no sense of acknowledgement of God in their hearts. 'You do not delight in sacrifice, or I would bring it; you do not take pleasure in burnt offering' (Ps. 51:16). They had not repented from their sins. The sacrifice was merely the artefact. God has no delight in such sacrifices. There is only one sacrifice that God accepts, and that is the holy sacrifice of His Son, Jesus Christ.

There is within the Godhead a perichoretic relationship where one is responsive to the other. Man is created in the image of God and therefore is a responsive creature. His response is not merely a reaction to his environment like an animal or vegetable. What distinguishes man from the rest of God's creation is his capacity to relate as subject to subject recognising the other in the relationship. 'What is it to be human?' we need to ask. Our humanness is defined not by our objectivity or rationality though these are important facets within our being but by our relatedness. Therefore, our relationship with our Creator and fellow creation constitute the distinguishing mark of our humanity. Being estranged from God in our fallen status, it is only in Jesus's perfect humanity that we will find fulfilment in our restored humanity.

As created beings, the possibility of our response lies in what God as creator has given to us. He has created us within limits and provided for our response. Our response lies within these limits. We cannot go outside of these limits as if we can respond 'in our own right'[277] and in ways that we consider appropriate. God has given us the enabling to respond through Jesus Christ and in the Spirit. He is indeed our response to God, and we

---

[277] R Anderson, *Historical Transcendence and the Reality of God* (Grand Rapids: Eerdmans, 1975), 132–145.

are responding to the response.[278] We are all called to share or participate in the merits of Jesus Christ.

Now in Jesus Christ becoming man, He has taken up our sinful humanity in Himself and as the representative of humanity made that perfect response to God—a response that we are not able to make. Jesus came to reveal God to us. He is indeed the God who is for man. There is more to that. Jesus Christ is also the Man who is for God. Becoming man is not a foreign thing to God. God created mankind in the first place. There is incorporated within the divine Godhead a humanity with whom God relates. John says, 'He came to that which was his own, but his own did not receive him' (Jn. 1:11).

In Jesus becoming man, He not only revealed to us the Father but also as a man responded to the Father in perfect obedience. He is the second Adam and made the response on our behalf. In standing beneath that man Jesus Christ and relying on His meritorious humanity, we now can approach God not in a direct manner but only through Jesus Christ, the mediator between God and man as Paul puts it, 'for there is one God and one mediator between God and men, the man Christ Jesus' (1 Tim 2:5).

8.4. Unitarian or Trinitarian

Our evangelical dogma has rightly emphasised the mediatorial role of our Lord Jesus Christ in redemption. However, when it comes to considering our response to the Father, we switch to our pietistic mode. In other words, it is the 'I' who is responding to God. We come before God to worship Him. We pray to Him and serve Him. We offer ourselves to Him. In these responses, where is the place of Jesus Christ? We have treated Christ in a utilitarian manner as if to say that when He has got us back to God, then His function is over. It is then over to us. We then pay lip service to His role in concluding our prayers with the words 'In Jesus's Name'. This is basically a unitarian approach, i.e. it is between me and God. Jesus Christ is the mediator between God and man, and this mediation is necessary and present in both the pathways from God to man and from man to God.[279]

---

[278] That is the response of Jesus Christ to the Father.

[279] This issue is dealt with very succinctly in the article by J B Torrance, 'The Place of Jesus Christ in Worship', *Theological Foundations for Ministry*, ed. R Anderson (Grand Rapids: Eerdmans, 1979), 348–369.

8.5. The Continuing High Priesthood of Jesus Christ

Many years ago, I was asked the question, 'What is Jesus Christ doing today?' It drew a blank. Of course, there was a blank to the question as it was something that I had not thought much about or was taught as far as I could remember. In the churches in which I had worshipped, there had been a great emphasis on the finished work of Jesus Christ, and that is rightly so. The words from the cross 'It is finished' gave the impression that there is nothing more to do on the part of God and Christ. The writer to the Hebrews emphasised the 'once and for all' sacrifice of Jesus Christ, which is fully sufficient and is not to be repeated. Again this is the right emphasis and needs to be reinforced again and again. Hebrews also mentioned Jesus achieving the 'rest' for the people of God. We also read that Jesus is now ascended into heaven and seated on the right hand of God on high, giving us a picture of a very relaxed pose. So what more is there to do? The rest is up to us and perhaps with the assistance of the Holy Spirit of God! Jesus Christ has asked us to continue His work and sent the Holy Spirit to assist us. This is far from the truth, as I will try to explain. We can be forgiven to have deduced from the above that there is nothing more to do on the part of Jesus Christ. Nothing is further from the truth. We need to consider the continuing ministry of Jesus Christ.

8.5.1. A Man in Heaven: Our Forerunner (Heb. 6:20) and High Priest in Heaven (Heb. 4:14)

Heb 6 [19]We have this hope as an anchor for the soul, firm and secure. It enters the inner sanctuary behind the curtain, [20]where **Jesus, who went before us, has entered on our behalf.** He has become a high priest **forever**, in the order of Melchizedek.

Heb 4 [14]Therefore, since we have **a great high priest who has gone through the heavens, Jesus the Son of God,** let us hold firmly to the faith we profess. [15]For we do not have a high priest who is unable to sympathize with our weaknesses, but we have one who has been tempted in every way, just as we are—yet was without sin. [16]Let us then approach the throne of grace with confidence, so that we may receive mercy and find grace to help us in our time of need.

There is today as it has been for the past 2000 years, a man in heaven. Jesus is incarnate in human flesh and His humanity remains with Him. We are not to think that Jesus Christ took pity on us and came as a man and now that He has done His job as a man left His humanity behind and went back to heaven. It is not with cold detachment that Jesus took on the form of a man and left it when the job is done. He identified with humanity, and He has now taken that humanity with Him into heaven as Heb. 4:14 tells us 'a great high priest who has gone through the heavens, Jesus the Son of God'. And as our great High Priest in heaven, He understands us and is able to sympathise with us in His humanity.

8.5.2. Intercession on Our Behalf (Heb. 9:24)

> **Heb 9** ²³It was necessary, then, for the copies of the heavenly things to be purified with these sacrifices, but the heavenly things themselves with better sacrifices than these. ²⁴For Christ did not enter a man-made sanctuary that was only a copy of the true one; he entered heaven itself, now to appear for us in God's presence. ²⁵Nor did he enter heaven to offer himself again and again, the way the high priest enters the Most Holy Place every year with blood that is not his own.

Jesus Christ continues to be our great High Priest in heaven. He intercedes on our behalf. While it is true that we can approach God the Father with confidence, it must be remembered that it is only through the accepted work of Jesus Christ on our behalf. We need to be reminded of the model of the temple in ancient Israel. There are priests in the outer courtyard of the temple where they accept the sacrifice from the people and make the appropriate offering to God for repentance and consecration. However, on the Day of Atonement once a year, the High Priest entered into the most holy inner chamber of the temple into the presence of God. The priests are not given that special service. That special service belongs only to the High Priest.

Now we have a High Priest who has done that for us, and He continues that ministry of intercession on our behalf before God. Our acceptance before God is only on the merit of our High Priest and not on how we have performed. If my ministry is considered on its own merit, then it counts for nothing. What I am doing is only acceptable to God on the merit of Jesus Christ, and I need to trust in that in my ministry. This takes me away from any arrogance on my part and causes me to acknowledge what others are doing because our services are not acceptable on account on how perfectly we have performed it.

8.6. The Law and Our Response

Now we can be free from any bondage or yoke that demands we come up to some man-made standard. All of us stand covered by that perfect response of Jesus Christ, whether one is a great theologian or missionary or serving locally at home. Some of us may be called to one kind of service or another, some given more prominence than others, but none of these services merit any more or less in the sight of God. It is that perfect humanity of Jesus Christ that counts, and we stand as beneficiaries of His perfect response.

The law and the cult do not constitute the centre of the covenant.[280] God is the centre of the covenant. The cult forms the covenant response through the enabling of God. They are the divinely provided way of covenant response. While we consider the covenants made with Abraham and his descendants as covenants of grace, our dualistic mind halts at the Sinaitic covenant; and to our delight, we find something contractual to feast on! This is not so. The Sinaitic covenant is also a covenant of grace. Within the laws given to Moses is the covenanted way of response to the God of grace, and He has graciously provided for us in the cult and ceremony the response that He desires. The cult and the law is the enabling of God in our response to Him. It is from beginning to end the grace of God.

When the creational covenant is interpreted in a legalistic manner, the result is the concept of a covenant of works. However, the obedience expected of Adam was the response to grace that was first imparted to him. Within the limitation placed upon Adam was the enabling of God to effect that response. David in his prayer understood this very clearly when he said, 'Everything comes from you, and we have given you only what comes from your hand' (1 Chr. 29:14).

So in the transaction of the new covenant, God provided the perfect response for us in the person of Jesus Christ. We often only think in terms of His substitutionary death as an act external to us. We also need to think in terms of the incorporation within His vicarious humanity as He continues as our Great High Priest in heaven.

Our response to God consists of what He has first provided for us in grace. 'Give what Thou commandest and command what Thou

---

[280] R Anderson, *Historical Transcendence*, 139.

wilt'—this prayer from Augustine landed him into endless troubles with his contemporary Pelagius. Augustine understood the priority of grace.

Just as ecclesiology is determined by pateriology, Christology, pneumatology, soteriology, and eschatology, so ministry and our response are determined by the same considerations.

8.7. Conclusion to the Theology of Ministry and of Response

1. The community of the church must be grounded in the community of the Trinitarian Godhead.
2. The ministry of the church must be grounded in the ministry of the Father, and this ministry is effected by the Son and continued by the Holy Spirit.
3. The ministry of the church then is our participation in God's ministry as a result of our union with Christ. This is a faith union achieved through the vicarious humanity of Jesus Christ and not a mystical union through some external transaction on the cross.
4. Thus, the ministry of the church as the continuation of the ministry of the Father is assured of its outcome, and we do not engineer imitations on the grounds of human possibilities.

Part Three, Chapter 9

COVENANT AS IT RELATES TO OUR CULTURE

This paper would not be complete without mentioning some specific issues in our culture and commenting on them in the light of the Trinity and the covenant. Where appropriate, reference will be made to the Chinese culture. In our global village, there is a gradual merging of the cultures, and especially with the overseas Chinese, many have taken on much of the culture of their adopted country. The distinction between the culture of the overseas Chinese and the culture of their adopted country is not great. The comments made here will be of a general nature, as they will apply to the overseas Chinese and equally well to the Anglo-Western culture. The treatment will be brief, as numerous authors and books have written much in these areas. The comments will be kept to key aspects in the interface between theology and culture.[281]

Our understanding of the covenant will cause us to rethink some of our core assumptions leading to the external expressions of our culture. Martin Luther King, writing on the social injustice in the Deep South,

---

[281] Numerous works have appeared recently in this area such as the following: C Kraft, *Christianity in Culture* (New York: Orbis, 1979); R Jenson, ed., *Essays in the Theology of Culture* (Grand Rapids: Eerdmans, 1995); G R Hunsberger and C van Gelder, eds., *The Church between Gospel and Culture* (Grand Rapids: Eerdmans, 1996); W A Dyrness, *The Earth Is God's* (New York: Orbis, 1997); K Tanner, *Theories of Culture* (Minneapolis: Fortress, 1997).

remarked, 'I have heard so many ministers say, "These are social issues with which the gospel has no real concern."' His criticism is right, as so many, including Christians, have separated the spiritual and the social. This form of thinking is the result of the dualism that pervades our society. It is a thinking that has subordinated the gospel to the prevailing culture. It fails to realise that at the core of our culture is the concept of God. It is a denial of the fact that whether God is acknowledged or not, lying at the core of our assumptions is the way we conceive of the ultimate reality. The gospel is concerned with the way in which we see the world and the society around us. We need to wrestle with the way our theology impacts upon our sociology.

It goes without saying that we can only come to comprehend a new thing in terms of what we know. It is no different when it comes to our understanding of the things of God. Our approach is basically an approach from below, i.e. we impose upon spiritual issues the framework that we have developed from the human life that we know. However, we need to start somewhere, and Jesus Christ took that earthly approach when He tried to reveal spiritual truth to His disciples. However, that was intended to move them over to a new framework,[282] or in the words of John, we need new wineskins. When we come to the things of God, we need to develop a new framework or a new starting point. This new starting point is the incarnation of Jesus Christ from which we gain an understanding of the triunity of God.

If we do not reason out these issues on the grounds of the Trinity and the covenant, then any other basis of approach will only reflect the cultural stance. In the latter case, we would still be in a state of cultural captivity. This is what L Newbigin means when he wrote his book *Truth to Tell: The Gospel as Public Truth*.[283] He argues that the thought forms of our society must be judged by the truth of the gospel. This chapter seeks to review our thoughts on various cultural issues in the light of our understanding of the triune God and His covenant.

9.1. The Culture of Narcissism

The problem with our communities is that our culture today emphasises self-realisation and self-fulfilment. It is narcissistic. We have seen the trend towards self-sufficiency and isolation in the Chinese culture. This is a trend

---

[282] See section 5.1, 'A Recovery of the Trinitarian Faith'.

[283] L Newbigin, *Truth to Tell: The Gospel as Public Truth* (London: SPCK, 1991).

that is common in all cultures. It is seen to varying degrees in all cultures in our global village.

Narcissism takes its name from a handsome young man, Narcissus, in Greek mythology. The son of the river god Cephissus and the nymph Leiriope, he was told by his mother that if he did not look on his features, he would have a long life. He was so attractive that all the maidens longed to be possessed by him. He ignored them all, even the fairest of the nymphs, Echo. One of the maidens prayed, 'May he who love not others love himself.' One day, Narcissus bent over a pool and saw the reflection of his own image. He fell in love with it straight away. He burned with love for his image and continued to gaze at it. Once, he bent over too far by the edge of the pool and fell into it and drowned. They could not recover his body, and at the spot where he drowned grew a lovely flower which was named after him, Narcissus.

Our society teaches us that we need to seek self-fulfilment and self-esteem. Our newsstands are full of glossy magazines telling us that we are somehow falling short of our potential and advocating means and ways by which we can arrive at that fulfilment. They are also full of apparent success stories to show us what we can become.

Therefore, there has developed one particular trait of our modern-day culture: introspection. This is much evident in the Chinese culture as we have discussed the ethnocentricity, egocentricity, and isolation of the Chinese. In the West, this self-awareness movement has its root back in days of Descartes when he taught, 'I think therefore I am' (*cogito ergo sum*). It teaches us an awareness of our own existence. This existentialist approach has been prevalent in the interpretation of the scriptures. All knowledge is derived from one's awareness of one's own self-existence. The philosophers from the Enlightenment emphasised the supremacy of reason. So the intellectual faculty of man was elevated, and together with the rise of empiricism, man then set about to define and manipulate the natural world to his advantage. If man is able to investigate the natural and biological world objectively, then he must also be able to examine himself in an objective way and get to 'know himself'.[284] This trend to self-analysis becomes one of man's foremost preoccupations.

In the field of psychology and psychotherapy, humanistic self-theories prevail.[285] It assumes the intrinsic goodness of the human person. This unipolar self-analysis is prescribed as the answer to man's relational ills.

---

[284] Pope's *Essay on Man* (1733–34): 'Know then thyself, presume not God to scan, The proper study of Mankind is Man.'

[285] P C Vitz, *Psychology as Religion* (Grand Rapids: Eerdmans, 1977), xviii.

The problem is that the self as subject is trying to analyse self as object. This introspection cannot lead to a discovery of self. What one sees is merely the reflection or image of one's own consciousness. The self sets up a framework by which it seeks to discover itself, and only those perceptions that fit into that framework are received. This only reinforces the presuppositions set up by the initial framework and leads to a further isolation of the self.

Writing on the Trinity, Moltmann made this remark for the release of self from its own prison:

> The modern culture of subjectivity has long since been in danger of turning into a culture of narcissism, which makes the self its own prisoner and supplies it merely with self-repetitions and self-confirmation. It is therefore time for Christian theology to break out of this prison of narcissism, and for it to present its 'doctrine of faith' as a doctrine of the all-embracing 'history of God'.[286]

This unipolar analysis of self is non-relational. What we need is a bipolar approach, i.e. we only know ourselves as we exist in community. John MacMurray writes, 'I need you to be myself.'[287] We only come to know ourselves through the eyes and mind of the other. We only know ourselves in relationship. To withdraw from relationship and retreat into our very self only leads to a loss of self-knowledge.

This introspection in our culture breeds much of the problem in our marriages, churches, and society. It is a loss of the covenant in our relationships. There is only the acknowledgement of self and not of the other. So our relationships with others are turned from the covenantal to the contractual, and therefore, the 'other' has become functional and utilitarian. When the function is over, the relationship can then be disposed of.

Of course, our secular culture has been calling to us all the time to consider the fulfilment we get from our careers, our marriage, and in all areas of life. This has led to an intensification of the isolation of the self. It is a culture where the first question is 'What is in it for me?' It is a totally individualistic, narcissistic culture. Therein lies much of the difficulties we

---

[286] J Moltmann, *The Trinity and the Kingdom of God*, trans. M. Kohl (London: SCM, 1981), 5.

[287] Quoted in A Torrance, 'The Self-relation, Narcissism and the Gospel of Grace', *Scottish Journal of Theology* 40 (1987): 501.

have in our churches and marriages. It is only a change to a new framework of thinking in terms of the covenant that will help to rid our culture of its predicament.[288]

Our materialistic and technological culture emphasises the things that are outside of us. It concentrates on tasks and achievements and very little on the being and relationship issues. Our churches also are involved in this culture of numbers and achievements. We need to change over to the covenantal framework in working out our relationship.

We need to rediscover what it is to be in community. The giving and receiving in community is the only means to self-knowledge. We need to come away from the dualism that is so deeply engraved in our core assumption to embrace the gospel of grace once again. Writing on the subject of narcissism and the gospel of grace, Dr A Torrance says:

> Conceived in these terms, there is no dualism between faith and works, between the self and the world. Neither is there any divorce between grace and law, between what we are in Christ and our summoning to be Christ-like. Living by grace is a structured mode of personal being—it is 'being' in accordance with the law of one's reality already realised.[289]

Much of the effort to overcome this deep dualism is at the level of the artefact. This is to deal only with the peripheral issues. Unless the core assumptions are changed, the artefactual alteration remains only a facelift. The problem remains. Just as Christ started with the earthly[290] in an effort to move them to the heavenly, we need to work towards a change in the underlying framework of thinking. It has already been pointed out in chapter 7.5 the need to change over to another framework of thinking if we are to embrace the covenantal God of grace.

Christ has already accomplished the reconciliation to this new framework. He came to establish the new covenant and this new relational framework based on the covenant we are to embrace in our life and in all that we do, i.e. our culture.

---

[288] This issue has been dealt with very adequately in A Torrance, 'The Self-Relation, Narcissism and the Gospel of Grace', *SJT* 40:481–510.

[289] Ibid., 509.

[290] Examples are in Jesus's encounters with Nicodemus and the Samaritan in John 3 and 4 respectively.

9.2. Worship: What We Are or What We Do?

T F and J B Torrance have done much of the work on the theology of worship.[291] I refer to their work and will provide a brief summary here. Many of the issues raised in this area have already been touched on earlier in this paper.

There is much controversy on the subject of worship. This centres mainly over the form, i.e. the way we do it. If worship is to show the worth of God, then it must reflect what His nature is and the way He relates to us. Our God is the triune God existing in a covenant relationship as Father, Son, and Holy Spirit, and is in a covenant relationship with us—a covenant made through His Son, Jesus Christ. Within the covenant, He has provided for us the covenant response in His Son Jesus Christ, 'the God who is for man and the Man who is for God'.[292] He is indeed our mediator, the Great High Priest who is continuing to offer intercession for us.

Much of our worship is self-centred and does not reflect the covenant response that God has provided for us in His Son. The pertinent question for us is 'Where is Jesus in our worship, and what role has He?' He is the true worshipper, and our worship is only acceptable insofar as it is offered through Him as covenanted. The prophets of old fought hard to dissociate worship from its external forms and put it where it ought to be: the covenanted response.[293]

9.3. Church Life: Pastor-Congregation Relationship

This is an area where there have been many unhappy endings. I need to curtail my remarks here and present the view as seen through the eyes of

---

[291] T F Torrance, *The Mediation of Christ* (Edinburgh: T&T Clark, 1992); J B Torrance, *Worship, Community, and the Triune God of Grace* (Carlisle, UK: Paternoster, 1996).

[292] This is to quote R Anderson's well-known expression.

[293] I also refer you to the works by T F Torrance and J B Torrance on worship as our covenant response. T F Torrance, 'The Word of God and the Response of Man', *Theological Foundations for Ministry*, ed. R Anderson (Grand Rapids: Eerdmans, 1982), 111–134; J B Torrance, 'The Place of Jesus Christ in Worship', *Theological Foundations for Ministry*, 348–369; J B Torrance, 'The Vicarious Humanity of Christ', *The Incarnation*, ed. T F Torrance (Edinburgh: Handsel Press, 1981), 127–147.

the laity[294] rather than through the clergy's. It seems very strange to me that so many denominations have advocated a contractual arrangement between the minister and the congregation. This is particularly so with the Chinese congregations as many of them are independent, standing on their own and run by a few families. I have no doubt that this is because of the many complicated scenarios that have caused difficulties in the relationship. Based on management principles, contracts and job descriptions have been drawn up in order to manage the difficulties. What has happened to the covenantal framework in the meantime?

As one who had been involved in such a difficult occasion on the side of the laity, I am aware that the issues relate to an almost total lack of appreciation of the covenant in the life of the church. The laity do not seem to understand the implications of the covenant. This may reflect a deficiency in the clergy in not communicating these issues more succinctly to the congregation.

A core assumption of many in our congregations is that of absolutism, i.e. as they perceive the absolute God, they transpose that image onto the minister. Perhaps many ministers give that impression of themselves as well thereby reinforcing the error among those whom they seek to minister. Furthermore, many ministers seek security of tenure and it is not an unreasonable request, but the congregation then expresses this security in terms of a contract rather than a covenant because that is all the only way they know how.

In today's world of achievement and results, many ministers are forced by the prevailing culture to produce what can be clearly seen. As a result, the peripheral issues are emphasised and the primary relationship with the congregation suffers.

I see the need for our congregations to be taught the triunity of the Godhead and the nature of the covenant and follow that through with the implications of a covenant relationship and the priority of grace and forgiveness. As there will be weak areas in each of us, these areas should be highlighted right at the beginning of the relationship between the clergy and the laity rather than for the clergy to present a perfect image. As part of the laity, I see the role of the lay leadership is to back up those weaker areas in the clergy so that the body works as an efficient whole. I see the minister-congregation relationship as one of mutual building up. I am not giving the impression that this is an easy thing to get across as I had failed on my part to get my fellow lay leaders to take this line, and it may even be more difficult for the minister to get it across.

---

[294] I am not an ordained minister of the church but a member of the lay leadership.

9.4. The Workplace

Our Western economy embraces the 'hire and fire' labour system. It is a system of the free market forces. We need to go out there to prove our worth and find acceptance. So in a slowdown in the economy, many people are laid off because the company needs to balance its books. It has no option because it has a fixed-wage cost structure based on a contract worked out bilaterally.

Let me relate something that has happened in Japan and Singapore[295] in recent years. The Japanese has a 'lifetime employment' system. So when there is a downturn in the economy, people are not laid off but continue to be employed. With the extra labour, the company then concentrates more on providing service for its customers. It is a strength in the Japanese economy, though this trend is slowly moving towards the contractual framework. This restricts competition for labour with the unwritten 'no-poaching rule'. Strike action is seldom taken as it strikes against the long-term future of the worker. A Japanese union idea of a strike is an 'one hour' stop work meeting during the lunch break. While the company continues to keep its labour force and to trade itself out of the difficult period, it also has the flexibility of reducing the bonus payment to the workers. This bonus payment can amount to 30–40 per cent of the annual salary. This is a secular model, but it speaks to me more of a covenantal relationship than the Western contractual model we have here.

So too in Singapore many years ago when the island state went through a very bad recession, the workers accepted a reduction in their wage packet in exchange for continued employment. Many people were able to keep their jobs, and this prevented the recession from becoming even worse. During the pickup stage a few years later, they were rewarded with a thirteenth-month wage packet. And so the bonus system has come to stay in the wage structure in Singapore.

These models, though not perfect, are closer to the idea of a covenant in the workplace than what we have here in this country. Our workers are not merely there to service the company and to create profits. On the contrary, we need to see the workplace as the environment where the workers are given opportunities for service according to their abilities and for their development. In the process, there has to be some income generated to keep those opportunities available. There ought to be a covenant relationship

---

[295] The comments here do not relate to Japan and Singapore in a universal way. They relate to trends in the work relationship in those two countries. However, there is also an evolving trend where the industrial culture of the West is being adopted by some quarters in these countries.

between employers and employees. Each does not treat the other as a means to an end. In the workplace, the primary objective should be an investment in the development of those who work there. The financial consideration is necessary to keep the business of people's development going. This may be too much for some to accept, but experience shows that those businesses that invest in their personnel are the businesses that do well.

I do not speak here as an economist, but one does not need to be an economist to see the inconsistency with a covenant relationship within our labour system and indeed our whole social structure.

If this is so, then questions need to be raised regarding the way we adopt the culture or the workplace. Is the workplace merely for the accumulation of profits? Or is it the place for the development of those who work there? Is the so-called Protestant work ethic a Christian principle to apply in the workplace? Is efficiency and productivity the only criterion to judge the performance of a workplace? Are those employed merely the servants of the masters? If so, we are back to a monarchian theology. Is it possible to experience the interpenetration of persons within the workplace? Can we not continue to keep in employment an inefficient worker because of a covenant relationship? Could not the workplace be the place for the development or redevelopment for these workers? These are important questions for the Christians engaged in organisational culture.

Our culture has put the emphasis on structure above people. In so doing, we have ignored the dignity of the human person. Such a dignity is conferred. We confer this dignity onto the human person not by lording it over him or by contorting him into a rigid structure but in empowering him.[296] God confers upon us our dignity by the empowerment of the Holy Spirit in our lives.

9.5. Family Relationships: Covenant or Contract?

When we say those words at our wedding 'For better for worse, for richer for poorer, in sickness and in health, to love and to cherish, till death do us part', we are expressing unconditionality in the relationship. However, marriage today is clothed in the language of companionship and fulfilment, so we go around seeking the right partner. Worse still, marriage is approached with contractual obligations. When we run into difficulties in our marriage, we talk in terms of incompatibility and therefore separation.

---

[296] H Thelicke, 'The Evangelical Faith' in *Theological Foundations for Ministry*, 63 ff.

Rather, 'the first sign of contradiction in committed relationships is not the end but the beginning of covenant love'.[297]

When we move out of communion, we withdraw into self and therefore sink into our narcissistic culture. 'A person is a person only because of others and on behalf of others.'[298] We need to see marriage as a covenantal relationship. 'Because humanity is originally and essentially co-humanity, the fundamental affirmation of human existence is surely one of relatedness. . . . Covenant is the theological paradigm for co-humanity experienced as relatedness.'[299]

In applying the concept of covenant to the family and marriage, Ray Anderson concludes,

> It is covenantal love that provides the basis for family. For this reason, family means much more than consanguinity, where blood ties provide the only basis for belonging. Family is where you are loved unconditionally, and where you can count on that love even when you least deserve it.[300]

---

[297] R Anderson and D Guernsey, *On Being Family*, (Grand Rapids: Eerdmans, 1985), 45.

[298] John MacMurray, *Persons in Relations*, p. 150. An African proverb.

[299] Anderson and Guernsey, *On Being Human*, 168.

[300] Ibid., 40 (Italics mine).

```
              Degree of
              Commitment
                  |
     Initial Covenant ─ ─ ─
                  |
                  |
Degree of  ─────  Mature   ─────  Degree of
Intimacy          Covenant          Grace
                  |
                  |
              Degree of
              Empowering
```

Figure 1. The Marital Relationship

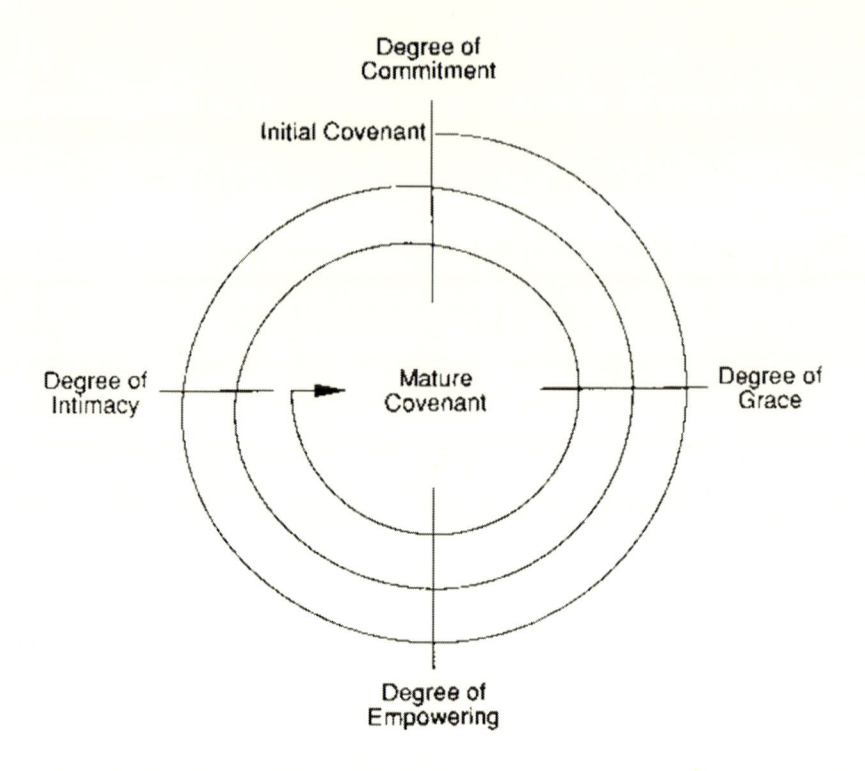

In attempting to spell out the sociological implications of the family relationship, the Balswicks in their book *The Family*,[301] presented a model to depict the family relationship in graphic form (see figure 1). It is a helpful working model.

Figure 1. The Marital Relationship

The model is depicted in a spiral rather than in a linear fashion. It tries to highlight a dynamic relationship and the presence of struggles and difficulties are implied. Otherwise, there is no need for grace. It is a model that seeks to factor in reconciliation and restoration as a continuing process in the relationship rather than at a single point in time. There is no mention of the law or regulation in the model; but a progression from covenant, grace (forgiveness implied), empowering to intimacy, and therefore a deepening of the relationship. It is a model that assumes the unconditionality of the relationship.

---

[301] J Balswick and J Balswick, *The Family* (Grand Rapids: Baker Book House, 1991), 21.

They have also tabulated the sociological differences in various models of marriage relationship.[302] They traced the differences between the traditional patriarchal and the modern model of marriage relationship and compared them to the biblical model. These are helpful for us to understand the different cultural expressions in our multicultural society.

God provided a 'helper' for Adam (Gen. 2:18). It speaks here of an assistance to man.[303] The marriage ordinance brings together the created maleness and femaleness of our cohumanity to its full realisation in its interdependence and cooperative interaction.[304]

9.5.1. The Aftermath of the Fall

While we often focus on the ideal marriage relationship, the 'living together happily ever after' happens only to the prince and princess in fairy tales. In real life, all too often, it does not. We need to take into account the fall; and that is the reality of the relationship that we are in, whether it be marriage, church, societal, etc.

The conflict within the marriage relationship is prefigured in Genesis 3:16:

> To the woman he said, 'I will greatly increase your pains in childbearing; with pain you will give birth to children. Your desire will be for your husband, and he will rule over you.'

There is a misunderstanding in the way we translate and interpret the Hebrew word *teshuqah*, rendered *desire* in the above passage. The use of the word *teshuqah* in the only other two passages in the Old Testament makes the usage clearer:

> If you do what is right, will you not be accepted? But if you do not do what is right, sin is crouching at your door; it desires to have you, but you must master [*mashal*] it. (Gen. 4:7)

> I belong to my lover, and his desire is for me. (Songs 7:10)

---

[302] Ibid., 80.

[303] G. von Rad, *Genesis*, Old Testament Library (London: SCM, 1961), 82.

[304] Balswick and Balswick, *The Family*, p. 20.

The usual interpretation of Genesis 3:16 is that of male dominance *mashal* (Heb.) and that the woman will 'desire' the man, much to the pleasure of the male species. Now we need to spend just a little time on the text and examine the word used. A comparison with Genesis 4:7 will show that the word *desire* is used in the sense of possession and control. Just as sin in crouching at the door, it wants to 'possess' you or 'desire' to have you. In other words, the woman wants to control the man and the man wants to dominate the woman. Now that sets up the eternal tussle in the marriage, each wanting the other for himself or herself. It is no longer the giving relationship where one lives for the other but rather to posses the other for oneself.

What should be noted here is that Genesis 3:16 is not a model for the marriage relationship but rather the result of the fall and therefore not the norm for true humanity. Christ has come to bring about the change to normality. The Christian gospel brings about reconciliation[305] and restoration of a person, i.e. from self-seeking to a turning towards 'the other'.

So often the tendency is to seek legal help when relationship problem arises because the basis is contractual. Our culture teaches us to stand on our rights and to seek self-fulfilment. We set up the framework on which we judge ourselves, and when we look at ourselves within that framework, we are always in the right. The other party does the same, and we have a stalemate and no longer a helpmate.

Much of today's marriage counselling deals with the artefact and does not really address the core of the problem. In other words, the counselling does not start from a biblical and Trinitarian perspective. As we are created in the image of God, our relationships are derived from the relationship within the triune Godhead. It is not often that marriage is talked of in terms of 'a prophetic foretaste and forecast of the Ultimate Marriage of the Bride and the Lamb (Christ)'.[306] It is indeed a profound mystery, and I refer you to the book of the same title for a theological exposition.

---

[305] This has been discussed in chapter 7.5.

[306] G Bingham, *The Profound Mystery: Marriage Love, Divine and Human* (Blackwood, South Australia: New Creation Publication Inc., 1995), xiv.

9.5.2. On the Matter of Headship[307]

Headship is part of the structure of our community. Many have put forward the idea of an egalitarian society as man's ideal. Proponents of such ideals have been disillusioned. We are all aware of the story in *Animal Farm*. One only needs to see a group of young children gathering together to play to appreciate that headship is part of our societal structures. As soon as the children start on their game, before too long, one of them will start to lay down some rules: 'Let us play it this way' or 'Why don't we do it like this?' One of them then plays the role of the leader. This role may pass on from one to another, but there will always be someone at the helm.

Every community has an authority structure. Our churches, our families, and our institutions have authority structures. Even in a relationship between two persons, usually one takes the leading role. In our fallen humanity, this authority structure is often abused leading to authoritarianism. It is what Peter labelled as 'lording it over those entrusted to you'.

> ²Be shepherds of God's flock that is under your care, serving as overseers - not because you must, but because you are willing, as God wants you to be; not greedy for money, but eager to serve; ³**not lording it over those entrusted to you**, but being examples to the flock. (1 Peter 5:2–3)

Against this authoritarianism the Balswicks spoke in their book. The chart that they tried to put together says many things in a shortcut fashion. They speak as sociologists rather than as theologians. What they have put forward in the chart is a sociological framework for relationship. They do not deny the male headship in the marriage covenant; but they see that the patriarchal model of male headship, i.e. authoritarianism, does not accord to womanhood the dignity as created in a cohumanity. If humanity is to be understood as cohumanity, i.e. as male and female, then there is a mutuality to be acknowledged and experienced. To contrast the authoritarianism of the patriarchal model, the chart is structured this way.

Our problem here is like the debate on the Trinity in the fourth century. We base our framework on the prevailing culture of the day. In the West today, we emphasise democracy and egalitarianism. We read this

---

[307] I am indebted to Rev Dr G Bingham for his invaluable insight into the subject here.

back into the Trinity, i.e. a social Trinity based on these principles, and from which we work out our Trinitarian theology.

Many theologians, over the centuries, shipwrecked when embarking on the discussion on the Trinity. Many said what should not have been said, and others have not said what should have been said. What I mean is this: one can so emphasise the oneness of the Godhead that one obscures the distinction of the Persons, or one can so emphasise the uniqueness of the Persons of the Trinity that one can be charged with tritheism. The perichoretic relations within the Godhead can be so emphasised in a social Trinity that one loses the sense of the hierarchy within the Trinity.

When we talk about mutuality, we do not infer the absence of authority. Just as the Father is the *fons divinitatis* and there is also a mutuality within the threeness of the Godhead in perichoretic love, so also in our marital or church relationship. There is a headship, and there is a mutuality. We cannot assume an absolute headship in our fallen humanity. While I exercise the headship in my marriage and family as well as in my church, I accept the correction that comes from my wife and children, as well as from my fellow believers in the church. In that process, I submit to what they say without loss of my authority. It is possible to experience mutuality in the context of a hierarchy.

Much of our concept of headship is derived from the doctrine of monarchianism. This has to be rejected, and when emphasised strongly, the pendulum may swing to a democratisation of the Trinity. This can so easily happen. To do so would be to read into the Trinity our cultural framework. There is a divine hierarchy in which the Father is fons divinitatis in the triune Godhead. This is not to infer a superordination or subordination within the Godhead. I refer to a comment by G Bingham in the New Creation Teaching Ministry 1994 pastors' school:

> Popular today in the interests of the establishing of certain social mores is the democratisation of the Trinity. . . . It is conceivable that there is a Trinitarian hierarchy and we may miss the love-dynamics such Divine hierarchy may hold—and thus the love-dynamics the human equivalent may hold—in dismissing hierarchy because, as is the case with all ontological categories, there has been misuse and abuse of it. The ineradicable (fallen) human idea that superordination and subordination mean superiority and inferiority is countered by Christ's loving subordination to

the Father whilst being 'one' with Him, and his teaching of the greatness of the one being the servant.[308]

Our understanding of the perichoretic relationship within the Trinity prevents us from embracing a static model in our community relationship. There is a movement from one person to the other in the Trinitarian Godhead, a movement of giving and receiving in love. So too there is this movement of giving to and receiving from one another in our communal relationship. The movement in these relationships is expressed for us as the covenant.

We do not need to accentuate or make an issue of the headship that is accorded to us. If we do, then we have a real problem of authority in our societal structures. In my church, we do not talk about who is in authority in the church. The church acknowledges me in the leadership, and I do not need to make an issue of it. Rather, I go to them and acknowledge their contribution. There is mutuality in our relationship without any loss of authority. In some instances, authority became a problem, and that was when the issue was highlighted just as it was in some of Paul's letters when he opened with the words 'Paul an apostle of the Lord Jesus Christ'.

Some of us see headship in a linear, static contractual way. We need to see headship as part of our covenantal relationship. It is dynamic. Man is head of the woman, but he is also in a covenantal relationship with her, and both are part of the body of Christ and need to submit to Him as Lord. Our relationship with each other is not perfect. There is a time where we submit to each other in our covenantal relationship because we are not perfect, but that does not mean that we relegate our authority. 'Submit to one another out of reverence for Christ' (Eph. 5:21).

We all do not live with the ideal situation all the time. When there is a loss of relationship, there is always resort to power structures and legalism. What does one do when the husband is abusive or the pastor becomes authoritarian? These are difficult situations and not easy to resolve. I will not attempt any suggestions as one can only get into more complicated problems. When we relate in love, authority, and mutuality, these are part of the spectrum of our relational experience. When the focus is on authority, there is loss of mutuality; and when there is a preoccupation with mutuality, there is already a loss of authority.

[21]Submit to one another out of reverence for Christ.
[22]Wives, submit to your husbands as to the Lord. [23]For the

---

[308] G Bingham, 'The Law of the Triune Godhead', *Relationships: Divine-Human*, New Creation Teaching Ministry Pastors' School (1994), 7.

> husband is the head of the wife as Christ is the head of the church, his body, of which he is the Saviour. [24]Now as the church submits to Christ, so also wives should submit to their husbands in everything. [25]Husbands, love your wives, just as Christ loved the church and gave himself up for her [26]to make her holy, cleansing her by the washing with water through the word, [27]and to present her to himself as a radiant church, without stain or wrinkle or any other blemish, but holy and blameless. [28]In this same way, husbands ought to love their wives as their own bodies. He who loves his wife loves himself. (Eph. 5:21–28)

There are several ways of conducting a relationship. It may be on economic grounds, utilitarian, and so on. For example, many marital relationships in the past have been stable because the woman of the house adopts a submissive role in exchange for economic security. In that context, the relationship may be fulfilling for both parties because of the assumptions that each holds. However, if those assumptions are altered, then the way in which they relate has to change. It then needs to find a new form of expression. For our understanding of relationships, we need to come back to what we know as the covenant.

Even in the secular world, there is a sense of a finality and unchangeableness in the understanding of the covenant. For a corporation, the constitution can be changed with a stated majority of its shareholders or members. In order to preserve something that cannot be changed in any way by any subsequent generation of members, this has to be stated in the constitution as a 'covenant clause'. This clause then cannot be altered in any way at subsequent meetings of the corporation regardless of support given at the meeting. It will stand forever as long as the corporation exists.

9.6. The Fringes of Life (Euthanasia)

In this subsection, the fringes of life should really take in the unborn as well. In my medical practice, I do not have much involvement in that area and feel that I should leave the discussion to my more learned colleagues. As a medical practitioner, this issue is close to my heart, and I have many occasions to treat the terminally ill and would like to reflect on my understanding and experience in this area. However, the title of the dissertation will restrict my comments to the Trinitarian framework.

Euthanasia is now a hotly debated topic in Australia and indeed in most countries. The Northern Territory of Australia has put this into law and has already claimed several 'victims'. This has a ripple effect all over the country. The pro-euthanasia and the pro-life sections are lobbying hard through various legal channels to foster their vested interest. This is a matter of concern not only for those in the medical profession but also for pastors and counsellors.

Many would want to sidestep the issue and argue the case for euthanasia on the basis that this is a matter of personal judgement. I beg to differ when the right to euthanasia becomes enshrined in legislation. We have all seen the slippery slopes when this legislation was passed in Holland where, initially, the legislation for euthanasia was instituted for the terminally ill; but increasingly, the right-to-die legislation is being transformed to a duty to die so that the individual would not be a burden to society. The so-called safeguards in the legislation for euthanasia are no safeguards at all as we have seen what has become of those safeguards when the legislation for abortion was introduced many years ago. The right to die for the terminally ill is the thin edge of the wedge. It will soon extend to nonvoluntary euthanasia. Euthanasia is a simplistic solution to a very complex situation, and we will explore some of the issues involved.

Our concern here is not so much with those legal issues but to examine the grounds from which this debate has been initiated and critically to evaluate some of its arguments. Much of the agenda for the debate has been determined from a Western philosophical viewpoint.

9.6.1. Definitions

Euthanasia comes from the Greek roots, *eu* meaning *happy* or *good* and *thanatos* meaning *death*.[309] Euthanasia may simply be defined as 'a gentle and easy death'. It may also refer to the means or action by which this process of gentle and easy death is brought about. The word is now used to refer to 'the killing of those who are incurably ill and in great pain or distress in order to spare them further suffering'.[310] Euthanasia is conventionally classified into three subtypes:

1. Voluntary, i.e. at the request of the person killed.
2. Non-voluntary, i.e. when the person killed is incapable of understanding the choice between life and death.

---

[309] G Abbott-Smith, *A Manual Greek Lexicon of the New Testament*, 3rd ed. (Edinburgh: T&T Clark, 1937).

[310] P Singer, *Practical Ethics* (Cambridge: Cambridge University Press, 1979), 127.

3. Involuntary, i.e. when the person killed is capable of making that choice but was not asked.

9.6.2. The Chinese Outlook

The Chinese equivalent of euthanasia is *an le si*. *Si* means death, and *an le* is translated *peace and happiness*.[311] It connotes a sense of satisfaction with life's accomplishment. It is a preparedness to depart from the earthly scene, knowing that the life that one has lived has been lived to its fullness.

The Chinese think of death more in terms of the cessation of cardiorespiratory function rather than in terms of brain death. In the past, when there is little or no chance of recovery for the patient, doctors and family members, together with the patient, through a process of consultation would then withdraw all passive treatment. The patient would then be kept as comfortable as possible and allowed to die a good death—an le si. This is considered a natural death with great harmony for all.[312] The capacity to harmonise conflicting issues is a great asset of the Chinese mind.

This is all quite straightforward when death is understood in terms of the cessation of cardiorespiratory function. It is more difficult for the Chinese and indeed for many people in other cultures to come to terms with the concept of brain death where there is spontaneous respiration and a continuing heartbeat. This difficulty is compounded in the Chinese mind by many factors of which I will comment briefly on only two, namely, longevity and filial piety.

Longevity has always been an important goal in the Chinese family tradition. The crane is the Chinese symbol of longevity. The goddess of mercy, kuan-yin, is the bestower of such blessings as health, long life, wealth, and, most important of all, children. There is also the god of longevity, Shou Hsing. They are important deities in the Chinese tradition.

Some aspects of filial piety have been discussed above.[313] This is the interconnecting golden thread of Chinese society. The reverence for one's parents is the beginning of Chinese societal structures. This is derived from the principle of benevolence, which is demonstrated in the love of all human beings. While the principle of autonomy rides high in Western thinking, the Chinese mind thinks more in terms of benevolence rather than autonomy. When Confucius was asked about benevolence, he replied,

---

[311] *Times Chinese-English Dictionary* (Hong Kong: Federal Publications, 1980).

[312] J Zhang, *Bioethics Research Notes* (Southern Cross Bioethics Institute, South Australia, Dec 1992).

[313] See section 2.3.2.

'It is to love all human beings.'[314] Thus, the emphasis on humanism in Confucianism is supreme.

Western forms of ethical thinking have been preoccupied with the issue of right and wrong. It is based on a theoretical contractual system. Chinese ethical philosophers strive for practice. It links the practice to the thinker. It is a matter of conduct or praxis rather than mere principles.[315]

9.6.3. Pain Management

This subsection may be more medical than theology, and indeed, it is. However, this is the cornerstone of the pro-euthanasia lobby, and one has to remove the footing on which the whole of their argument stands.

Of course, a terminal illness is an unbearable situation when there is an inadequate management of pain. As medical practitioners, we recognise that there are conditions that are we not able to cure, yet it remains our duty to relieve pain and to accord to the patient a reasonable level of comfort. Though no active medical or surgical therapy is appropriate at that juncture, the cessation of medical treatment does not mean the cessation of all care. The focus simply shifts from treatment to care, and that means making the patient's remaining time as comfortable and as meaningful as possible.

The euthanasia debate focuses on the inadequacy of this care. The pro-euthanasia lobby assumes that the medical fraternity is not able to provide for the adequate relief of pain in the terminally ill and therefore the assisted death of the patient in a humane way is the solution to the problem.

This assumption by the pro-euthanasia lobby is falsely based. They have ignored the expertise that has developed by our colleagues[316] in anaesthesia for pain relief in the terminally ill. Numerous pharmaceutical agents in varying combination are very effective in the control of pain. The route of delivery may vary, and the subcutaneous continuous infusion pump is a most useful apparatus in management. Techniques have developed for various kinds of nerve blocks, which are relatively noninvasive. Minimally invasive techniques in nerve blocks by laparoscopy have been developed.

The issue at stake here is not so much a right to euthanasia but the kind of care given to those in the terminal stages of their illness. We are

---

[314] *Analects*, XII.22.

[315] C Moore, *The Chinese Mind* (Honolulu: University of Hawaii Press, 1967), 169.

[316] I write here as a surgeon working in close liaison with my anaesthetist colleagues.

not arguing against disconnecting the respirator when it is beyond doubt that there is brain death and it is shown beyond doubt that there is no possibility of recovery. We are not arguing against the discontinuation of treatment when that situation is present.

The case for euthanasia rests solely on this ground, i.e. that of unrelieved pain. In some cases this is true. It is a reflection not of the inability to care and to relieve pain but of the inadequate health care services provided, though in some areas these services may have been ignored in favour of vested interest. As the medical profession shows less care to the terminally ill in the face of increasing technological advancement, this will give more grounds for the proponents of euthanasia. As doctors, we need to be carers first and technocrats second.

9.6.4. Cultural Relativity

We live in an age of cultural relativity. This is the view that moral practices vary with and depend on human needs and social conditions of particular cultures so that no moral beliefs can be universally true. They maintain that there can be no universal 'oughts'. This attitude is representative of the view of an individualistic society where each person is allowed and encouraged to 'do what is right in their own eyes' (Judges 17:6 KJV). Such an attitude will only lead to a breakdown of morality and order and ultimately to the disintegration of society. Society, in order for it to exist without any unbearable strain, needs to have clearly defined guidelines from those in responsible positions, especially in issues affecting the margins of life.

It has been argued that we live in a pluralistic society with a diversity of cultural norms and sociomoral values. It is therefore not possible to have one ethic as it would mean domination by some groups over others. However, mankind shares a common destiny, and questions of morality affect people of all religious backgrounds and cultures. The moral questions do not affect a particular group of people alone but are dealing with universal human problems. As such, there need to be principles that are applicable, without exception, to all human beings. Ethical principles must have universal applicability and cannot be restrictive. What is right for one person must be right for all persons in similar circumstances.

Hans Kung, writing in the introduction to his book *Global Responsibility*, says,

> It has become increasingly clear to me in recent years that the one world in which we live has a chance of survival

only if there is no longer any room in it for spheres of differing, contradictory and even antagonistic ethics. This one world needs one basic ethic.[317]

Such an ethic must also be rationally defensible. Gustafson goes so far as to say that the foundation of ethics must be reason and not religion.[318] In the search for these universal principles, researchers have approached the problem from various angles. Some have looked at the essential facts of life and survival and used them to mount a proposition of certain ethical principles. Others have tried to trace the basis of social values inherent in various cultures and societies. Still, others have looked at comparative religion and cultures. These are attempts to discover some universal areas of ethical agreement that are fundamental to all mankind.

That there is a unity in ethics is an important basis from which ethical thinking should proceed. The dualism evidenced in an ethical thinking that is compartmentalised cannot realise the ideal of an ethics with universal applicability. There have developed principles of ethics that we use from time to time. These are:

1. The principle of respect for autonomy
2. The principle of nonmaleficence
3. The principle of beneficence
4. The principle of justice

Personal autonomy has been elevated to an absolute right. It has overridden all other principles. However, these principles are not absolute in themselves, though some proponents have tried to argue from that standpoint. One cannot apply the principle of autonomy to the exclusion of other principles. None of the above principles can be applied exclusively on its own without acknowledgement of other principles involved. We have seen above that the principle of beneficence is paramount in the Chinese mind. Yet above these principles is the principle of life. The principle of the sanctity of life rides above all other principles. We will discuss this a little later in this section.

---

[317] H Kung, *Global Responsibility*, trans. J. Dowden (London: SCM, 1991), xvi.

[318] J M Gustafson, 'Can Ethics be Christian? Some Conclusions', *Readings in Moral Theology*, no. 2, ed. C Curran and R McCormick (New York: Paulist Press, 1980), 146–147.

9.6.5. Relatedness

Of course, it is a hopeless situation when there is no one around the terminally ill to talk to and care for them and to relate to them at that stage of their illness. Of course, life is not worth living when one's immediate relations are not around to support and to care. The movement to legislate on euthanasia is a reflection of the disintegration of the family and societal network.

The true humanist approach to the situation is not in euthanasia but in the restoration of relationship in our fractured society. It is not even in the provision of better health support services, though this will certainly help to ease the pain of the terminally ill.

There are many problems that need to be managed in the care of the terminally ill. As is so often in our society, we seek resolution of our problems in a legalistic manner. We fail to identify the relational problems in our society and to deal with them. We allow issues peripheral to the person to determine the outcome rather than to rectify the many personal and relational issues involved.

We are in a disposable society, and we project onto the human person the same values as we apply to material things. We look at the economic worth of the person as we do to material things. We look at the utility of the person as we do to material things and make an evaluation on those grounds. Of course, the answer when we apply those formulae in the terminally ill is euthanasia. It is the logical conclusion. But there is a higher principle involved—that of the givenness of life and its sanctity. There is a relatedness of the human person in life, and that cannot be assessed in terms of economy and utility.

9.6.6. The Givenness of Life

We cannot ignore the move towards legislation that so blatantly disregards the sanctity of human lives. The human person did not ask for the right to be born. Each of us is given life. That is the gift of life. I did not choose life. I did not choose to be a Chinese. I am a Chinese. I did not choose my parents. Some would wish they could. They are my parents whatever shape or size they may be. Each of us is given life as a human being to share in a common humanity. While we enshrine the principle of freedom of choice, in the very event of being born, we had no choice at all. Recently, a certain premier in this country publicly inferred that we have the right to choose life and so therefore the right to choose death. He needs to rethink his premises for that statement. We did not choose life.

We did not have a say in the baggage of chromosomes and genes that we carry around with us. We have to accept all that we are given at that very point in the commencement of life. We then live out that life and begin to make some choices in the way in which we choose to live it. When we are given life, it allows us that freedom of choice. To choose to terminate life is to choose to terminate that which accords to us the freedom to choose. It is therefore contradictory to say that we have the freedom to choose death. It is equally meaningless for one to say that he or she chooses to be born. Life chooses us. We did not choose life. Death will choose us in its time, but we will not choose death. Life and the relatedness in living are far too precious for us not to be in it.

When a person would rather die than to live with a disablement, then the gift of life is seen as getting into the way of the pleasures of life. It speaks of the breakdown of the relationship that that life was created for. We live in a world of absolutes. It is deeply embedded in the core assumptions of our minds. We cannot accept anything that is less than perfect. So when the in utero ultrasound or blood screen shows up a defect in the foetus, we demand an abortion. A learned man of God, John Cardinal O'Connor, offered this guidance, 'Speak from the heart of the experiencing of human vulnerability and wear your disabilities like a mantle about your shoulders.'[319]

9.6.7. The Sanctity of Life

The value society places on human lives today is seen in the continuation of a tradition for medical graduands in which they have to acknowledge the Hippocratic oath, a section of which says, 'I will give no deadly drug to any, though it be asked of me, nor will I counsel such, and especially I will not aid a woman to procure abortion.'[320]

In the declaration of human rights, a charter of the United Nations (1948), is the reaffirmation of 'faith in fundamental human rights, in the dignity and worth of the human person, in the equal rights of men and women and of nations large and small'.[321] This declaration is affirmed by

---

[319] M J Owen, 'The Wisdom of Human Vulnerability (Disability: The Tie that Binds)', *Dolentium Hominum* VIII, no. 22 (1993): 171.

[320] J W Todd, 'Medicine and Surgery, Practice of', *The New Encyclopedia Britannica*, vol. 11, 15th ed. (Chicago: Encyclopaedia Britannica, Inc., 1984), 849.

[321] E Schwelb, 'Human Rights', *The New Encyclopedia Britannica*, vol. 8, 15th ed. (Chicago: Encyclopaedia Britannica, Inc., 1984), 1185.

all members of the United Nations, which comprise about 97 per cent of the world's population.[322]

In a statement from the World Medical Association, the acknowledgement of the value of human lives is made clear in a clause that obligates the physician to 'maintain the utmost respect for human life from its beginning.'[323]

In Buddhism is enshrined the principle of the sanctity of life. Christianity taught that life is sanctified. It can be seen that this principle is enshrined in all cultures and all religions. It is also a principle that all the professional medical bodies have etched into their code of practice. It has indeed universal acceptance.

9.6.8. Conclusion

It is quite meaningless to talk of euthanasia as a dignified death when one actively takes a life. It is life that needs to be dignified. A life that is dignified is lived in its relatedness and not in isolation. The dignity that should be accorded to the terminally ill is the provision to that person of the best degree of care and comfort that the medical profession is capable of with the technology that is made available today. We as carers must be in the forefront of caring and pain relief. Our inadequacy in this area only leaves the door wide open for the proponents of euthanasia. We need to think logically about the givenness of life and the sanctity of life itself.

The medical body of this country and its member associations must take a lead in these difficult ethical issues. Sections of the community will have different views because of their vested interests. It is easy to take one factor and build a whole system of thinking around it. However, not everyone is able to take all the issues involved and hold a balanced view. We need to educate the public, but first of all, the medical profession must put this on its agenda and ensure we are able to consider all the issues involved. We do this by maintaining a dialogue within our profession and association. I believe the medical profession is able to hold such a balanced view. Complex issues such as abortion and euthanasia cannot be just personal issues based on one's subjective judgement.

---

[322] J Fleming, *Principle of the Sanctity of Human Life*, Dietrich Bonhoeffer Institute Study Booklet, no. 14, (Adelaide, July 1990), 11.

[323] The declaration of Geneva is appended to the International Code of Medical Ethics, World Medical Association, Nov 1983, doc. 17A.

9.7. Ethics

In ethics today, the language of right dominates. In particular, it is the right to freedom that seems to rise above all other rights. So it is the right to express our freedom in sexual preference. It is the right to die.

The Sermon on the Mount is very commonly quoted in any discussion on ethical issues. Indeed, it is a challenge to us to reconsider many of the ideals we hold. This section of Matthew's gospel is held by many to contain the ethical standard of the Christian faith. Indeed, it does. It challenges us to reconsider the standards that the law demands of us. Are they just and adequate? Jesus acknowledged those standards but insisted that they did not go far enough. He has come to inaugurate the new covenant, which is sealed in His blood. This new covenant will be in the hearts of the people as Jeremiah told us.

Jesus wants to move beyond the external legalities of the law to the inner sanctum of our being where the Spirit of God dwells. There the Holy Spirit inspires and motivates us, bringing our whole being into line with His will.

When we are devoid of the inner reserve, which the Holy Spirit of God brings, then we will seek justification in terms of the demands of the law. We see that happening everywhere in society and even in the church. When the Spirit is the driving force, the obstruction from the legal code will be challenged and a new code brought in to facilitate the new awakening. That will be the dawn of another new day.

So often the Sermon on the Mount is taken as a rigid moralistic code to judge and to condemn. Rather, it is a call to us to enter into the reality of life with the Spirit. It is not a code that tells us what to do but rather a call to remind us of what we should be and who we are. It shows us where and why we should be different from the conventions of society. It tells us to go where our heart leads us because the Holy Spirit is there to do the leading.

We need to come out of our legal enclave and accord the human dignity to our fellow beings as participants in the one eternal covenant of God. We have lost the sense that we are only created beings and do not have any right to an existence except that it be given from above. We share that givenness with all others that God has brought into being.

In our relationships today, we often come into it with a contractual framework rather than the biblical covenantal framework. The contractual framework celebrates the idea of mutuality and is based on a given set of laws or regulations. So the church's relationship with the pastor, sadly, has become a contractual rather than covenantal one. Our marital relationship has also become contractual. This is a tragedy for our churches and families today.

It is in terms of one's distinctiveness as well as interpenetration that we formulate a model of relationship. Here I want to shift over to the sociological equivalents of cohesion and disengagement. These terms are used in sociological models. In a relationship, there is cohesion and disengagement. Where the two individuals or units are so cohered that they cannot be disengaged, that is referred to enmeshment. It is not a healthy relationship. It is the loss of one's distinctiveness or identity. On the other hand, to be so disengaged that there is no cohesion whatsoever is also an unhealthy state. It is the loss of interpenetration of persons.

This model of interlocking circles can be applied in marriage and family. It can also be applied in intrachurch and interchurch relationship. All cultures have their assumptions in the relationship formed in these basic units of society.

Part Three, Chapter 10

CONCLUDING REMARKS

I have covered quite some ground in this paper, from the Chinese culture to church history and the present-day economic system, from marriage and family to ethics and euthanasia. Though the coverage is only brief, I have attempted to demonstrate perhaps barely adequately that the basic problem in our churches today is that we have subordinated the gospel to our culture. We need to return to the Trinitarian Godhead to see that the concept of the covenant needs to pervade our culture. It will cause us to appraise our present strategy quite differently. It will cause us to come away from our deeply dualistic approach and start thinking from the One Eternal Covenant and see the way it ought to influence the way we live, the things we do, and the way we relate.

All that has been said in this paper is best summarised by an event that I experienced in a dream some years ago.

It was some time during the year 1987. It was a stressful time in my life. I had many concerns regarding the church. Many things had happened, and they did not fit the gospel that I had been taught, but I could not say precisely what. One night, I had a dream.

I was worshipping with my family in the church one Sunday. It was the usual worship service that one would expect on a Sunday morning. There was a fairly lively praise and worship in song led by a member of the church, which was the usual practice in the church that I went to. The worship seemed to be progressing well with the congregation responding to the songs and prayers. Then suddenly a strange thing happened. There arose from within the congregation a large number of people bearing firearms. They got up from all over the pews and threatened the congregation with their firearms. They held the church captive. What their demands were, I did not know. It was not clear in my dream. All I remembered was that these people held the congregation captive. My only concern then was to get out of the church hall to get help. I knew that I could not, as an individual or in concert with anyone else in the congregation, overcome them. A few tried to resist but were suppressed very quickly by their captors. To get out and call for help was the only course of action I could think of then.

I did not know how it happened, but in my dream, I found myself outside the church hall free from the captives. I could have sneaked out without their notice, or I could have been taken out in a way that I did not know how. All I remembered from my dream was that I found myself outside the hall and freed from the captivity of the gunmen. But my family was still inside the church hall, and so were many of my friends who were close to me. I needed to do something to get them out. I felt for them as I did not want to see them harmed in any way by the captors. Yet I was helpless. I was powerless against those people with their firearms. There was an agony within me that I could not describe.

I just felt so helpless. I tried to raise the alarm in some way, but again I could not remember what I actually did then. I might not have even done anything at all to raise the alarm. I just wanted to. What was amazing in my dream was that even before I could raise the alarm, help was at hand. There was an army of people right there as soon as I found myself outside the church building. They could have been military personnel, I could not be sure. Whatever they may be, they inspired the confidence in me that they could help in the situation, and they looked confident in going about their task. They were all ready to mount an assault from outside. I felt relieved. Somehow I had the confidence in these men and knew that they would deliver the church from the captivity. They would free my family and friends who were held captives within that building. What eventuated after that I did not know as the terror of the ordeal woke me up.

That has been my concern for the church for many years. The preparation of this dissertation reminded me of this dream. I had not understood what the dream meant then, but I do in some measure now. It was the church in cultural captivity. My freedom from it was in a way that I do not know how. I was delivered by the grace of God. I realised that I needed to disengage from the church in order to be of some assistance in her release. The release of the church from its cultural captivity again was in ways that I would not understand. All that I can do is simply to raise the alarm. In translating this into terms used in ministry, this is to proclaim the *kerugma*, the good news of Christ's coming. I have to disengage from the church in order to re-engage the church in some ways. The disengagement is to free myself from the cultural captivity. The re-engagement is to assist the church in achieving freedom from her cultural captivity. However, the re-engagement is not solely the effort on my part. The re-engagement is with the assistance of those who were there even before I could raise the alarm, and the release happened in ways beyond my knowing.

I had talked about this with Rev Dr Geoffrey Bingham, executive director of the New Creation Teaching Ministry in Adelaide. I shared my concern with him regarding the church and asked what I can do to aid the release of the church from her cultural captivity. He said this to me, and I quote:

> By the preaching of the cross. We will never free people from culture by pointing out the bondages they represent: we will do it only by a pure preaching of the gospel. It is Christ who transforms men and women, and he cannot do it by a theology of the cross, a detached, objective set of ideas, though they may be correct doctrine.'[324]

I have to learn this in order to understand the meaning of my dream.

---

[324] Personal communication.

Appendix

BY THE PREACHING OF THE WORD

I feel that this appendix to the book is necessary as the concluding remark at the end of the last chapter left the issue suspended. The reply from the late Rev Dr Geoffrey Bingham, 'By the preaching of the word', needs some explaining as it can be understood in a variety of ways. Since presenting this thesis to the Fuller Theological Seminary in 2000, I have reflected on those words, and it is necessary to elaborate on what is meant when we say that this change can only come about 'by the preaching of the word'. This may mean different things to different people depending on the way we understand the word and preaching. Furthermore, as I have been arguing in the preceding chapters, this understanding is also dependent on whether we come to it from a Trinitarian framework or not.

The popular understanding of this phrase comes from our secular education. Put simply, the process of understanding or digesting a text or a paper is like this. We read it and analyse it, often reducing it to a few basic tenets. From there, we reorganise the data to fit somewhere around the framework we have in our minds. For most people, when they come to the church and listen to the sermon preached, that is what goes on in their minds. That is why many preachers have a take home two or three pointers or principles so that the parishioners have something to work on to reorganise their thinking and their lives. Sometimes this is a good thing for people to have some kind of a handle to hold on to as they grapple with the difficulties in their lives. However, that is not the sole function of preaching.

I am reminded of a story told to me by a pastor friend of mine many years ago. After preaching a sermon on a Sunday morning, one of the parishioners, a young man, came up to the pastor and said, 'Reverend, that was a good sermon this morning. I have heard many good sermons over the years that I have been in this church, but I don't remember most of them.' The pastor took a good look at him and smiled before responding. He said, 'That is so true, and my experience is similar. You know, over the years, your mother must have cooked many good meals for you, and I don't think you remember many of those meals, but they have done you a lot of good. I have seen you grown over the years.'

Coming to the Word of God or listening to the sermon takes on a different dimension from our secular learning. The Word of God does its work within us when we have taken it in. What it does within us is not controlled by our conscious mind just as the body autonomously continues with the digestion of the ingested food while we are oblivious to the process that is going on within. This is so because though the Bible is a text, it is not simply a text for our analysis. It is the Word of God, and it demands our submission to it. This is where our discussion must start. We will also later on consider the way we hear the preached word.

The Word of God

We have come to refer to the Bible as the Word of God. It is the written Word of God, but it is also the living word. We will explore the relationship between the written and the living word. We have come to revere the revelation given to us in the Bible. We acknowledge that the Bible is the authoritative and inspired word and we are to submit to it. We also acknowledge that the Bible has come to us by the Holy Spirit (2 Tim. 3:16), and our understanding of the Bible is by the illumination of the Spirit. We are taught by God (Jn. 6:45). What do all these statement mean?

We have regarded the Bible as a text or a book that we can learn from, and though that is still true, there is something more beyond that. We call it the scriptures, and we often understand that in terms of the scriptures of other religions—i.e. a book of illumination—and if we know enough of it, we will become enlightened. Some have even regarded the Bible so highly that they have gone so far as to worship the book, a practice that we refer to as bibliolatry.

On the other hand, there are also people who have little understanding of the text and gone their way to impose their own ideas on the text with disastrous result. Yet the Word of God is not merely a text, though it demands scholarship in deciphering the ancient writings just as we would with any ancient Chinese or Egyptian texts. Without this scholarship, we would merely be projecting our twenty-first-century ideas onto these ancient writings. It demands that we should apply the historico-grammatical approach to these ancient texts in order that we may not distort the meaning. We must not be reading our own assumptions into the texts.

However, when we have done all that, it is not yet the end of the process. There is still a fundamental problem with that acknowledgement. And it is this: we have come to it with our secular training. In our educational system, we have been given assignment, and we then go to the resources at our disposal, whether it be the internet or a set of books or encyclopaedias. We go to the library or sit at the computer to research the topic. So when one comes to the religion, we are told that the knowledge of God is given to us in the Bible. We then transfer the training we have in research to the Word of God. We analyse the Bible and resort to various criticisms developed by scholars with their respective expertise to uncover within the Word of God what we consider to be the truth.

Now this may be an acceptable approach with our research into various disciplines in life. In this approach, we have subordinated the information to our intellect and the framework we have constructed in our mind. From the information we have obtained in this way, we then critique that pool of knowledge and form our opinion as to its validity. Now one cannot subject the Word of God to our intellect in this way. By this, I do not refer to the critical analysis of the written word. There is a literary skill involved in the writing, and in our reading we need to be conversant with the way the ancient literature has come to us. There is nothing wrong with looking at the text in that way. In fact, text criticism has brought to us through its analysis of the various ancient documents a very reliable text of scripture.

My objection is the way we have subjected the understanding of the Word of God to our analysis and our culture. The written text is the written word. Somehow in our reading of the written word, there is the transformation of that into the living word. We will explore the way this comes about.

The Bible was neither written for historical records nor merely for our enlightenment. Jesus did many more things that were written in the New Testament, 'but these are written so that you may come to believe that Jesus is the Messiah, the Son of God' (Jn. 20:30–31). We all know that, and believing is a big thing in Christianity so much so that it has become the end of all that we seek to achieve. That is to stop short of the purpose for which the Bible is written. John made this plain in his gospel, 'Now Jesus did many other signs in the presence of his disciples, which are not written in this book. But these are written so that you may come to believe that Jesus is the Messiah, the Son of God, and that *through believing you may have life in his name*' (John 20:30–31, italics mine).

The framework of sections of Christianity is by and large a matter of knowing and believing. That is not a God-given living process. It is controlled by us. It is static, and in that process, one can only fall back onto the self to make it work. The self becomes the centre of the process. Christ and the Spirit are left on the periphery. That is why some Christian 'communities' are so fragmented as they are only associations of individuals and not yet a community bonded in the body of Christ. It has yet to experience the true life that is in Christ.

The Word of God Is Alive in the Old Testament

The Word of God is not a static word. It is alive, and this theme is well displayed in the Old Testament. The Old Testament writers often referred to the word as a person. It does not see the scriptures simply as writings that give us some illumination, though the psalmists referred to that process at work in us. The word is personified. The writers relate to the word as if it has a life of its own. In the Old Testament, some of the authors personified the word. Consider the following:

> ⁴For the word of the LORD is upright,
> and all his work is done in faithfulness.
> ⁵He loves righteousness and justice;
> the earth is full of the steadfast love of the LORD. (Ps. 33:4–5)

> ⁴In God, whose word I praise,
> in God I trust; I am not afraid;
> what can flesh do to me? (Ps. 56:4)

> ¹⁰In God, whose word I praise,
> in the LORD, whose word I praise (Ps. 56:10)

These verses speak of the word in a two-way relationship. The word is spoken of as part of the being of God. At times, the word and God are used almost synonymously as in the testing of Joseph.

> ¹⁸His [Joseph's] feet were hurt with fetters,

his neck was put in a collar of iron;
¹⁹until what he had said came to pass,
The word of the LORD kept testing him. (Ps. 105:18–19)

Again here, the Word of God has a life of its own and tested Joseph. The Hebrew word here for *testing* is *tsaraph*, a word meaning to refine as by a goldsmith.

This synonymous usage of the word, and God was seen time and again in the psalms. We know that it is God who revives and strengthens us, but here the psalmist attributed it to the word.

²⁵My soul clings to the dust;
revive me according to your word.
²⁶When I told of my ways, you answered me;
teach me your statutes.
²⁷Make me understand the way of your precepts,
and I will meditate on your wondrous works.
²⁸My soul melts away for sorrow;
strengthen me according to your word. (Ps. 119:25–28)

The prophet Isaiah also wrote in the same vein when the weary is sustained by the word:

⁴The Lord GOD has given me
the tongue of a teacher,
that I may know how to sustain
the weary with a word. (Is. 50:4)

The Word of God sustains the weary. The word translated sustain is of uncertain origin. It is *uwth*, which means 'to help' or 'to succour'.

The doctrine of creation is best treated in the psalms, and here the psalmist put it most clearly in referring to the creative word:

6By the word of the Lord the heavens were made,
and all their host by the breath of his mouth. (Ps. 33:4–6, NRSV)

This last reading is certainly the most revealing of all the passages in the Old Testament. The Word of God creates. It gives life where there has been no life. The doctrine of creation is best expounded in the Psalms. The Word of God is not an impersonal physical force that gave rise to the universe. The Word of God that comes from His breath gives life to the universe. The Word of God is life. This theme was taken up by John in the opening of the gospel he wrote.

The Word of God Is Alive in the New Testament

The theme of the living word is sustained in the New Testament. Jesus put it plainly in the parable of the sower (Lk. 8:11). The Word of God has life. It is likened by Jesus as the seed in the parable of the sower. It may look dormant, but it has life in it. It is capable of growing into a large tree and then gives life to others.

In his gospel, John makes it absolutely clear in the first few verses. He is the creative Word. 'What has come into being in him was life.' The Word of God gives life, and 'the life was the light of all people'. The light is the result of the life and not the reverse. It is not that the light gives life, but the life gives light. It is not an enlightenment that gives us life. In our keenness to achieve enlightenment, we have reversed the process. That is our fallen nature. It is the union with the word, which is life, and it is this that gives the enlightenment.

> [1]In the beginning was the Word, and the Word was with God, and the Word was God. [2]He was in the beginning with God. [3]All things came into being through him, and without him not one thing came into being. What has come into being [4]in him was life, and the life was the light of all people. (Jn. 1:1–4)

This theme is sustained in the letters of John. Jesus is the word of life. John gives testimony to the humanity of Jesus, a life which he had encountered in a physical way. It was not just a physical encounter. There was more. In that encounter, something transpired. It was the 'word of life'. In a similar way too, we have communion with that life.

> We declare to you what was from the beginning, what we have heard, what we have seen with our eyes, what we have looked at and touched with our hands, concerning the word of life. (1 Jn. 1:1)

This theme comes to a crescendo in John 1:14 when he expressed the theme in the words 'the Word became flesh'. What follows is the communion with the created order when 'the word lived among us'. It is oneness with created humanity, though we cannot read this into the verse here.

This theme of life is carried on in the gospel of John. The hearing and the believing is not the end of the process. If that is so, then it would be merely intellectual. There is more to the hearing and believing. It is the giving of new life. The believing as a result of the hearing frees one from judgement to enter into the new life. This is the work of the word of Jesus.

> [24]Very truly, I tell you, anyone who hears my word and believes him who sent me has eternal life, and does not come under judgement, but has passed from death to life. (Jn. 5:24)

The New Testament continues to refer to the Word of God as living and active in the lives of the believers. It lives in us. It cleans us. It does not fail. It grows in us. The following is a list of some of the references to this theme:

> and you do not have his word abiding in you, because you do not believe him whom he has sent. (Jn. 5:38)

> You have already been cleansed by the word that I have spoken to you. (Jn. 15:3)

> So the word of the Lord grew mightily and prevailed. (Acts 19:20)

> It is not as though the word of God had failed. (Rom. 9:6)

> Let the word of Christ dwell in you richly; teach and admonish one another in all wisdom; and with gratitude in your hearts sing psalms, hymns, and spiritual songs to God. (Col. 3:16)

> We also constantly give thanks to God for this, that when you received the word of God that you heard from us, you accepted it not as a human word but as what it really

is, God's word, which is also at work in you believers. (1 Thess. 2:13)

But the word of the Lord endures forever." That word is the good news that was announced to you. (1 Pet. 1:25)

The Word of God is life. It fulfills the purpose of God. It is at work in us. It demands our humility and obedience to the word.

A Theology of Word and Spirit

The way the written word becomes the living word in us is not the result of our intellectual activity or our discernment. It is by the work of Jesus Christ on the cross and the subsequent resurrection, ascension, and the giving of the Holy Spirit. So often we regard the Holy Spirit as an adjunct for the work of ministry when it is the Spirit that ministers to us. He takes the things of Christ and makes that a reality in our lives. Jesus puts this repeatedly to the disciples in His farewell discourses:

> [26]But when the Counselor comes, whom I shall send to you from the Father, even the Spirit of truth, who proceeds from the Father, he will bear witness to me. (Jn. 15:26)

> [13]When the Spirit of truth comes, he will guide you into all the truth; for he will not speak on his own authority, but whatever he hears he will speak, and he will declare to you the things that are to come. [14]He will glorify me, for he will take what is mine and declare it to you. (Jn. 16:13–14)

The word without the Spirit is not the living word. It will remain as the written word, a text. It is the Spirit that gives life. The Spirit without the word cannot be the Spirit of God. The Word of God must come from the breath of God. There is no breath of God without the Word of God. We cannot conceive of that. The breath without the word does not give any direction. The imagery of the breath and the word is consistent in the Old Testament. It is a powerful imagery for our understanding of the Word and Spirit.

So what do all these mean for us?

1. We must not treat the Word of God as if it needed a boost from us. The Word of God is the primary agent in the conviction and transformation of humankind. We are the adjuncts for the Word of God. It is not so much as our efforts that are the primary work. The work of the Word of God is the primary effort. We are the supportive staff.
2. We must not think that we need some form of gimmick for the Word of God to be effective. It is effective on its own. An audiovisual presentation in preaching can sometimes be somewhat gimmicky. However, as long as it is used as an adjunct to the preaching of Christ, it is probably acceptable. But we must not go beyond that.
3. It is not that Christ needs our preaching but that our preaching needs Christ.
4. That is why Paul could say that he did come to the Corinthians with excellence of speech because it is not the presentation that counts, but the word spoken in the power of the Holy Spirit.

> [4]My speech and my proclamation were not with plausible words of wisdom, but with a demonstration of the Spirit and of power, [5]so that your faith might rest not on human wisdom but on the power of God. (1 Cor. 1:4)

So as Paul says, 'Let the word of Christ dwell in you richly; teach and admonish one another in all wisdom; and with gratitude in your hearts sing psalms, hymns, and spiritual songs to God' (Col. 3:16).

Further references to the living word in the Old Testament.

> [3]He humbled you by letting you hunger, then by feeding you with manna, with which neither you nor your ancestors were acquainted, in order to make you understand that one does not live by bread alone, but by every word that comes from the mouth of the LORD. (Deut. 8:3)

> [34]I will not violate my covenant,
> or alter the word that went forth from my lips. (Ps. 89:34)

> [9]How can young people keep their way pure?
> By guarding it according to your word.

[10]With my whole heart I seek you;
do not let me stray from your commandments.
[11]I treasure your word in my heart,
so that I may not sin against you. (Ps. 119:9–11)

[25]My soul clings to the dust;
revive me according to your word.
[26]When I told of my ways, you answered me;
teach me your statutes.
[27]Make me understand the way of your precepts,
and I will meditate on your wondrous works.
[28]My soul melts away for sorrow;
strengthen me according to your word. (Ps. 119:25–28)

[13]Those who despise the word bring destruction on themselves,
but those who respect the commandment will be rewarded. (Prov. 13:13)

[11]so shall my word be that goes out from my mouth;
it shall not return to me empty,
but it shall accomplish that which I purpose,
and succeed in the thing for which I sent it. (Is. 55:11)

[2]All these things my hand has made,
and so all these things are mine,
says the Lord.
But this is the one to whom I will look,
to the humble and contrite in spirit,
who trembles at my word. (Isa. 66:2)

Hearing the Word

When we speak, it does not mean that others will hear. We have this technique of selective hearing loss. We will only hear what we want to hear, and we do not need to teach our children that. It comes naturally.

There is a grid in our brain that acts as a filter to what we accept or reject. In our upbringing, we have developed a grid or framework that filters out what we cannot accept or do not want to accept. So if we have a framework that will allow the things we hear to latch on, then we accept that. If there is no such framework, then the brain rejects that.

As an example, it is like what Christopher Columbus faced in his days. There was the assumption that the world was flat. So when Christopher Columbus proposed to reach the East Indies by going west, he was ridiculed. The people could not accept his assumption as they just cannot hold to the proposition that the world could be round. So it is with us when we face issues like the triune God, worship, and service. We use our secular concepts or framework to work those out rather than developing new framework to understand those things.

There is also a problem when we try to teach these things. It is an axiom in teaching that we work from the known to the unknown. It is a good principle that we all use. However, the assumption in that principle is that the unknown can be reached by what we know. We just need to go a bit further to reach it. Now what happens when the unknown cannot be grasped by what is known? Can the people in the days of Christopher Columbus work from known principles to the fact that the world is round? It took something different. In other words, there is nothing in what is known to help to explain what is unknown. We need a new principle, a new pair of lenses. We need that quantum leap. This is because there is nothing in the universe that will explain the Creator. The Creator cannot be explained by what He has created. If that can be done, then it would mean grounding God on the things that He has created. That is not the case. That is why the principle of moving from the known to the unknown cannot work in our approach to the creator God. At best, they can only give us some kind of a handle on things.

It was reported that when Henry Ford started to market his car, he said that he did go to the people to find out what they wanted. He said that if he had done so, they would have told him that they wanted a faster horse. He had something much faster and better than that.

We need the creation of a new framework to take us there. This requires the work of the Spirit of God within us. It is a revelation and not a deduction. Like all Chinese, we have built within us the Great Wall that will keep out everything that we don't like or can't comprehend. God has to break down this wall within us.

<u>Psalm 40</u>

⁶Sacrifice and offering thou dost not desire; but thou hast given me an open ear.1	Burnt offering and sin offering thou hast not required. ⁷Then I said, 'Lo, I come; in the roll of the book it is written of me; ⁸I delight to do thy will, O my God; thy law is within my heart.' (Ps. 40:6–8)

I gather that this text from Psalm 40 is not easy to translate. It looks straightforward, but we need to do some work in order to understand what it is saying to us. The psalm denounces the sacrifice and offering that the people were bringing to God. We often assume that God will accept what we offer to Him. Not so. There is something beyond the offering, and that is the state of our hearts. We cannot simply go our own way and then think that we can appease God with some kind of offering to Him. That wouldn't work.

In contrast to the rejection of the offering, the psalmist says, 'Thou has given me an open ear' or 'My ears you have pierced'. Why is this contrasted with the offering? The literal translation of this runs like this: 'You have dug two ears for me.' What does this mean? It has obviously something to do with hearing. That is what ears are for.

However, we need to work a little harder in order to draw out the meaning of this passage. One tool that we can use is by means of tabulation (see above). We can use this very often in the psalms because in poetry, the poet often used parallelism, i.e. saying the same thing twice or saying the same thing again in a different way. This is effective communication. So we have the rejection of offering mentioned twice, and in contrast to that is the digging out two ears for us. The parallel saying points to the obedience that is required. In other words, the offering is contrasted against obedience. It is obedience firstly, then the offering. There is no point in making the offering without the obedience to God in our lives. The writer to the Hebrews took this verse to apply to Jesus, the one who obeyed the Father perfectly.

The Word of God

It is not just a text for us to analyse or to study. People often do that and ridicule the Bible without even knowing the premise on which the Bible comes to us. Yes, we need to study the word and use all the literary skills to understand the text, but that is only the beginning. After that, the Word of God does something is us.

We need to realise first of all that the Word of God is the creative word (Ps. 33:6). When God created the world, the creation responds to the command of God. He commanded, and it came into being. Creation is not independent of the Creator, though often we think that it can. Creation is dependent on the Creator and responds to the Creator.

Straight after the completion of creation, Genesis records for us that the command of God or the Word of God came to created humanity.

> [16]And the Lord God commanded the man, saying, 'You may freely eat of every tree of the garden; [17]but of the tree of the knowledge of good and evil you shall not eat, for in the day that you eat of it you shall die.' (Gen. 2:16–17)

The response to the Word of God from humanity is obedience, but Adam and Eve subjected the Word of God to their own evaluation and analysis. The end result of that is disobedience because humanity has put its own understanding above the Word of God. God relates to His creation by His spoken word, and the creatures are to respond to His word in obedience.

The Model of Jesus

Jesus is both God and man. We cannot know what humanity ought to be by observing humanity. This is because humanity is fallen. The nature of the human race is disobedience to God, and thus, its natural history cannot be taken to be normality. Jesus came as the perfect man, and His life and practice are the norms of what humanity ought to be. This is what Jesus said of how He went about doing the things He did. He said, 'I can do nothing on my own authority; as I hear, I judge; and my judgement is just, because I seek not my own will but the will of him who sent me' (Jn. 5:30).

The hearing precedes the doing. The learning comes before the practice. I cannot preach until I have heard. I cannot do before I get my instructions.

Obedience

It is interesting to look at the Greek word for *obedience*. It is a compound word: *hypo-akouō*. The two words: *hypo* meaning *under* or *submit*, and *akouō* meaning 'to hear'. So to obey is to put oneself under or to submit to what one hears. We cannot separate the hearing and the doing.

We must insist on the priority of hearing. Unless we hear, we cannot obey. Unless we hear, our doing would only be the expression of our self-will. That is why Jesus said, 'I can do nothing on my own authority; as I hear, I judge.'

The Word of God is the creative word. When we hear, the word goes to create the framework that we need to respond to Him. The Word of God works in our lives, transforming and refashioning us to be His people. That is why Paul wrote, 'Consequently, faith comes from hearing the message, and the message is heard through the word of Christ (Rom. 10:17 NIV).

In what Jesus said to the churches in Revelation, He warns them repeatedly on the way they hear. 'He who has an ear, let him hear what the Spirit says to the churches' (Rev. 2:7 RSV). See also Rev. 2:11, 17, 29; 3:6, 13, 22; 13:9.

We may think that we have ears and we will hear in a natural way. That is not so. The one who has an ear is the one whom God has dug out two ears to enable the person to hear. It is a God-given understanding and not merely intellectual. That is why we need to take heed how we hear. We need our brains but not that only. We need also the enabling of the Spirit's revelation. Jesus warned us on the way we hear, 'Take heed then how you hear; for to him who has will more be given, and from him who has not, even what he thinks that he has will be taken away' (Lk. 8:18).

What to Do with the Nonhearers?

We like to have a method to deal with the nonhearers, but the truth is that there is not a great deal one can do if people do not want to hear. As they say, you can bring a horse to the water, but you cannot make the horse to drink.

What we want to do is to look at the reasons for the non-hearing. The theme is quite confronting as it assumes that there are those who will not hear the Word of God. Some of us may quite readily acknowledge that.

There will always be those who will not hear the Word of God, but not me. Let me correct that right away as we are all nonhearers for a start. God's word cannot be heard unless He digs two ears for us.

So does that mean that God sometimes prevents us from hearing? We will have to say yes to that question. But why should that be so?

There are three ways of hearing. One is the hearing that goes to the brain. That is intellectual. The other is the one that goes straight through. That is when we do not want to hear. The third is the one that goes to the heart. That comes by the Word of God. He digs two ears for us. It turns the hearing into action. What are the reasons for the nonhearing?

The First Reason: Opposition to the Word from the Beginning

It was the Word of God that brought humanity into being, and as a result, humanity is to respond to the creative word. It is this creative word that was opposed right at the beginning. God spoke to the human pair in the garden (Gen. 2:16–17). However, the Word that God gave was doubted and challenged. It was put to the primal pair whether God did really say, 'You shall not eat of any tree of the garden' (Gen. 3:1).

The seed of rebellion was planted with the words 'Did God say?' and followed by the command that was given. This formula casts doubt on the Creator and shifted the fulcrum onto the self and the individual assessment of what God really intended. In so doing, humanity wants to reverse the creational order of humanity's dependence on the Creator to that of independence from, and assessment of, the Creator. In so doing, humanity wants to turn from being a responder to the creative word to an initiator.

A Short History of Opposition

This passage from Luke's gospel summarises the plight of the prophets since God raised them to speak forth His word.

> [47]Woe to you! for you build the tombs of the prophets whom your fathers killed. [48]So you are witnesses and consent to the deeds of your fathers; for they killed them, and you build their tombs. [49]Therefore also the Wisdom of God said, 'I will send them prophets and apostles, some of whom they will kill and persecute,' [50] that the blood of all

the prophets, shed from the foundation of the world, may be required of this generation, [51] from the blood of Abel to the blood of Zechariah, who perished between the altar and the sanctuary. Yes, I tell you, it shall be required of this generation. (Lk. 11:47–51)

'From the blood of Abel to the blood of Zechariah'—that is the awful history of the fallenness of Israel. While this is said of Israel, yet it is also the sad commentary on humanity. The opposition to the prophetic word is part of the fallenness of humanity. It is inherent within us because of our sin.

The Second Reason

The call of Isaiah in the sixth chapter of his book is often used to challenge people to respond to the call of God with those words, 'Here am I. Send me.' Yet this commissioning was accompanied with the revelation that Isaiah would be sent to a hardened people who did not want to hear the word.

> [8]And I heard the voice of the Lord saying, 'Whom shall I send, and who will go for us?' Then I said, 'Here am I! Send me.' [9]And he said, 'Go, and say to this people: "Hear and hear, but do not understand; see and see, but do not perceive."' [10]Make the heart of this people fat, and their ears heavy, and shut their eyes; lest they see with their eyes, and hear with their ears, and understand with their hearts, and turn and be healed. (Isa. 6:8–10)

Why did God do this? We find this difficult to understand, but if we see that the fall was the result of the distortion of the word, then this will be the way humanity responds to the Word of God.

We should also need to see this as the judgement of God upon the people who had rejected His word. This judgement is not a trigger mechanism set in the law. It is the actual presence of God in that judgement. Since the Word of God is His grace to His people, and they have rejected that word, then their blinding is God's judgement upon them. And it is to this situation that we are sent.

The Prophetic Word and Repentance

This judgement of God is a warning to all of us. If we continue to reject His word, the judgement will come. This will cause blinding of our eyes and deafness of our ears. God does not sit there and tolerate the arrogance of humanity. The blinding and deafness will come upon us for sure.

The prophetic word calls for a turning to the Lord as our destiny is hid in Him. Zephaniah spoke of the judgement to the people during the time of King Josiah, and in that judgement is the promise of restoration.

> ³Seek the Lord, all you humble of the land,
> who do his commands;
> seek righteousness, seek humility;
> perhaps you may be hidden
> on the day of the wrath of the Lord. (Zeph. 2:3)

The prophetic word brought about repentance and with it the promise of restoration.

The Third Reason: False Priests and Prophets

As the prophetic Word of God is rejected by the people, the natural consequence is the acceptance of the false word. Scripture warns of the false word to which people will flock. This false word appeals to the self-assertion of the individual as it allows them to be in control rather than to live in faith and in dependence on the Creator. We see that there were false priests and prophets in Israel and in New Testament times. Micah gives this warning:

> ¹¹Its heads give judgement for a bribe,
> its priests teach for hire,
> its prophets divine for money;
> yet they lean upon the Lord and say,
> 'Is not the Lord in the midst of us?
> No evil shall come upon us.' (Micah 3:11)

The false word is to say what the people want to hear so that they feel justified in their cultural norm. Better still, in the process they get paid for it. The formula that the false prophets use is to assure the people that all is well with them because God is in their midst. Or is it? It is the affirmation that what is culturally accepted is all right. It is a false assurance. It is a kind of bunker mentality. The true prophet will be opposed because he speaks the words of judgement from God and forces the transformation of the cultural norm.

We have got used to the Mary Poppins's formula for taking strong medicine: a spoonful of sugar makes the medicine goes down. The false prophets give us the medicine with a spoonful of sugar to make it more palatable and in the process masks the truth of God.

The characteristics of the false word are:

- It is close to the truth.
- It is soothing.
- It is not confrontational.
- It does not demand repentance, i.e. a turning around.

Some of the theology of the first world is a theology that preserves and justifies its affluence and lifestyle. It does not come through the cross—the central and crucial point of theology.

The Church Exists in this Opposition

In one of his moving farewell speeches, Paul spoke to the elders of the church at Ephesus from Miletus, and he said,

> [28]Take heed to yourselves and to all the flock, in which the Holy Spirit has made you overseers, to care for the church of God which he obtained with the blood of his own Son. [29]I know that after my departure fierce wolves will come in among you, not sparing the flock; [30]and from among your own selves will arise men speaking perverse things, to draw away the disciples after them. (Acts 20:28–30)

And again to Timothy:

> [1]Now the Spirit expressly says that in later times some will depart from the faith by giving heed to deceitful spirits and doctrines of demons, [2]through the pretensions of liars whose consciences are seared. (1 Tim. 4:1–2)

The church of God exists in the midst of this deception, and this is the reality that confronts our ministry. Our commission is to speak the truth of

God and to continue speaking it. We can only pray that God will dig the ears and give the hearing. Let us not reject the word that we have heard. It is only by the mercy of God that we are given hearing and understanding.

Ministry of the Word

We have discussed the curious verse from Psalm 40:6 that God is digging two ears for us to hear. Obviously, it is not referring to the way we hear naturally. In other words, God needs to give us hearing ears in order to hear His word. I also pointed out that the Word of God is not to be regarded as a text to be subjected to our intellectual analysis. It demands a response from us. This response is created by God. The way the response is of God is like this. He first dug two ears for us so that we can hear Him. Then the Spirit of God creates within us a framework to hold on to the things of God. Thus, the understanding is a revelation given by the Spirit. This is a simplistic way of getting a handle on things. What goes on is perhaps more involved like the molecules that interact in the digestion process in the body.

We want to see the way the Word of God works in us. The early apostles regarded the Word of God very highly. We can see this from Acts 6. They had devoted themselves to the word. We will see what that means.

First of all, I want to show to you from the book of Acts, the way they regarded the Word of God. It is very different from the way we see it. We need to see the way the apostles regarded the Word of God as something living and active in some of the passages in Acts. Clearly, they do not see the word as merely a text for us to learn or even to memorise.

> [4]But we will devote ourselves to prayer and to the ministry of the word. (Acts 6:4)

> [7]And the word of God increased; and the number of the disciples multiplied greatly in Jerusalem, and a great many of the priests were obedient to the faith. (Acts 6:7)

> [14]Now when the apostles at Jerusalem heard that Samaria had received the word of God, they sent to them Peter and John. (Acts 8:14)

> 24But the word of God grew and multiplied. (Acts 12:24)
>
> ⁴⁸And when the Gentiles heard this, they were glad and glorified the word of God; and as many as were ordained to eternal life believed. ⁴⁹And the word of the Lord spread throughout all the region. (Acts 13:48–49)
>
> ²⁰So the word of the Lord grew and prevailed mightily. (Acts 19:20)

In these passages, it is quite obvious that the word that is referred to in the book of Acts is not just the word spoken. There is a personification of the word as in the Old Testament. The word takes on a life of its own. Luke did not consider the word as a text but as something that is alive and growing. We want to explore what this means.

In most of our churches, our congregations consist of people who can read and write. More than that, we have congregations of scholars, professional people, people with tertiary qualifications and not only just one but several. They would have read millions of words and unfortunately, many have come to the scripture with the same mind-set. The Bible or the Word of God is, of course, the written word on a printed page. But of course we know that it is more than just that. And though we know that, we need to respond to that knowledge accordingly.

In the Old Testament, the Word of God is the creative word. We saw that earlier on. The word is closely related to the breath of God. Of course, it is not difficult to see that as when we speak the word, there is the breath exhaled required in the speech. The two go hand in hand (Ps. 33:6).

The Greek philosophers have understood the word as the reason or the force for the beginning of the world. That is the Logos. In the modern-day big bang theory, that is also an impersonal force at work. They are both denial of the creative word or the God who creates in a personal way.

However, the excellence of the thought of John brought together the word of Greek philosophy and the creative acts of God in the creative word, and not only that, but the word became flesh. So the understanding is not only a matter of personification as a figure of speech. It is the reality of the word alive and active. This word is Jesus Christ. So when we receive the word, we are not just receiving an idea or a principle in order to remember or to apply it. No, when we receive the word, we are receiving Christ into our lives. It is the word in us.

- So when we proclaim the word, we are not proclaiming a philosophy or merely principles that we can apply but proclaiming Jesus Christ.
- When we teach the word, we are not teaching a text or literature but teaching and presenting the Lord Jesus Christ to the people.
- When we come to study the word, we are not absorbing information. We are absorbing the Lord Jesus Christ.
- When we speak of the ministry of the word, we are speaking of the ministry of Jesus Christ in the lives of the people.

When we say that the word grew and multiplied, we are saying that the life of Jesus Christ is taking on more and more people into His. We should not understand this is in an institutional sense. The Word of God is growing by leaps and bounds in the world today, and that is taking place in the hearts of men and women. When the people receive the word, they are not subscribing to a philosophy of life. They have received the Lord Jesus Christ into their lives and have become incorporated into the body of Jesus Christ.

Having said all these, our starting point is still the printed page and the Bible that has come down to us. We need to acknowledge this. God speaks to us from this text, and we need to know this text. I am not saying that we all should be Greek and Hebrew scholars. But for a start, we should know at least the books of the Bible. So often when the scripture is read, some of us do not even turn to that because we do not know where that book is. So under the pressure of being a 'user-friendly church', we put the text of the scripture on the screen. We should not have to do that. How about we all learn the name of the sixty-six books of the Bible for a start—thirty-nine in the old and twenty-seven in the new. Make that a family exercise.

The next thing that we should do is to have some idea of the contents of the books whose names we have learnt. That is again not too difficult. We can do that very simply in a matter of a few hours. Get together and form a group and we can go through that. We do not need to know the details, but it is good to get a panorama of the scriptures and from that we can build up a little detail as we go along. But if you do not have the broad picture, then how are you going to fit in the details. It will become airy fairy.

Our God is the God of history, and some details of the history of the acts of God are necessary for us to comprehend the way God has dealt with His creation and His people. How do we comprehend what God is doing in China if we have no idea of the imperial kingdom and the rise of the Nationalists and the Communists and their bitter struggle?

Furthermore, we have been taught that we need only to read a verse or a couple of verses a day to get us going. We call that the morning devotion. Well, that is better than not doing it at all. We need to do more than that. If we really believe the scripture as the living word and it brings to us Jesus Christ, then I think we ought to do more than just reading a few verses a day. However, that should come from the love of God and His word and not merely a routine that we need to conform to. If that is so, then there could be a sense of guilt if we neglect the practice.

One further problem with us is that when we come to be familiar with the Bible or certain books or passages, we get the attitude that we have known the word. If we get into that frame of mind, then we will not learn anything more from the word. The Word of God ceases to speak to us because we have closed our mind to what it is saying. We have put God's word into a box, a neat little package that we then can use. Don't do that.

God's word is always fresh to us no matter how many times we have heard it. This is because it is the living word. We have our family stories, and no matter how many times we tell it, each time it brings back that happy memory of what we have done together. Those family stories have taken on a life of their own. Jesus is the Word of God, and no matter how many times we have heard the word, Jesus continues to speak to us in new ways if we are open to hear Him.

The Continuing Ministry of the Word

We have said enough on the hearing and the nonhearing. I want to start from the point where God has done His work in us and we have submitted and heard the word not only through the ears that God has dug but also when He opens the eyes of our hearts.

When that has happened, we often assume that that will be a constant state. In other words, it is like when one becomes an engineer or an accountant or attain to any other qualification, we assume that one is qualified forever. No, that is not the case. We are all aware of the need of continuing education and updating in all our profession. The constant state is an outdated principle in physics. All states are subject to change and all states are subject to entropy, i.e. to decay, unless there is an input to maintain that state.

Let me give an example of this. Take the case of secular humanism. We call it secular, but that was not the case when it all started. Humanism has its roots in Christianity. In the days of the Enlightenment, there was a revolt against the oppression of the day. Humanism has a Christian base. That is, the proponents were people who had embraced the Christian gospel or affected by its teaching. However, there was one problem, and that is they had extracted the teaching and ostracized the teacher. They took the teachings of the scriptures and discarded the author of the scriptures. They had the teachings, but Christ was no longer in it. It is like when you have received the gift, and if you are a materialist, you then forget about the giver. It is the material above the relational. The relational ceases after the gift is used or forgotten. That is our fallen state, i.e. the sinful state, when we have rebelled against the Creator.

The problem in the church is this: there was initially the work of the Spirit of God or we may call it the visitation of the Spirit. The Spirit does His work, and the church of Christ came into being. The leaders then think that they have the expertise, and Christ became an adjunct to the process. When we do that, then we have degenerated into the state of self. We then create the cultural church where Christ takes second place and the culture became all important. That state is no different from the state of unbelief. The cross has been moved to the side in preference to human determination.

That is why in the letters to the church, Christ told the church at Ephesus that they have abandoned their first love, i.e. they have substituted a system for Christ. 'But I have this against you, that you have abandoned the love you had at first' (Rev. 2:4).

We are all aware of the need to hear and to do. In our fallen state, we have separated the hearing and the doing, and that is why James wrote to rectify the problem. A person of integrity is one who does what he says. Now to hear and not do is the same problem as to do and not hear.

> [23]Anyone who listens to the word but does not do what it says is like a man who looks at his face in a mirror

> [24] and, after looking at himself, goes away and immediately forgets what he looks like. (James 1:23–24 NIV)

It is easy to pretend that you have heard and then forget about it. That is really not hearing. The proof of the hearing is in the doing. James is not teaching that we should only be doers. The hearing and the doing is one continuous process. It demands the input of Christ and the Spirit in our lives. To hear and not to do is just as wrong as to march out to do without hearing the voice of the Spirit. We need to emphasise the relational in what we are doing and the continuing leading and input from Christ and the Spirit.

We need to avoid thinking of the ministry of God like some kind of a mechanical robot. That is because we often think that God created this universe and left it to run on its own steam and then have a good rest. God is working and continues to oversee His creation. He is not watching us from a distance. He is intimately involved in our lives and all that we do.

The Word in the world
(Or Is It the World in the Word?)

I have emphasised that the word is alive. The Bible refers to both the written word as well as the word that is alive. However, what we have before us is the written word, and we need to know how to deal with it. That is not put quite right. It is really the way the word deals with us, but for our purpose, what do we do with the word before us? I will deal with the way we handle the word. Paul said to young Timothy:

> Do your best to present yourself to God as one approved by him, a worker who has no need to be ashamed, rightly explaining [*orthotomounta*] the word of truth. (2 Tim. 2:15)

The NIV has 'correctly handles the word of truth' and the KJV 'rightly dividing', which I think is the preferred translation. The word used is a compound of *orthos*, meaning *straight*, and *tomoteros*, a derivative of *temno* meaning *cut*. It implies that when we analyse the word, we need to present the word as it really is without distorting it, cut it straight as one might say. Paul was acutely aware of this responsibility of presenting the word as it really is. He saw it as an awesome responsibility. He said, 'For we are not peddlers of God's word like so many; but in Christ we speak as persons of sincerity, as persons sent from God and standing in his presence' (2 Cor. 2:17). Here we have the concept of God's word in the presence of God.

Psalm 19 talks about the written Word of God:

> [7]The law of the LORD is perfect,
>   reviving the soul;
> the decrees of the LORD are sure,
>   making wise the simple;
> [8]the precepts of the LORD are right,
>   rejoicing the heart;
> the commandment of the LORD is clear,
>   enlightening the eyes;
> [9]the fear of the LORD is pure,
>   enduring forever;
> the ordinances of the LORD are true
>   and righteous altogether.
> [10]More to be desired are they than gold,
>   even much fine gold;
> sweeter also than honey,
>   and drippings of the honeycomb. (Ps. 19)

And so is Psalm 1:

> [2]But their delight is in the law of the LORD,
>   and on his law they meditate day and night. (Ps. 1)

We live in a tension between the word and the world. 'We are in the world but not of the world.' The way we read and hear the word is affected by our upbringing in whichever part of the world we may find ourselves. We must not equate the thinking of the world with the word. There is a tendency to do just that as ultimately that process will justify us. We are in the world but not of the world. The world has rejected the word, but we are the people of the word. John wrote, 'I am not asking you to take them out of the world, but I ask you to protect them from the evil one. They do not belong to the world, just as I do not belong to the world' (Jn. 17:15–16).

We do not have Christ with us in person. He is absent, but in some ways, He is present with us. This is not easy to comprehend. What we have with us is the word—the written word that takes us to the living word. We have to start with the written word because that is what God has given to us.

> [8]The words that you gave to me I have given to them, and they have received them and know in truth that I came from you; and they have believed that you sent me. (Jn. 17:8)

What we often do is to bypass this written word to Christ Himself, we think, if that is at all possible. That is not the purpose of God. That is a false notion. So often, we have put the word under our culture, our preferences, and our social connections.

The Practical Word: The False Word

While we are in the world, there are practicalities that we need to deal with. We cannot avoid that. It has often been said that our preaching do not relate to the real world in which we live. The cry is that we need a practical word. I do not deny this, but there is a danger that in so doing we may be returning to the days of the Pharisees where everything that we do is spelt out; and the more we do it, the more detail there will be. What that does is to obscure the reality of the word in us and substitute that with the practical word that will justify our actions.

The message of the Bible that we bring across must make sense to us in our daily living. It must not merely remain in the realm of the theological and do not engage our daily lives. However, we must not disregard the theological, i.e. our understanding of God, because that is where we must start. We need to know who God is, and we cannot be true to our calling if we do not know the one who has called us. The problem cannot be resolved by merely dwelling on the practical or by doing more of theology. It is a problem of our rejection of grace. It is as we understand the grace of God that we can truly live out the word in the world.

Some churches feel that the theological is not of much relevance to daily living and that they should dwell on the practical. So the preaching dwells on the things that people should do, the so-called practical things. There is a problem here. When we have a rule for a certain practice, then that practice takes over from the leading of God. Put it in a question form. Do we make the man-made rule above the leading of the Spirit, or is the rule subordinate to the leading of the Spirit? People then argue that the rule becomes the leading of the Spirit. That may be so for a time. However, that is a dangerous line to take. That puts our judgement on equal terms with the Spirit's leading. What happens when the situation has changed or the rule becomes not relevant? What do we do then? What becomes of the rule? Who makes the rules? I am not talking about daily administrative issues like when do we start the service or when do we have our lunch, etc. When we make a rule absolute, then we have lost the sense of our life together in the Spirit.

Being and Doing

We need to differentiate the 'being' and the 'doing' in life. Our doing is the result of our being, i.e. what we are. As redeemed creatures, our doing follows from the redeemed life in Christ. We have the leading of the Spirit within us, and that is the way we are to live if we are in Christ. Therefore, the emphasis in preaching is on the being, and there is not much we can do about the being because that is the creation of God and remains in the province of the work of God, i.e. in the realm of the work of the Spirit which God has given to us. If that is not the way we live, what then is the purpose of the pouring out of the Spirit at Pentecost?

Creation is the work of God, and the new creation in Christ is also the work of God. Our ministry is not to effect the new creation. It has been effected by Christ and the Spirit. Our task is to preach the word. Therein lies our problem. What is the word that we preach? That word is Christ, and our preaching is to hold out Christ to the people. We can do no other. There is a place for the instruction of people and that instruction is subject to the word, both written and living. We need to point them to the Christ.

The World in the Word

The problem with us is that we have so much of the world in us and we want to justify our existence. That is why we twisted the word to suit us and to preserve the culture that we so enjoy. So the world is in the word; and when that word is preached, though it may be understandable and sound good, it is the false word. It is the rejection of grace. When we have a rule and we follow that, it makes us feel good. It also makes us feel that we have attained to the standard of God, but really have we? Can we see the false confidence that preaching on the practicalities gives to us?

The word is often subordinated to the world and its culture. It does not matter where we come from—be it from the West or East. Christmas is very much a cultural event. I wonder how it would be celebrated if we were to remove all cultural vestiges from it! It would be difficult and may even upset many people.

Chinese New Year is another. Many Chinese churches celebrate the event as part of their church service. When there is a New Year or Christmas celebration, many ethnic churches finish the service with a meal and everyone brings something along. The service and the celebration are held together, one after the other, because for convenience they do not want to make that on two separate occasions. What happens there is that the meal becomes the primary event. Some do not even come for the service but spend the time at home preparing the meal. The preaching of the word was not heard. Satan has hijacked the service by the cultural event.

I heard that in China some ten years ago, during Christmas one shopping centre put up a Santa Claus crucified on the cross. I don't blame the Chinese as the Western church has so linked Santa with Christmas and continue to preach the cross. It becomes difficult for people outside to hear the real message. We need to maintain the primacy of the word and make that clear. We must be conscious that it is very easy to subordinate the word to a good idea because the idea becomes an ideology and that takes over from the word. We have then sold ourselves to the evil one.

The World: A False Reality

We are in the world, but we are not of the world. The things of the world are there for us, but we need to see beyond the material to the God who has given to us the world to sustain us. But when the things of the world rule over us, then we are slaves to them and no longer servants of the God who has given to us these things. To enable us to live in the world that has so long enslaved us, God has given to us the word in order for us to know Him and to be free from that enslavement. The written word is given to us so that through it, we 'may have life in his name'. That is the power of the word.

Today there is a teaching of the Holy Spirit that bypasses Christ. There is also a teaching on Christ that bypasses the word. We must not do that. If we do that, then we will be all over the place with no grounding. We need the Word of God to reveal the will of God to us. When we make a statement like 'This is the will of God', what we are really saying is that we think that this is the will of God. We must not put on equal footing the will of God and what we think to be the will of God. If we do, then if others disagree in some way, then it makes us right and them wrong. That puts us equal with God, and that is not right. How then can we know? God has given us the word, and He has given us the family of God. The unity of the two will give us greater assurance that it is the will of God. That is in essence what the life in the body of Christ is all about.

We cannot bypass the word to get to Christ. Jesus prayed, 'And now I am no longer in the world, but they are in the world, and I am coming to you' (Jn. 17:11). Jesus is not here in person with us. We can only come to know Christ through the word. However, the word is not just a text for us to decipher. It is the living word capable of bringing us to God. We are not people of the word, the written text, but people of the word—the living Word. Christ is absent in our world, i.e. He is not here in person, but yet He is present. We live in this tension. What we have is the written word, and that is where we must start.

We cannot come to scripture asking questions like how or why. These are speculations of our mind. There is only one question we take to scripture and that is the *who* question. Who is the God behind the text? Unless we do that, then the word will remain beyond us and beyond our intellect too. John did not say, 'But these are written so that you may *know how to live or why this is so.*' These are legitimate questions, but they are not the primary questions and certainly not what scripture is about. He said that these are written so that we may know who God is and that we may have life in Him. This comes through the word.

How then do we understand the Bible? We can talk about various methods of interpretation, but I won't go into those technical matters. Ultimately, it is reading the word. It is no use knowing the methods of interpretation and only uses it sparingly when we come to certain passages. The Bible is not to be used that way. The Bible is the way to God. In other words, the Bible speaks to us about who God is, and it is this knowledge that governs the way we read it. One can be a Bible scholar like any other pursuing a literary career. The Bible becomes merely a text to be deciphered. Obviously, with such an approach, one will come to a very different conclusion that way.

I don't think that there is anyone who seriously comes to word and do not understand it. The Bible is the Word of God, and the Word of God speaks to us, i.e. if we read it. If we only come to the word occasionally, then we would have problems of understanding.

The first problem is not coming to the word seeking God. What I mean is that we come to the word seeking answers to lots of things other than who God is. The second is our rejection of grace. The latter is a more serious problem. When we reject grace, we reject God; and so when we come to word, we will not be able to see God and hence will not understand what is written. This is because the Word rightly interpreted (divided) shows us the God of grace, and if we reject grace, then there is no way we can see this God. Therein lies the biggest problem in reading the Bible.

The Bible is about God's saving action in the world. This is the primary underlying principle in interpretation. Unless we have this as our anchor, then any interpretation will be off focus, and that includes even scholarly interpretations. We may use textual principles, and these can be helpful in difficult passages. We should see these as adjuncts to interpretation, i.e. tools at our disposal rather than tools that controls us. What I mean is this: if a method of interpretation gives us an understanding that is contrary to the salvific story of the scriptures, then we need to reconsider its application.

If we come to scripture and we understand the text, then so what? What does that do for us? That has been a problem in Christian groups when we argue about the text. The question we need to ask is what the purpose of scripture is and what should be the intended result when we come to it. Unless we get this right, then all kind of problems will result.

God's purpose in this regard is made clear. He is the creator, and He sustains His creation. He is in covenant relationship with His creation, and because of sin, He has given His Son to redeem His creation and to bring His creation back to Himself. Any departure from what has been made clear in scripture is not of God. Whatever the method of interpretation we may use, should it depart from this clear line of scripture is fallacy. Methods of interpretation are tools in our hands and not the master of our destiny. This quotation from Paddison is helpful:

> This means that biblical interpretation has the knowledge of God as its ultimate objective. Understood theologically, biblical interpretation must conform itself to the object of the Bible's own testimony. The aim of interpretation is the

> creation, nurturing, and sustaining of participation in, and covenant relationship with, the God to whom these texts direct us. Put otherwise, the question of how we can speak of God is decisively answered by appeal to the practice of biblical interpretation. The work of biblical scholarship, as one particular form of the interpretative task, is therefore to be regarded as theological method, dogmatic content, a spiritual discipline, and even perhaps a form of prayer. . . . The aim of reading a text written by a biblical author like Paul is not to seek out the putative historical circumstances behind this or that pronouncement, but to look towards the reality which so radically reorientated Paul's life. (Angus Paddison, *Scripture: A Very Theological Proposal* (London: T & T Clark International, 2009), 2.)

I have said that I do want to engage the technical aspect of interpreting scripture except to mention the old and time-honoured dictum of scripture interpreting scripture. What is not clear in one passage will be made clear in another. That is why we need to read the whole of scripture and not just the few passages that we like.

Therefore, our reading of scripture must take us away from the present to what is beyond us, i.e. to the God of creation and His redemptive work. It must take into consideration our sin and rebellion against the creator. It must accept the work of grace in our hearts by the Spirit of God. The two problems in understanding scripture are the rejection of grace and the reliance on the human intellect. That is not to say that the intellect is not to be used, but the intellect must be submissive to the Spirit of God and not make judgement against the Spirit of God. The intellect must allow the truth of scripture to transform it so that it can then in submission to the Spirit of God redetermine the way this life is to be lived.

I have mentioned the falsehood when the world is in the word, i.e. using the notions of the world to interpret the word and hence justify the life we live instead of transforming it. Reading the word takes us to the one beyond us, i.e. God the Creator. When we read the word and it doesn't do that but instead take us to the things of this world, like health and wealth, then there is a problem in its interpretation. The things of this world are gifts from God, and as such, we must be stewards in its use. I am still relatively fit and healthy, and thus, I can run and go about various things. If I have a bad knee, then I will be restricted in what I can do. What God has not given, I will not be able to do. What God has given is a gift and to be used for His glory.

I do not say that there are no difficult passages in scripture. There are but very few. Let us not take those passages to justify our lack of reading the Bible. You won't encounter many of them when we come acknowledging the grace of God in our lives. If you don't acknowledge the grace of God, then you will have lots more of those difficult passages. Our rejection of grace blinds us to the truth of scripture.

Bibliography

Anderson, G H, ed. *Asian Voices in Christian Theology*. Maryknoll, New York: Orbis Books, 1976.

Anderson, R. *Historical Transcendence and the Reality of God*. Grand Rapids: Eerdmans, 1975.

_____. *On Being Human*. Grand Rapids: Eerdmans, 1982.

_____. *Ministry on the Fireline*. Downers Grove: IVP, 1993.

_____, ed. *Theological Foundations for Ministry*. Grand Rapids: Eerdmans, 1979.

Anderson, R and D Guernsey. *On Being Family*. Grand Rapids: Eerdmans, 1985.

Balswick, J and J Balswick. *The Family*. Grand Rapids: Baker Book House, 1991.

Barth, K. *The Humanity of God*. Translated by J Thomas. USA: John Knox Press, 1960.

_____. *Church Dogmatics*, vol. 1.1. Translated by G W Bromiley. Edinburgh: T&T Clark, 1975.

Bavink, J H. *The Impact of Christianity on the Non-Christian World*. Grand Rapids: Eerdmans, 1948.

Bingham, G. *Liberating Love*. Blackwood, South Australia: New Creation Publication Inc., 1960.

_____. *The Everlasting Presence*. Blackwood, South Australia: New Creation Publication Inc., 1990.

_____. *The Profound Mystery: Marriage Love, Divine and Human*. Blackwood, South Australia: New Creation Publication Inc., 1995.

_____. *Love's Most Glorious Covenant*. Castle Hill, NSW: Redeemer Baptist Press, 1997.

British Council of Churches, *The Forgotten Trinity*, volume 1: The Report of the BCC Study Commission on Trinitarian Doctrine Today. London: BCC, 1989.

British Council of Churches, *The Forgotten Trinity*, volume 3: A Selection of Papers presented to the BCC Study Commission on Trinitarian Doctrine Today, ed. A Heron. London: BCC, 1991.

Bromiley, G. *Historical Theology: An Introduction*. Grand Rapids: Eerdmans, 1978.

Brueggemann, W. *The Psalms and the Life of Faith*. Minneapolis: Fortress Press, 1995.

Calvin, J. *Institutes of the Christian Religion*, 2 volumes. Edited by J T McNeill. Philadelphia: Westminster Press.

Carson, D A and J D Woodbridge, eds. *God and Culture*. Grand Rapids: Eerdmans, 1993.

Covell, R R. *Confucius, The Buddha, and Christ*. New York: Orbis, 1986.

Creel, H G. *Chinese Thought*. London: University Paperbacks, 1954.

Donovan, V. *Christianity Rediscovered*. London: SCM, 1982.

Dudley, C S. *Building Effective Ministry*. San Francisco: Harper and Row, 1983.

Dumbrell, W J. *Covenant and Creation*. Great Britain: Paternoster, 1984.

Dyrness, W A. *The Earth Is God's*. New York: Orbis, 1997.

Ferguson, S B and D F Wright, eds. *New Dictionary of Theology*. London: IVP, 1988.

Finlayson, R A. *The Story of Theology*. 2nd ed. London: Tyndale Press, 1969.

Franklin, R W and J M Shaw. *The Case for Christian Humanism*. Grand Rapids: Eerdmans, 1991.

Frost, P J. *Organisational Culture*. Newbury Park, CA: Sage, 1985.

Fung, Y L. *A Short History of Chinese Philosophy*. New York: MacMillan, 1948.

Gilliland, D S., ed. *The Word Among Us*. USA: Word Publishing, 1989.

Green, M. *Evangelism in the Early Church*. Grand Rapids: Eerdmans, 1970.

Gunton, C and D Hardy, eds. *On Being the Church*. Edinburgh: T&T Clark, 1989.

Hanko, H. *God's Everlasting Covenant of Grace*. Grandville: Reformed Free Publishing Association, 1988.

Hart, T and D Thimell, eds. *Christ in Our Place*. Great Britain: Paternoster, 1989.

Hunsberger, G R and C Van Gelder, eds. *The Church between Gospel and Culture*. Grand Rapids: Eerdmans, 1996.

Jenson, R W, ed. *Essays in the Theology of Culture*. Grand Rapids: Eerdmans, 1995.

Jinkins, M. 'Elements of Federal Theology in the Religious Thought of John Locke'. *Evangelical Quarterly* 66:2 (1994): 123–141.

Kelly, J N D. *Early Christian Doctrines.* 5th ed. London: Adam & Charles Black, 1977.

Kettler, C D and T H Speidell, eds. *Incarnational Ministry.* Colorado Springs: Helmers & Howard, 1990.

Kraft, C. *Christianity in Culture.* New York: Orbis, 1979.

Kung, H. *Global Responsibility.* Translated by J Dowden. London: SCM, 1991.

Kung, H and J Ching. *Christianity and Chinese Religions.* London: SCM Press, 1989.

Lausanne Consultation on Gospel and Culture. *Down to Earth.* Eds. J Stott and R Coote. London: Hodder and Stoughton, 1981.

Leys, S, trans. *The Analects of Confucius.* New York: W W Norton, 1997.

McKinney, R, ed. *Creation, Christ and Culture.* Edinburgh: T&T Clark, 1976.

Moltmann, J. *The Trinity and the Kingdom of God.* Translated by M Kohl. London: SCM, 1981.

_____. *Creating a Just Future.* Translated by J Bowden. Philadelphia: Trinity Press International, 1989.

_____. 'Covenant or Leviathan? Political Theology for Modern Times'. *Scottish Journal of Theology* 47 (1994): 19–41.

Moore, C A. *The Chinese Mind.* Honolulu: University of Hawaii Press, 1967.

Newbigin, L. *Foolishness to the Greeks.* Grand Rapids: Eerdmans, 1986.

_____. *The Gospel in a Pluralist Society.* London: SPCK, 1989.

_____. *Truth to Tell, the Gospel as Public Truth.* London: SPCK, 1991.

Niebuhr, H R. *Christ and Culture.* New York: Harper and Row, 1951.

Packer, J I and T Howard. *Christianity: The True Humanism.* England: Word Publishing, 1985.

Padilla, C R, ed. *The New Face of Evangelicalism.* London: Hodder and Stoughton, 1976.

Parsons, M. 'Being Precedes Act: Indicatives and Imperative in Paul's Writing'. *The Evangelical Quarterly* LX, no. 2 (April 1988): 99–127.

Rahner, K. *The Trinity.* Translated by J Donceel. Great Britain: Burns & Oates, 1970.

Ro, B R and C C Albrecht, eds. *God in Asian Contexts.* Taiwan: Asia Theological Association, 1988.

Ro, B R and R Eshenaur, eds. *The Bible and Theology in Asian Contexts.* Taiwan: Asia Theological Association, 1984.

_____, eds. *The Bible and Theology in Asian Contexts.* Taiwan: Asia Theological Association, 1984.

Schaller, L E. *The Change Agent.* Nashville: Abingdon Press, 1972.

Schein, E. *Organisational Culture and Leadership*. San Francisco: Jossey-Bass, 1985.

Singer, P. *Practical Ethics*. Cambridge: Cambridge University Press, 1979.

Tanner, K. *Theories of Culture*. Minneapolis: Fortress, 1997.

Thompson, L G. *Chinese Religion: An Introduction*. California: Dickenson Publishing Company, 1975.

Torrance, A. 'The Self-Relation, Narcissism and the Gospel of Grace'. *Scottish Journal of Theology* 40 (1987): 481–510.

Torrance, J B. 'Covenant or Contract'. *Scottish Journal of Theology* 23 (1970): 51–76.

_____. 'The Contribution of McLeod Campbell to Scottish Theology'. *Scottish Journal of Theology* 26 (1973): 295–311.

_____. 'The Place of Jesus Christ in worship.' *Theological Foundations for Ministry*, ed. R S Anderson, 348–369. Grand Rapids: Eerdmans, 1979.

_____. 'The Vicarious Humanity of Christ.' *The Incarnation*, ed. T F Torrance, 127–147. Edinburgh: Handsel, 1981.

_____. 'The Covenant Concept in Scottish Theology and Politics and Its Legacy'. *Scottish Journal of Theology* 34 (1981): 225–243.

_____. 'Interpreting the Word by the Light of Christ or the Light of Nature? Calvin, Calvinism and Barth.' *Calviniana: Ideas and Influence of Jean Calvin*, Sixteenth Century Essays and Studies, vol. X, ed. R V Schnucker, 255–268. Kirksville, MO: Sixteen Century Journal Publishers, 1988.

_____. 'Contemplating the Trinitarian Mystery of Christ.' *Alive to God*, eds. J I Packer and L Wilkinson, 140–151. Downers Grove: IVP, 1992.

_____. *Worship, Community, and the Triune God of Grace*. Carlisle, UK: Paternoster, 1996.

Torrance, T F. *Space, Time and Incarnation*. Edinburgh: T&T Clark, 1969.

_____. *Reality and Scientific Theology*. Edinburgh: Scottish Academic Press, 1985.

_____. 'Karl Barth and the Latin Heresy.' *Scottish Journal of Theology* 39 (1986): 461–482.

_____. *The Trinitarian Faith*. Edinburgh: T&T Clark, 1988.

_____. *The Mediation of Christ*. Edinburgh: T&T Clark, 1992.

_____. *Theology in Reconstruction*. Eugene, OR: Wipf and Stock Publishers, 1996.

Vitz, P C. *Psychology as Religion*. Grand Rapids: Eerdmans, 1977.

Yen, C H. *A Social History of the Chinese in Singapore and Malaya 1800–1911*. Singapore: OUP, 1986

Edwards Brothers Malloy
Thorofare, NJ USA
January 15, 2016